The Multinational Enterprise Revisited

The Multinational Enterprise Revisited

The Essential Buckley and Casson

Peter J. Buckley
Professor of International Business, University of Leeds, UK

Mark Casson
Professor of Economics, University of Reading

palgrave
macmillan

First published 2010 by
PALGRAVE MACMILLAN

Palgrave Macmillan in the UK is an imprint of Macmillan Publishers Limited, registered in England, company number 785998, of Houndmills, Basingstoke, Hampshire RG21 6XS.

Palgrave Macmillan in the US is a division of St Martin's Press LLC, 175 Fifth Avenue, New York, NY 10010.

Palgrave Macmillan is the global academic imprint of the above companies and has companies and representatives throughout the world.

Palgrave® and Macmillan® are registered trademarks in the United States, the United Kingdom, Europe and other countries

ISBN: 978-0-230-51599-4   hardback

This book is printed on paper suitable for recycling and made from fully managed and sustained forest sources. Logging, pulping and manufacturing processes are expected to conform to the environmental regulations of the country of origin.

A catalogue record for this book is available from the British Library.

A catalog record for this book is available from the Library of Congress.

10 9 8 7 6 5 4 3 2 1
19 18 17 16 15 14 13 12 11 10

Printed and bound in Great Britain by
CPI Antony Rowe, Chippenham and Eastbourne

Contents

List of Figures   vi

List of Tables   viii

Acknowledgements   x

1   The Future of the Multinational Enterprise after 30 Years   1

2   The Optimal Timing of a Foreign Direct Investment   25

3   A Theory of Cooperation in International Business   41

4   Multinational Enterprises in Less Developed Countries:
    Cultural and Economic Interactions   68

5   Organising for Innovation: The Multinational Enterprise
    in the Twenty-First Century   96

6   An Economic Model of International Joint
    Venture Strategy   118

7   Models of the Multinational Enterprise   147

8   Analysing Foreign Market Entry Strategies: Extending
    the Internalisation Approach   177

9   The Moral Basis of Global Capitalism:
    Beyond the Eclectic Theory   205

10 Strategic Complexity in International Business   239

11 Edith Penrose's Theory of the Growth of the Firm and
    the Strategic Management of Multinational Enterprises   277

Index   301

List of Figures

2.1 Derivation of minimum average cost   27

2.2 The discontinuous marginal revenue curve   28

2.3 Optimal switching of modes   29

2.4 Direct switching from exporting to FDI   31

2.5 Dynamics of switching   33

3.1 Forward integration into a JV   54

3.2 Backward integration into a JV   54

3.3 Buy-back arrangement   55

3.4 Multistage arrangement   55

3.5 The dominant partner in networks   65

4.1 The development of international trade between
     developed countries   86

4.2 The role of developed countries in the development
     of LDCs   89

5.1 Schematic summary of the innovation process   105

6.1 Schematic illustration of four IJV configurations
     generated by the sharing of technology and
     marketing expertise contributed by two firms   122

6.2 Schematic illustration of IJV configurations 5–9 based
     on a single shared production facility   124

6.3 Configuration after Firm 2 has been acquired and
     rationalised by Firm 1   126

6.4 Configuration when Firm 1 licences in technology
     from Firm 2   127

6.5 Influence of market size on strategic choice   135

6.6 Impact of volatility factor on strategic choice   136

6.7 Combined impact of market size and volatility on
     strategic choice   137

6.8	Impact of cultural heterogeneity, protection of independence, economies of scope and technological uncertainty on strategic choice	139
6.9	Comparative analysis of the international business environment in the 1960s and 1980s	141
8.1	Twelve entry strategies and their variants	190
10.1	Diagrammatic solution of the entry strategy under uncertainty	248
10.2	Strategy for information gathering	250
10.3	Comparison of decision trees with and without research	252
10.4	Decision tree for integrated research/waiting/switching problem	255
10.5	Diagrammatic solution of an entry problem encompassing research, deferment and switching	257
10.6	Schematic representation of a simple international business system	260

List of Tables

4.1   Factors in the long-run economic success
      of a nation   74

6.1   Typology of IJVs according to the kind of
      knowledge shared   121

6.2   Key determinants of the costs of alternative strategies   129

6.3   Impact of market size and volatility on strategic choice   138

6.4   Impact of key explanatory factor on strategic choice   144

8.1   Twelve entry strategies and their variants   188

8.2   Costs of alternative strategies compared with the
      profit norm   191

8.3   Comparative static analysis of the effects of changes in the
      values of the explanatory variables on the choice between
      the three dominant strategies   196

8.4   Comparative static analysis of the effects of changes in the
      values of the explanatory variables on the propensity to
      adopt each possible entry mode   197

9.1   The rhetoric of moral manipulation: Five views of human
      nature compared   216

9.2   Who benefits most from self-control? A comparative
      analysis by type of control   218

9.3   Two dimensions of a socio-economic system:
      Degree of decentralisation and degree of altruism   221

9.4   Winners and losers from the globalisation of capitalism   228

10.1 Two possible errors in strategic choice under uncertainty   248

10.2 Foreign entry strategy set encompassing research,
      deferment and switching, assuming that it is always
      profitable to serve the market   256

10.3 Tabular representation of flows illustrated in Figure 10.6   262

10.4 Structure of location costs for the flows illustrated in
      Figure 10.1 (excluding sunk costs of marketing
      and distribution)   265

10.5	Dominant locational strategies	266
10.6	Alternative contractual arrangements for linking domestic R&D to foreign distribution	270
11.1a	Sequential entry into national markets with a fixed product range	288
11.1b	The innovation diffusion model sequential product innovation with overlapping sequential local entry	288
11.2	The Buckley and Casson model: Sequential product innovation with simultaneous local entry	290

Acknowledgements

Peter J. Buckley and Casson M. *The Future of the Multinational Enterprise* after 30 Years – the Continued Relevance of the Book (unpublished paper, written especially for this volume).

——. 1981. The Optimal Timing of a Foreign Direct Investment. *The Economic Journal*, Vol. 91, No. 361, March, pp. 75–87.

——. 1988. A Theory of Cooperation in International Business, in F. J. Contractor and P. Lorange (eds), *Cooperative Strategies in International Business*. Lexington, MA: Lexington Books, D. C. Heath & Co.

——. 1991. Multinational Enterprises in Less Developed Countries: Cultural and Economic Interactions, in Peter J. Buckley and Jeremy Clegg (eds), *Multinational Enterprises in Less Developed Countries*. London: Macmillan.

——. 1992. Organising for Innovation: The Multinational Enterprise in the Twenty-First Century, in Peter J. Buckley and Mark Casson (eds), *Multinational Enterprises in the World Economy: Essays in Honour of John Dunning*. Aldershot: Edward Elgar.

——. 1996. An Economic Model of International Joint Ventures. *Journal of International Business Studies*, Vol. 27, No. 5, pp. 849–76.

——. 1998. Models of the Multinational Enterprise. *Journal of International Business Studies*, Vol. 29, No.1, pp. 21–44.

——. 1998. Analysing Foreign Market Entry Strategies: Extending the Internalisation Approach. *Journal of International Business Studies*, Vol. 29, No. 3, pp. 539–61.

——. 2001. The Moral Basis of Global Capitalism: Beyond the Eclectic Theory. *International Jounal of the Economics of Business*, Vol. 8, No. 2, July, pp. 303–27.

——. 2001. Strategic Complexity in International Business, in Alan M. Rugman and Thomas L. Brewer (eds), *The Oxford Handbook of International Business*. Oxford: Oxford University Press.

——. 2007. Edith Penrose's Theory of the Growth of the Firm and the strategic management of multinational enterprises. *Management International Review*, Vol. 47, No. 2, pp. 151–73.

1
The Future of the Multinational Enterprise after 30 Years

1.1 Methodology: Multilevel analysis

This book presents the results of more than 30 years of research collaboration. The achievement is quite modest. We began with a problem – how to explain the existence of the multinational enterprise (MNE) and the way that it behaves. We found an answer, in conjunction with other scholars. But the answer to that question only raised new questions. As these questions were answered, so new questions multiplied, and we soon found ourselves with many more questions than we had started with.

Was this progress? Well, it was progress of sorts, because the questions that we are now asking – 30 years on – are much smarter than the ones that we were asking to begin with. They are certainly more tightly focused. Instead of a single general and rather ill-defined question, we now have a set of specific well-defined problems. The big problem has been broken down into little problems that are easier to solve. We know how to tackle the specific problems, but it still takes a long time to work through all of them.

Progress of another kind has been achieved as well. Just as every problem consists of a set of more specific problems, so that problem itself is a special case of an even bigger problem. If we can understand the bigger problem then we can solve lots of different specific problems in a single step. But how do we find out what the bigger problem is? One way is to explore analogies and metaphors. We may be able to find seemingly unrelated problems which are nevertheless fundamentally similar so far as their logic is concerned. By extracting the common logic of these problems, and examining it carefully, each individual problem can be viewed in a new light.

There are, therefore, two distinct problem-solving techniques: one is to break down a problem into smaller and more manageable sub-problems, and the other is to embed the problem within a more general problem of which it is a special case. These two approaches are often regarded as conflicting. Thus 'detail addicts' who focus on the specifics distrust 'big picture thinkers' who go for generality, on the grounds that their speculations go way beyond the available evidence, while big-picture thinkers distrust detail addicts on the grounds that 'they cannot see the wood for the trees'.

In our view, the two approaches are complementary. It pays the problem-solver to go up to a higher level of generality in order to solve the fundamental issues, while at the same time driving down to a greater level of specificity in order to address practical outcomes. Looking at a problem simultaneously at different levels helps to put it into perspective, and thereby makes it easier to solve.

These methodological principles are illustrated by the research reported in this book. In pursuing our research agenda, we have engaged with several distinct but related problems. Each problem has been analysed as a subset of a wider problem. This produced an answer – but an answer of a very general nature. Having solved the problem in general terms, we then resolved the problem into a set of specific subproblems that addressed particular issues arising at the empirical level. Using the solution to the general problem, these specific problems were then addressed in turn.

The main fundamental problems we have addressed are as follows:

The nature of the multinational enterprise (MNE): the reasons why it exists, the functions it performs, and the way it behaves when performing them. This problem is addressed by the theory of internalisation, which explains the boundaries of the MNE; this theory draws upon a general theory of the boundaries of firms in a market economy developed by Ronald Coase (1937).

The determinants of the international division of labour – which explain why multinationals locate different activities in different countries (and avoid some countries altogether). Our account of the international division of labour draws upon the classical analysis of the subject developed by Adam Smith (1776), chiefly in the context of the national economy. We encapsulated some of Smith's key insights into a 'systems view' of international business, based on a schematic model of a global production system.

The rationale for joint ventures; the reasons why joint ventures are chosen in preference to exclusive ownership, or to arm's length agreements. Joint ventures represent a partial form of internalisation. They tend to be popular at times of industrial restructuring, because they allow two or more firms to share access to a key resource without merging their entire business operations. The ambiguity of control involved in a joint venture had led some scholars to question their value. We argued, however, that the costs incurred by ambiguity of control are finite, and can be offset by a range of significant benefits. These benefits are linked to the flexibility of joint ventures, which is particularly valuable at times of global volatility; joint ventures allow firms to make incremental changes in one field of their operations without disturbing their other fields of operation. By embedding the theory of joint ventures within a general theory of the costs and benefits of alternative contractual arrangements, we were able to show that joint ventures are chosen, like any other arrangement, in response to a trade-off between their costs and benefits. These trade-offs are governed by the same factors that affect other internalisation decisions.

The nature of trust in international business transactions. Without some minimal degree of trust, international business activity could not take place. Yet for many years it was implicitly assumed that the requisite level of trust was always available. Trust is costly to engineer, however, and economic efficiency requires that it is engineered in the most appropriate way. The scarcity of trust was most apparent when economic logic began to favour joint ventures; this conferred competitive advantages on groups of firms that were able to trust each other to a high degree. Our analysis of trust drew upon general principles of rational action sociology, and were inspired partly by the work of Knight (1935). Trust can be engineered through law or through society, or some combination of the two; it also needs to be supported by reputation. The level of trust is determined both by the demand for trust – as reflected in the types of business organisation that need support – and the supply of trust, as determined by wider social, cultural and institutional factors in the societies in which business activity is embedded. The market in trust encourages business structures to evolve in ways that build on existing legal systems and social networks, whilst at the same time legal systems and social networks evolve to better support existing business structures. Due to global volatility, business, law and society are constantly changing: international business is affected by new technologies, international law by political integration and international society by changes in cultural values, as disseminated through jet travel, television and the Internet. In response to these changes, the boundaries of legal systems and the boundaries of social networks are redrawn, as are the boundaries of firms themselves. With suitable modification, the theory of internalisation can explain these shifting boundaries. The analysis of change in the entire global system is thereby placed on a single coherent footing with a generalised theory of internalisation playing a central role. The systematic exploration of the links between business, law and society in an international context connects the research reported in this book with our research agenda for the future.

We have not pursued our research agenda single-handed, of course. In tackling the bigger problems we were able to 'stand on the shoulders of the giants' – writers who have addressed big issues that transcend the specific issues in international business that have been the focus of our work. As already indicated, the giants we have in mind include not only the eighteenth-century economist Adam Smith (1776) but also the twentieth-century economists Ronald Coase (1937), Friedrich Hayek (1937, 1945), Frank Knight (1921, 1935) and George Richardson (1960). It is interesting to note that all of these economists took a philosophical stance, and in the cases of Smith and Hayek actually contributed to philosophy as well; in addition, Knight contributed to sociology, and Coase to legal studies. We hesitate to include any of our contemporaries in a list of intellectual giants, in case it should 'go to their heads', but they will know who they are (or at least they will think that they know who they are, and should therefore be content).

We have also received a lot of support in developing specific applications of the theory. Our professional colleagues in the Academy of International Business have been a great help – most particularly the late John Dunning, who was a mine of useful information on all aspects of international business, and gave us his support and patronage throughout our careers. We also owe a great debt to our many doctoral students – past and present – who have worked on various aspects of the topics covered in this book. The papers reprinted here are purely those that we wrote with each other, and do not include the papers that we have published with our research students alone.

1.2 The nature of the multinational enterprise

By definition, an MNE owns and controls activities in two or more different countries. It may, for example, develop a product in one country, produce it in a second country and sell it in a third one. Such an MNE will have a research subsidiary in the first country, a production subsidiary in the second country and a sales subsidiary in the third country. It may be headquartered in any one of these countries – or in some other country altogether, for that matter. It owns and controls interdependent activities located in different countries, linked by flows of goods, services and know-how, and coordinated by management.

When economists first began to look seriously at the MNE in the early 1960s, they naturally focused on those aspects of the MNE to which existing theory drew their attention. The dominant theory in international economics at the time was Heckscher-Ohlin trade theory. According to this theory, each country had a fixed endowment of labour and capital, and specialised in producing a mix of products that made the best possible use of its endowments. Each country had access to the same technologies. Countries with relatively large endowments of labour specialised in producing labour-intensive products, while countries with large endowments of capital specialised in producing capital-intensive products. Each country exported the products in which it specialised. There was no room in this theory for the MNE; it was purely and simply a theory of trade.

The natural way to introduce MNEs appeared to be to relax the assumption that each country had a fixed endowment of capital. MNEs would then emerge as conduits of capital flow between countries. Capital would flow from countries with a low rate of return on capital to countries with a higher rate of return on capital, and MNEs would profit from the increase in the rate of return. The problem was that, on balance, capital flows involving MNEs flowed in exactly the opposite way – from countries with a high rate of return (such as the US) to countries with a low rate of return (such as the UK). A further complication was that capital flowed between countries in both directions at once. This conflict with the evidence was fatal to the theory.

Indeed, on reflection the theory made little sense anyway, as capital could be transferred between countries very easily by the purchase and sale of bonds in the international capital markets. There was no need to route capital transfers through MNEs – especially once post-war capital exchange controls had been abolished. In modern parlance, the capital flow theory had confused indirect (or portfolio) investment with direct investments made by MNEs.

Having ruled out capital as the explanatory factor, economists turned to technology. By the 1960s a number of investigators had identified a 'technology gap' between the US and other countries. Other countries needed to catch up with the US and close this gap, it was said, but they were finding it difficult to do so. This assumption of a technology gap clearly conflicted with the assumptions of Heckscher-Ohlin trade theory. Furthermore, economists who believed in perfect markets could not believe that a technology gap could persist because enormous profits could be made by closing it. In popular terminology, closing the gap looked like a 'free lunch'.

Two main lines of explanation were possible. The first was that the technology was country-specific, and so could not be transferred; US technology could only be used in conjunction with local US resources, such as abundant land or natural resources, or labour with special skills. The other was that the market in technology was imperfect. The intervention of the MNE could then be seen as a device for improving the efficiency of the market in technology. But how could a firm be seen as making a market more perfect than an existing market itself?

Although the idea that an MNE could improve upon a free market seemed somewhat counterintuitive to begin with, on reflection it made a lot of sense. It could explain other apparent anomalies too. Returning to our earlier description of the interrelated activities carried out by an MNE, it might well be asked why these different activities located in different countries needed to be coordinated by a firm. Why not use Adam Smith's 'invisible hand' to coordinate these activities through impersonal markets? Why is the 'visible hand' of management preferred to the 'invisible hand' of the market?

The argument for using market forces rather than management is reinforced by another consideration, namely that the knowledge required for successful coordination is often local. Successful research depends upon recruiting the right sort of researchers – and selecting the right researchers from the right local universities requires local knowledge. Successful production depends upon choosing an appropriate location for a plant – near to airports, say, or harbours, or centres of population; this again requires local knowledge. Marketing requires knowledge of local tastes and customs. How can someone sitting in the headquarters of an MNE possibly have the local knowledge required to make all of these decisions? They can delegate the decisions to subsidiary managers, of course; but how can they motivate the subsidiary manager to take the right decision when it is the headquarters that 'takes the rap' from the shareholders when things go wrong? Why not get independent local entrepreneurs to take these decisions: licence technology from an independent research laboratory with local knowledge of the first country, subcontract production to a plant owned by someone with local knowledge of the second country and franchise the marketing of finished product to an independent distributor with local knowledge of the third country? By playing off different entrepreneurs against each other, their services can be obtained at competitive rates. Production can be undertaken by the cheapest subcontractor, for example, and distribution undertaken by the cheapest distributor. These solutions may be cheaper than what could be achieved using a wholly owned plant or a wholly owned distribution facility.

This general line of reasoning suggested that the answer to specific questions about the technology gap and about the linkages within an MNE were embedded in the answer to a much wider question concerned with the fundamental rationale for the existence of the MNE. To construct a general rationale for the MNE, however, it was unnecessary to start from scratch. For the rationale of the MNE was in turn embedded in an even wider question, namely the rationale of the firm itself, and this was a question that had exercised Ronald Coase in the 1930s.

Coase had noticed that in lectures on price theory markets were said to coordinate the economy and in lectures on business studies managers were said to coordinate the economy. Furthermore, he might have added, in lectures on socialism, planners were said to coordinate the economy. There seemed to be 'overkill' where coordination was concerned. Coase concluded that, given the existence of alternative coordination mechanisms, economic principles suggested that the cheapest form of coordination would be selected in any given circumstance (Coase, 1937). In arriving at this verdict, he assumed that the economy was basically market-driven, and that firms would only arise when managerial coordination provided itself superior to the market. In a similar vein, as Cheung (1962) later argued, government would only emerge in a free society when state planning provided better coordination than either markets or private firms.

In Coase's world, all coordination mechanisms, including markets, are imperfect, but some are more imperfect than others. We used this idea to explain the emergence of the MNE. We began by noting that some markets are more prone to imperfections than others. For a variety of reasons, the market in technology was likely to be highly imperfect. To begin with, property rights in information were insecure. Although some inventions could attract patent protection, it was often possible for imitators to 'invent around' a patent. Under these circumstances, it was often better for an inventor not to register a patent in order to avoid drawing attention to his idea, but to exploit it as a trade secret instead. This would involve exploiting the technology itself. This was exactly what MNEs did when they invested overseas in order to exploit their inventions. Secondly, the cost of managing the transfer of technology overseas would discourage some firms from investing abroad; they would just exploit their invention at home instead; this explained the existence of the technology gap. Thus the theory was consistent with the evidence both that MNE were most common in high technology industries and that, despite the activities of MNEs there was still a residual technology gap in certain industries.

Because markets do not work properly, the cost of coordinating activities within the firm through the use of management may be lower than the costs of coordinating them using external markets. Under these circumstances, it pays to bring interdependent activities under common ownership and control. If these activities happen to be located in different countries then the integration of activities within a single firm creates an MNE.

Once market imperfections had been identified as the fundamental issue, it became clear that they could have significant ramifications for theory as a whole. There was no reason why such imperfections should be confined to the market in technology. They could, in principle, affect any market.

Markets for final products are difficult for firms to internalise, however. Final products are products supplied to households or to government, and firms are not in a position to take over households or government. It is, however possible for households and government to take over firms, or simply to organise their production in-house; in the case of households this is exemplified by the 'do-it-yourself' principle.

So far as firms were concerned, therefore, the main implications of internalisation concerned intermediate products. These are products that one business supplies to another. Technology is an intermediate product, as described above, because it is transferred from one business activity – namely R&D – to another – production. But there are many other intermediate products in international business; they include agricultural products supplied to food processors, raw materials extracted in mines and supplied to refiners and fabricators, components supplied to an assembly plant and a vast range of specialised business and consulting services, often supplied by small firms to large ones.

They also include finished products waiting to be passed on for marketing and distribution.

Many of these intermediate product markets suffer from problems relating to quality control. The quality of the technology may be uncertain so far as other firms are concerned – it may not be as good as the inventor claims. In order to be certain of the quality, it would be necessary for the user to have developed the technology themselves. Likewise with production and distribution. Customers may blame the distributor for supplying defective product when in fact the defect occurred in production; conversely, perfectly good product may be ruined by a distributor who fails to handle it properly. In each case one party suffers because of mistakes made by the other. If each party believes that the other will bear the cost of their deficiencies then they will have little incentive to take care. The same problem arises when they believe that if they do take care their efforts may be undermined. These imperfections in intermediate product markets explain why interdependent activities of many different descriptions may be encompassed by an MNE. In our earlier example, the MNE internalised not only the transfer of technology between R&D and production, but also the consignment of product from production to distribution, and as a result three different types of activity were encompassed by the firm.

Once the general problem of the existence of the MNE had been resolved, lots of different specific issues quickly fell into place. These specific issues included the timing of international expansion, the industries in which MNEs produced, the countries in which they were headquartered and the countries in which they invested.

A good example of a specific question is why the number of MNEs increased so dramatically after World War II. If there were substantial gains from internal coordination, why were MNEs not ubiquitous from the outset? The answer is that the gains from internalisation are greatest in technology transfer, as noted above, and that after World War II opportunities for technology transfer increased dramatically. This was because many of the new technologies created through defence-related research turned out to have civilian applications. In addition, mass-production consumer good technologies had been perfected in the US during the interwar period and were now sufficiently well codified to be transferred overseas. Because the new technologies had potentially global application, production plants were established in many different parts of the world, and MNEs proliferated as a result.

MNEs did not invest in all countries, however; and they invested much more heavily in some countries than in others. Countries in

Western Europe were very popular with MNEs, whereas others – particularly in Africa – were not. Technology was harder to transfer to some countries because their education system was not so good – it was difficult to recruit workers who could absorb technology quickly. Political risks in postcolonial societies meant that factories were prone to nationalisation or expropriation. In some Asian countries protection for patents was weak, and so on.

The importance of these different factors depended on the industry in which the MNE was engaged and the nature of the activity in which it planned to invest. When an MNE was planning to distribute its product to local consumers, the size of the market and the local standard of living were important factors. When an MNE was planning to serve a wider market, embracing neighbouring countries, then access to a local transport hub was important. When the MNE was planning a large export-oriented production plant then cheap labour was important, and so on.

1.3   The international division of labour in a global economy

As the study of MNEs has progressed, so new questions have continued to arise, but when these questions are very specific they are usually fairly straightforward to address. Every so often, however, a new question has arisen which is not so easy to deal with.

In the 1980s evidence began to suggest that some MNEs were evolving systematically into global firms. Instead of serving just a selected set of overseas markets, they were beginning to serve all the markets to which foreign governments permitted access. Some writers therefore asserted that the expansion of MNEs was the cause of globalisation. Others argued that the reverse was the case, and that the increasing reach of MNEs was a consequence, and not a cause, of globalisation; globalisation, they suggested, was a wider phenomenon than the growth of MNEs. Others 'hedged their bets', and claimed that globalisation and MNEs were 'co-evolving'.

Evidence also showed that during the early 1980s many mature MNEs had begun to restructure their operations. They acquired new facilities, often through mergers and acquisitions, and divested themselves of other activities – sometimes by selling them to rival firms. How were these changes to be explained and why they were occurring at this time? What was the link, if any, between globalisation and restructuring?

Because a number of changes were occurring simultaneously, there was plenty of scope for confusion. Unfortunately, little formal modelling was done in the international business literature, and so much of the discussion remained opaque. We therefore developed a 'systems view' of international business which was designed to provide greater clarity on these issues. We visualised a world production system, based on a configuration of facilities, including R&D laboratories, production plants and distribution warehouses, distributed across the world, and serving a range of different industries. Under a hypothetical socialist world system, all these facilities would be owned by a single world superstate. Under the kind of free-market capitalism that characterises modern globalisation, these facilities are owned instead by a range of different firms – mostly private, but some owned by individual nation states. Because the world is partitioned into separate states, many of these firms are MNEs because the facilities they own are based in different countries.

Internalisation theory was then applied to explain why certain clusters of related facilities were owned by the same firm. Different clusters, owned by different firms would interface through external markets where different firms would trade with each other.

A key insight of this systems view was that the internalisation decisions are interdependent. Furthermore, they are interdependent in two distinct ways.

Firstly, firms are typically involved in multiple internalisation decisions. These decisions are interdependent; the outcome of one decision cannot be fully understood without reference to other decisions. Consider, for example, the MNE described at the outset, which operates three facilities – R&D, production and marketing. Internalising one linkage, say between R&D and production, involves the firm in the ownership of two facilities, but internalising a second linkage – say between production and marketing – automatically internalises a third – between marketing and R&D. While acquiring a second facility internalises only one linkage, acquiring a third facility internalises two. This demonstrates that internalisation decisions taken as part of a restructuring operation need to be analysed holistically. Focusing exclusively on a single linkage, such as the link from R&D to production, rather than the full set of linkages, can create a misleading picture.

The second interdependency concerns the internalisation decisions of different firms. From a systems perspective, a facility that is wholly owned by one firm cannot be simultaneously wholly owned by another firm, because the principle of private property does not permit this. As a consequence, if one firm internalises a linkage to a given facility then other firms cannot internalise linkages to that facility because to do so they would have to own it as well. They may have linkages to it – but only external ones. Thus the internalisation decisions of different firms are interdependent when they compete to internalise linkages to the same facility.

Early writers on international business ignored this interdependency because they implicitly assumed that MNEs always invested in greenfield facilities. They ignored the fact that it is not always economic to add to capacity in an industry when expanding overseas, and that for this reason it is sometimes better to make acquisitions instead. When greenfield expansion is uneconomic, firms can gain strategic advantage by being the first to acquire a target facility. A pre-emptive acquisition benefits themselves and disadvantages their rivals at the same time. Such pre-emption is only possible when greenfield investment is not an option for rival firms.

Having set out the systems view, we then examined how the forces of globalisation shaped the world production system. Following the lead of other economists, we argued that globalisation arose from a combination of exogenous factors, the most important of which were policy changes and technological improvements in international transport and communications.

Abolition of exchange controls and the deregulation of domestic capital markets encouraged international capital flows, making it easier for MNEs to borrow in one country in order to finance investment in another. Relaxation of border controls promoted migration and gave MNEs greater freedom to post employees overseas. Most importantly, multilateral tariff reductions negotiated under UN auspices reduced the effective protection of manufacturing and encouraged the concentration of assembly in cheap labour locations. Advances in transport reduced the cost of shipping both intermediate and final products, while advances in communications made it easier to coordinate trade flows – whether internal or external to the firm. Social changes were important too, as explained in more detail below. As these factors changed, so the shape of the world production system changed as well. This induced changes in internalisation, which altered the boundaries of firms.

Some exogenous changes directly affected internalisation decisions. The spread of international manufacturing standards and the strengthening of intellectual property rights improved the performance of external markets relative to internal markets and led to a significant growth in international licensing, franchising and subcontracting. These were all policies that had been considered very risky in the 1960s.

This analysis showed how changes in the exogenous drivers of globalisation simultaneously affected the structure of the world production system and its degree of internalisation. It thereby explained both the growth and the restructuring of MNEs. It provided a logically coherent interpretation of the changing structure of the international business system from the early post-war period down to the end of the century.

According to our interpretation, the traditional high-technology MNE of the 1960s had a relatively simple structure. R&D was conducted in the home country, under the watchful eye of headquarters, and the technology generated was then diffused internally to production plants in each market. Each major market had its own production plant that used the technology in the same way, with only minor adaptations to suit local conditions. Exports from these plants were usually destined for smaller neighbouring countries. Tariffs on finished products were generally higher than on intermediate products such as components, and finished products were often bulkier and difficult to transport as well. As a result, there was a high level of 'effective protection' for assembly operations, and trade by MNEs was mainly confined to key components exported from the home country to foreign assembly plants.

By the early 1980s, all this was changing due to the exogenous factors described above. The consequent rationalisation of international production led to the run-down or closure of assembly operations in some of the larger and richer countries. With fewer assembly plants, the new generation of plants exported, on average, a much higher proportion of their output. These new generation plants helped to drive economic development in the 'newly industrialising countries'. Local firms in these countries began to take on component production too. South East Asia was particularly attractive to MNEs because of its good maritime links and a well-educated non-unionised workforce with a strong work ethic. Mass production of precision components migrated from MNE home countries to specialised overseas plants.

Strategic interactions between restructuring firms help to explain some of the apparent anomalies in international business behaviour at this time – such as 'follow the leader' investments. Business strategy in mature industries became more concerned with rationalising existing capacity than with building new capacity, and therefore favoured mergers and acquisitions rather than greenfield investments. The globalisation of capital markets facilitated the financing of large international mergers and acquisitions. Races therefore developed to acquire strategic facilities in newly liberalised markets, with firms acting defensively in order to avoid being locked out once all the target firms had been acquired.

During the 1980s a new elite of 'systems integration' or 'flagship' firms emerged in many industries. These firms expanded rapidly through merger and acquisition, building global procurement and distribution networks. These networks linked the integrator to an international supply chain of licensees and subcontractors on the one hand, and a group of distributors and resellers on the other. Sometimes described as 'network' firms, or as being 'hollowed out', these firms ruthlessly exploited the profit opportunities for restructuring created by globalisation. The scope of their operations, and their successful performance, is well explained by the systems view.

1.4   Joint ventures

The restructuring of the 1980s involved extensive use of joint ventures. Two or more firms would come together to share the equity in some facility. In some cases this would be a new facility, but in many cases it would be an existing facility acquired from another firm. An intriguing case arose when one of the joint venture partners was the previous owner of the facility. Many of the flagship firms described below had entire networks of joint ventures, some of which undertook core activities including R&D.

From the standpoint of internalisation theory, a joint venture is simply one of several institutional options for coordinating interdependent activities. It is a form of non-exclusive internalisation. When two firms jointly own a facility they can both establish internal linkages with it. They do not need to replicate the facility in order for them both to own it. All they need to sacrifice are the benefits of exclusive internalisation, which would allow them to deny all other firms access to the facility.

Non-exclusive internalisation is particularly important in the circumstances discussed above, in which greenfield investment is not an option and there are only a small number of existing facilities that can be acquired. Instead of investing prematurely in order to pre-empt their rival, two firms can acquire a joint stake in the target facility.

To some international business scholars in the 1980s, however, joint ventures looked like a recipe for disaster. At the heart of a joint venture there appeared to be an ambiguity over control – particularly in a 50:50 joint venture where, in principle, an enduring stalemate between the owners could emerge. To other scholars, however, the joint venture was an innovative response to new circumstances. As a new phenomenon, it was suggested that an entirely new theory was required to address it.

In fact, joint ventures were not a new phenomenon in the 1980s. Prior to the spread of joint stock company organisation in the nineteenth century, most medium-sized businesses were organised as partnerships, and had exactly the same ambiguity of control. Indeed, a joint stock company is itself a partnership between multiple shareholders. If anything was new about the 1980s joint venture, it was that the partners were not private individuals but were joint stock firms.

Even here, however, there were plenty of historical precedents. In the nineteenth century independent firms often partnered each other in consortia when bidding for large projects. It was a method of combining the complementary skills of the partner firms. These nineteenth century joint ventures were, in many respects, clear antecedents of modern joint ventures. Like many modern joint ventures, they were based on joint projects with definite completion dates, and were dissolved once the project was completed. The logic of the venture was to internalise the flow of knowledge from the partner firms that was to be synthesised in the implementation of the project. Once the relevant knowledge had been pooled, there was no further logic to internalisation, and so the joint venture could be dissolved.

There are clearly strategic risks in pooling knowledge in this way, however, as knowledge could leak out through the joint venture to rival firms. Internalisation theory predicts that joint ventures will tend to involve non-rival firms, for example, firms from different industries, or from different subsectors of the same industry. Where the firms are from the same industry, it is possible that one firm may be entering a particular sub-sector while its partner is planning to leave, so that the role of the joint venture is to transfer the technology to the entrant on terms satisfactory to both partners. For example, one partner may be diversifying into the sub-sector as part of a restructuring programme, while the other may be moving out in order to concentrate on areas of greater strength.

Once the basic logic of the joint venture process is understood, the analysis can be refined by examining other aspects of the situation. Joint ventures can also be a useful way of sharing the capital costs involved in the construction or acquisition of a new facility. A firm that invests in several joint ventures spreads its risks more effectively than a firm that puts all its resources into a single wholly owned venture. Although it is not the primary function of a firm to diversify its risks – since shareholders are better placed to diversify risks using investment funds – it can be a useful way for a firm to reduce the risk of bankruptcy, and for salaried managers to reduce the risk of losing their jobs as a result of a hostile takeover.

Joint ventures can also be used as a 'front' for collusion between rival firms. Anti-trust agencies and competition regulators police pricing behaviour in industries with a small number of firms in order to control informal or secret cartels. By forming a joint venture, rival firms can acquire a legitimate reason for cooperation, which may be extended from joint venture management to cartelised price-fixing.

From the standpoint of internalisation theory, therefore, a joint venture is an option that is always 'on the table'. Whether it is chosen depends upon whether there is another option that is more attractive. There is an entire spectrum of possible arrangements, with exclusive ownership at one extreme, arm's-length contracts at the other, and joint ventures and other arrangements, such as informal long-term contracts, in the middle. Which of these arrangements is chosen will depend upon which appears most attractive under the circumstances prevailing at the time.

The advantage of joint ventures tends to be greatest during periods of industrial restructuring because it is then that firms need to buy in to existing facilities in competition with other firms. Restructuring often occurs at times of adversity, when risks are high and balance sheets are weak, so that the advantages of risk sharing are also high. At times of adversity prices are often low due to excess capacity, and this encourages cartelisation to combat price warfare.

Joint ventures are useful when there are strict limitations on horizontal mergers. In principle, the ambiguity of control could be eliminated by the two partner firms merging before they acquired control of the target facility. The target facility would then be owned by a single firm from the outset. Even if horizontal mergers are permitted, however, this is not necessarily the best solution. Quite apart from conflict in negotiating the terms of the merger, consistent application of the horizontal merger principle would soon lead to industry domination by a handful of unmanageable giant firms.

While the advantages of joint ventures tended to be understated, the cost of joint ventures tended to be overstated, thereby reinforcing the analytical bias. Although ambiguity of control is a genuine problem, it can be mitigated in a number of ways. Firstly, the partners can agree to delegate day-to-day responsibilities to an independent manager. Although there may be conflict over his appointment, the manager may be able to retain his independence so long as the joint venture goes well. Secondly, the partners may have external sanctions against each other. They may be partners in similar ventures elsewhere. In any case, the joint venture is unlikely to be the only connection between them; they may compete for the same customers, or for the same employees, and can initiate reprisals by initiating a price war or headhunting key employees. Thirdly, each firm is likely to have a reputation to protect. Joint venture partners are often high-profile firms with strong brands. Gaining a bad reputation through a dispute with a partner may damage the prospects of making further partnerships with other firms. Put another way, a reputation for being a good joint venture partner can be a considerable competitive advantage under volatile business conditions.

1.5   Communication and trust

The problems created by ambiguity of control in a joint venture are greatest when communication between the partners is poor and trust is low. Communication problems caused by language differences may mean, in an extreme case, that the two parties cannot understand each other at all. Potentially more problematic, however, is the case where the two parties think that they understand each other but in fact do not. Such misunderstandings are often cultural rather than purely linguistic – the same word may have different meanings because it carries different connotations. It is often asserted, on this basis, that joint ventures are more likely to be successful when the partner firms share a common culture; this may refer either to the national culture of the country in which the headquarters is situated, or to corporate culture, or a combination of the two.

Even if two parties understand each other, they may not believe each other. This is a question of trust. Two parties trust each other when they each believe what the other says and are confident that they will act in an acceptable way. Trust is of economic value only when it is warranted; that is, the expectations on which it is based are valid. Unwarranted trust often leads to a person being cheated. Warranted mutual trust represents an economic equilibrium; each party's expectations are fulfilled by the other party and so neither party sees any need to change their behaviour. Unwarranted trust represents a disequilibrium because a person who is cheated will normally learn from their mistake and change their behaviour.

Trust has two major dimensions: competence and integrity. A person may be honest when they negotiate a deal, but may lack the competence to deliver. This incompetence may be due to a lack of technical skills, or simply due to the fact that they do not have the backing they require – they may not have the necessary authority to commit their firm, or their firm may not have the backing of shareholders and banks that is required to finance a deal. Reputation for competence is therefore important in setting up a joint venture.

Honesty is an ethical issue, concerning whether someone is deliberately trying to mislead the other party. In a free market economy it is relatively easy to lure people into transactions with the deliberate aim of cheating them. In some cases, this involves lying to them, but in many cases it does not. It simply involves supplying partial information and encouraging people to fill up the gaps for themselves in a particular way. This involves understanding the culture of the other party, in order to anticipate the assumptions that they will make in the absence of information to the contrary. Since deals such as joint ventures require a large amount of information to be exchanged, the problem of partial information is very real, and this makes it easy for firms to be misled. The risk of being misled is potentially greater when the partner shares the same culture, because they will know the assumptions that will be made in response to partial information. Thus while the risks of misunderstanding are potentially greater with cross-cultural joint ventures, the risks of being cheated are potentially greater where there is cultural similarity.

Where two firms share the same culture, the nature of this culture will also influence joint venture success. This is because some cultures discourage cheating more than others. Some cultures encourage a long-run view that cheating will sooner or later be punished, while others encourage a short-term view that cheating is worthwhile whenever it is possible to 'get away with it'. Some cultures encourage an 'insider-outsider' view, in which it is wrong to cheat insiders but acceptable to cheat outsiders, whereas other cultures encourage a universal view that does not discriminate but takes the same attitude to all.

Unfortunately, recent literature has tended to confuse issues of communication and issues of trust. The consequence has been a rather sterile debate about the role of opportunism in transaction cost theory, which centres on whether people are naturally cheats and whether all contractual problems ultimately stem from this. The assumption that cheating is natural had little to do with Coase's original insights into the boundaries of the firm. The rigorous application of internalisation theory shows that while cheating often occurs, it is not inevitable, and that while contractual problems are aggravated by cheating, cheating is not the only cause of them by any means.

Much of the recent literature in the 'new institutional economics' emphasises the rule of law in sustaining trust. The law builds 'institutional trust' – in contrast to 'personal trust' – which is based on the qualities of individual people and is generated by the social system. Much of the literature on arm's-length contracts emphasises the importance of institutional trust while the literature on joint ventures stresses the importance of personal trust instead. Personal trust is important in joint ventures because the ambiguity of control restricts recourse to the legal system for the settlement of disputes.

Personal trust is of wide significance because the costs of the legal system are so high. In any case, the effectiveness of legal institutions is limited by the personal qualities of legal professionals; thus if judges are corrupt the party with the deepest pockets usually wins the case.

While the importance of communication and trust came to the fore in international business studies through the study of joint ventures, issues of communication and trust are fundamental to all international business arrangements. Misunderstandings can arise, and cheating can occur, in any situation. But the insights into trust derived from the study of joint ventures have not been systematically applied to other international business arrangements. Our most recent work has attempted to remedy this defect.

To begin with, it was important to recognise that the global production system is embedded not only in a set of national legal systems but in a set of social systems too. These social systems facilitate communication and engineer trust, and thereby contribute to the coordination of the global production system. They can support the legal system, and where the rule of law is absent they can replace it.

Social systems have their faults, however. The existence of rival social systems can impair coordination; different social groups may standardise internal communications on different languages and may engineer internal trust by creating suspicion of rival groups. Nevertheless those new institutional economists who analyse institutions exclusively in terms of the law, and portray society as a negative factor that creates and sustains ethnic divisions, misrepresent the situation. For society is the foundation of law; law evolved from society, and not society from the law. Furthermore, law remains largely segmented by national boundaries, while many modern social movements transcend these boundaries, as did religious movements before them. Thus society remains an important instrument for reducing the costs of coordination by performing those functions that the law can only perform at a very great expense.

In principle, the concepts of internalisation theory can be used to explain the boundaries of social groups in much the same way as it can be used to explain the boundaries of firms. People join social groups because of the benefits they confer. Although everyone is born into a particular social group – namely their family and its local community – they can renegotiate their affiliations once they become adolescent or adult. In a free society they can relocate, choose a job that appeals to their sense of vocation and marry someone of their own choice. It is at this stage of the group affiliation process that internalisation factors come into play.

Two main types of social group may be distinguished; one of which is the analogue of a firm and the other an analogue of the market. The analogue of the firm is the formal group with an organisational structure. It is typically configured as a membership organisation. The analogue of the market is an informal group that meets at a one-off social event. The analogies are not exact, however, because, for obvious reasons, the relations promoted by social groups are more 'personal' than the relatively impersonal relations promoted by markets and firms.

Membership of a group normally involves a commitment of some kind – the minimum commitment usually being one year's subscription, with renewal of membership being expected. Attendance at a one-off event requires less commitment, although where such events are organised for 'social networking' purposes, there is often an expectation that participants will make commitments later once they have identified a suitable partner. The social event helps to reduce the risk of committing to an inappropriate partner.

People who join membership organisations are generally making a commitment to a partnership with many other people – namely all the other members of the organisation. Each person's commitment is important to the others because the performance of the group is directly related to the number of members and the effort that they commit to the group. In most cases performance is related to the average performance of individual members, although in some cases it may depend upon the person who is potentially the 'weakest link'. Members are expected to monitor, encourage and support each other, in order to raise other members' performance as well as their own. In this respect, the membership organisation resembles a firm because teamwork is key to success, although it differs from the firm in that it is members rather than shareholders that control it.

By contrast people who attend one-off networking events are often looking for a single partner. The role of the event is to introduce prospective partners to each other. In most cases the partners come from different groups – buyers and sellers, entrepreneurs and venture capitalists, men and women – although this is not invariably the case.

The organiser adds value by advertising a meeting point, providing hospitality, and in many cases by vetting the invitation or attendance list to exclude incompetent or untrustworthy people. To ensure accurate and impartial vetting, the organiser requires a high reputation.

Networking events are extremely useful for businesses contemplating complex transactions, which may include licensing, franchising, venture capital financing, or joint venture partnerships as discussed above. Networking events are like external markets in that they match up complementary pairs of people or firms. The partners may be interpreted, broadly, as the buyers and sellers of a particular type of product. Like markets, different networking events tend to focus on different types of product. Networking events, however, emphasise personal contact and intense communication, whereas conventional markets tend to emphasise impersonal contact and a minimal level of communication that is just sufficient to facilitate comparison of price.

Membership organisations tend to emerge whenever there are substantial benefits from regular meetings between the same set of people. By socialising with people who have similar leisure interests, for example, the members of a club can share their enthusiasm with others and collaborate on projects of mutual interest. People can also combine socially to promote a political agenda by joining a political party. They can derive emotional benefits from collective membership of churches and other religious organisations. Employees can also benefit from socialising with colleagues, and firms may sponsor such activity because it raises performance by improving internal communication and trust.

Many social organisations – whether formal or informal – are non-profit. This principle prevents the emergence of a specialised group of profit-taking members whose interests may conflict with others. It therefore provides assurance to members or participants that the motives of others are not purely venal. Non-profit organisations also tend to be inclusive; for example, the leader is recruited from and elected by the entire membership body, rather than from a specialised group of shareholders, as in the case of a private firm. This increases trust even further; by contrast, distrust within a private firm can be heightened by the dominance of absentee shareholders who are perceived as profit-claimants interested purely in short-term dividends or speculative capital gains.

Because of the ambiguity of social relationships within a private firm, it is useful for firms to strengthen internal cohesion by freeriding as much as possible on the 'social capital' provided by other groups. Thus individual firms may recruit employees from particular educational institutions, local communities, or ethnic groups. In this respect, the boundaries of firms may map onto social boundaries, as firms give preference to members of certain social groups as consumers, suppliers, or employees.

Social groups are in competition with each other too. Other things being equal, people will prefer to affiliate with groups in which other members may be useful to them in building their business or developing their career. There is a tendency, therefore, for social groups to adapt to meeting the needs of business because this helps to attract new members and fund the growth of the organisation.

As an illustration of these points, consider the relations between major MNEs and major business schools. Many MNEs recruit from a limited range of schools – even though they recruit managers of many different nationalities. Recruiting from a limited number of schools can improve internal communication and promote cohesion within the management team. Many business schools are educational charities – and many of those that are not charitable are still non-profit. They are expected to have a distinctive ethos, or to be part of a family of schools that shares such an ethos. Alumni networks strengthen the trust between fellow-graduates of the school. Nevertheless the schools are in competition with other business schools for student recruitment, and they must recognise that students join not only for the ethos but also for the contribution to their career. Thus while the MNEs adapt their hiring to the quality and availability of business schools with the appropriate ethos, so schools adapt their curricula, and to some extent their ethos, to the changing requirements of MNEs.

The same point can be made about the legal system. Some MNEs are headquartered in countries whose legal principles are Roman in origin, others in countries with Anglo-Saxon origins, and so on. As a consequence, MNEs have an incentive to concentrate their activities in countries with a common legal system, although in practice the effects of this have been mitigated by the emergence of specialised financial centres through which transactions can be routed in order to maintain them under a single jurisdiction. Despite the proliferation of international treaties in the post-war world, national legal systems have converged to only a limited extent.

Social systems, by contrast, have tended to globalise and converge. Professional associations are a case in point, with international associations taking over from national associations, or a national association globalising to take on an international role. As noted earlier, these changes are clearly explained by technological advances such as jet travel and the Internet. In this respect, the emphasis of new institutional economists on law rather than society is particularly misleading when studying the dynamics of change in international business, as it directs attention away from the most significant sources of change.

The religious and moral systems that guide societies have also changed. Loosely speaking, there is much less respect for traditional authority than before World War II, and less commitment to moral self-restraint; correspondingly, there is more emphasis on individualism, self-expression and the competitive pursuit of self-interest. These changes have encouraged able people to embark on careers in private business, to speculate financially, and generally to exploit the many business opportunities available in the post-war era. The downside is that it has become more difficult to know whom to trust, and this has led employers to place greater reliance on formal control procedures – inflexible bureaucratic systems that are poorly adapted to decision making in volatile economic environments such as those that prevail today.

When we first developed the systems view set out above, we had few qualms about assuming that the basic drivers of globalisation were exogenous. In reflecting on our recent work, however, it has become clear that this approach is not really tenable. The exogeneity of social, political and legal factors can certainly be justified as a simplifying assumption that is necessary in order to understand the changing configuration of the international business system at a particular time, but it is hard to justify when undertaking long-period analysis. In the long run the performance of the international business system has cultural as well as economic consequences which feed back to shape the social, political and legal environment in which the international business system operates. As indicated above, the principle of internalisation can help to address this issue, by analysing the boundaries of social, political and legal institutions, but integrating the results of this analysis with the analysis of the international business system itself is not an easy task. We expect to be preoccupied with this problem for some little time to come. This is therefore a good time to publish the present book, because our next joint paper may take somewhat longer to write than most of the others.

1.6   Conclusion

The approach to problem solving outlined above generates a progressive research agenda. This agenda has kept us busy with a succession of intriguing problems since we first entered the field over 30 years ago. A key point about this agenda is that each stage builds on what has been learnt at the previous stage. If mistakes have been made at earlier stages then sooner or later they will come to light. Logical inconsistencies will emerge, or evidence will appear that contradicts the theory. This feedback loop means that theory development can progress steadily, with the risk of diverging down 'blind alleys' being kept to a minimum.

The careful reader of the following chapters will note that we have changed our opinions on a number of issues as we have progressed. We have not changed our views on fundamental issues, however, because we have seen no need to do so. In some respects, the theory of internalisation is quite unusual as a social science theory in the sense that it really works. There is no need to disguise weaknesses, or obfuscate difficulties; weaknesses can be acknowledged because they can be remedied, and difficulties can be recognised because they can be overcome. Failing systems of thought often degenerate through steady attrition; qualifications and complexities are added to salvage the system until it becomes more complicated than the phenomena it claims to describe, and it no longer has any heuristic value. Internalisation theory, by contrast, has, in our judgement, retained its vitality. It is as incisive today as it was when first put forward by Ronald Coase.

This book is meant for readers who are interested, like we are, in problem-solving, and wish to build on the achievements of the past in order to tackle the new issues that emerge as the research frontier advances. Although this book reprints articles from previous decades, we have not prepared it because we like going over old ground, but because we believe that this earlier work provides foundations upon which future research can be built. It is as a resource for the future, and not as a celebration of the past, that this book is meant to serve.

References

Cheung, S. N. S. 1983. The Contractual Nature of the Firm. *Journal of Law and Economics* XXVI (1), April, 1–26.

Coase, R. H. 1937. The Nature of the Firm. *Economica* 4: 386–405.

Hayek, Friedrich von A. 1937. Economics and Knowledge. *Economica*, ns, 4: 33–54.

Hayek, Friedrich von A. 1945. The Use of Knowledge in Society. *American Economic Review*, 35(4), 519–30.

Knight, F. H. 1921. *Risk, Uncertainty and Profit*. Chicago: University of Chicago Press.

Knight, F. H. 1935. *The Ethics of Competition*. London: George Allen & Unwin.

Richardson, G. B. 1960. *Information and Investment*. Oxford: Oxford University Press.

Smith, A. 1776. *An Inquiry into the Nature and Causes of the Wealth of Nations*, Glasgow edition, Oxford: Oxford University Press.

2
The Optimal Timing of a Foreign Direct Investment

Analyses of the optimal timing of foreign direct investment (FDI) decisions have been curiously lacking in the general literature on multinational enterprises (cf. Buckley (1979a, b)). Although comparative static analyses exist, comparing exporting to the host country with market servicing from a production unit sited in the host country (Horst, 1971; Hirsh, 1976), the only attempt to predict the timing of the switch from exporting to foreign-based production is that of Aliber (1970) (although Vernon (1966) gives a cost-based rationale for the switch). This chapter attempts to fill this gap in the theory of FDI. Section 2.1 outlines and criticises previous attempts to deal with the problem, sections 2.2–4 present a simple model, which ignores set-up costs, and sections 2.5 and 2.6 give a more detailed analysis including such costs. Further extensions of the theory are considered in section 2.7, and the conclusions are summarised in section 2.8. The problem emerges as being more complex than had previously been appreciated.

2.1 Received analysis of the optimal timing of an FDI

Analyses which are concerned with the dynamics of the foreign expansion of the firm should be able to specify those factors which govern the timing of the initial FDI. Aliber's model covers exporting, licensing a host country firm and FDI.

Aliber assumes that the source country firm has a monopolistic advantage or 'patent' which it can choose to employ either in the host or source country, and either internally or externally, the latter by sale of a licence to a host country producer. The patent is a capital asset, the income from which is measured by the decline in the cost of production from the reduction in the amounts of various factors required to produce a given output. The value of the patent is the capitalised value of this cost reduction. In a world of unified currency areas but separate customs areas, Aliber argues, the FDI decision is merely one of the economics of location, although tariffs should be included as a type of transport cost. Initially, when location costs indicate foreign-based production, licensing would be the preferred alternative, for although Aliber includes 'cost of doing business abroad' as an extra cost for a foreign investor, he assumes that the licensor would be able to extract the full rent from the licensee (cf. Casson (1979)). However, at a larger market size 'costs of doing business abroad' decline and FDI is preferred. Aliber rather fudges this issue by claiming that at a 'certain point' in the growth of the host country market 'the inference is that the host country firm is no longer willing to pay the scarcity rent demanded by the source-country firm' (Aliber, 1970, p. 24), that is, the capitalised value of the patent to the source country firm is greater than its value to the host country firm.[1]

We now turn to a multiple currency world. Aliber suggests that interest rates on similar assets denominated in different currencies may differ, because of the premium demanded by currency holders for bearing the uncertainty that exchange rates may be changed. Financial markets therefore apply a different capitalisation rate to the same income stream according to its currency of denomination. A source country is one with a strong currency: a source country firm applies a higher capitalisation rate to the same income stream than a host country firm. Consequently, FDI becomes the preferred form of market servicing at a lower market size than in a unified currency area. The choice between licensing and FDI is determined by the balance of the 'costs of doing business abroad' (which favour licensing) and national differences in capitalisation rates.

In Aliber's scheme, the market servicing decision is dependent on (1) the relative costs of production in source and host countries, (2) transport costs and tariffs, (3) the 'costs of doing business abroad' – an extra cost which is relevant only to the FDI mode of market servicing, (4) different rates of capitalisation of income streams, depending on the currency of denomination and (5) market size and market growth in the host country which provides the main dynamic element in the theory.

2.2   A simple model of the market servicing decision

We begin by distinguishing three types of cost associated with a particular mode of market servicing (cf. Alchian (1959)):

(a) A non-recoverable set-up cost, which is a once-for-all cost incurred as soon as the mode is adopted;
(b) A recurrent fixed cost (i.e. independent of the rate of output) which is due to indivisibilities in the factor inputs hired in connection with the market servicing activity (e.g. the salary of the local manager);
(c) Recurrent variable cost (i.e. the usual output-related costs of labour, materials, etc.).

The simplicity of the first model depends on ignoring category (a) costs which are reintroduced in section 2.5. We assume throughout that there is no change in host country tax policy or in transport costs.

Let there be n modes of market servicing indexed $i = 1, 2, ..., n$. When costs (b) and (c) above are the only ones under consideration, we plot in Figure 2.1 the average cost curve for each mode and determine the least cost Viner envelope (Viner, 1931). The envelope, shown as a heavy line in the figure, tells us the average cost (AC) at each output when only the efficient mode relevant to that output is used.

For outputs less than q_1, mode 1 is efficient, for $q_1 \leq q \leq q_2$, mode 2 is efficient and for $q \geq q_2$ mode 3 is efficient. For any given output, a profit-maximising firm will select the efficient mode.

We now introduce further assumptions to make the analysis dynamic.

(i) In the foreign (or 'host') market, the firm is faced with a limit pricing situation, such that for a wide range of different cost conditions the profit maximising strategy is to supply exactly the amount

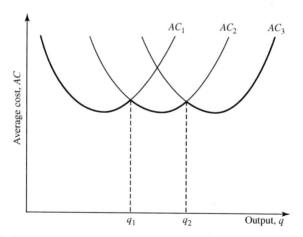

Figure 2.1 Derivation of minimum average cost.

demanded at the limit price. As shown in Figure 2.2, because of the discontinuity in the marginal revenue (MR) curve of the firm, the profit maximising output is q^* for any marginal cost (MC) in the range between p^* and p^{**}.

(ii) The 'size' of the market, q, is the quantity demanded at the limit price and exhibits autonomous growth over time. The pattern of growth is logistic, with size approaching a constant ('saturation') level after a certain time.

(iii) The different modes of market servicing are regarded as alternatives, so that only one mode at a time is used.

(iv) For any given mode average variable cost is constant (and so equal to marginal cost, which is also constant).

Superficially, this assumption rules out economies of scale in production. But if we are prepared to identify different modes according to the size or type of plant to be used, then economies of scale can be included by giving the mode 'production with large plant' higher fixed costs and lower variable costs than the mode 'production with small plant'.

(v) If all the modes are ranked in ascending order of fixed cost (type (b)) they will be in descending order of variable costs (type (c)). This assumption is weaker than it seems. It is bound to be true if we consider only modes which could possibly be efficient, for clearly if one mode had a higher fixed cost *and* a higher variable cost than

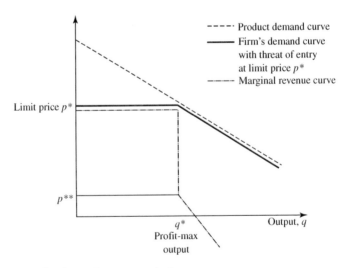

Figure 2.2   The discontinuous marginal revenue curve.

another, it would not be worth considering at any scale of output. If all such inferior modes are eliminated then condition (v) always holds.

Assumptions (i) and (ii) enable us to map from the static cost function $c(q)$ to the 'dynamic' cost function $c(t)$, where $t \geq 0$ is the time that has elapsed since the market was entered. Assumption (iii) tells us that only the cost functions for each mode need to be considered – 'linear combinations' of them can be ignored because it is possible to use only one mode at a time. Assumptions (iv) and (v) tell us that the total cost function for the ith mode is

$$c_i = a_i + b_i q \tag{1}$$

with fixed cost $a_i > a_{i-1}$ and marginal cost $b_i < b_{i-1}$ $(i = 1, 2, ..., n)$, where $b_1 \geq p^*$ and $b_n \leq p^{**}$.

Plotting the total cost functions $c(q)$ (quadrant 3, Figure 2.3) and determining the 'envelope' shown by the heavy line gives the outputs

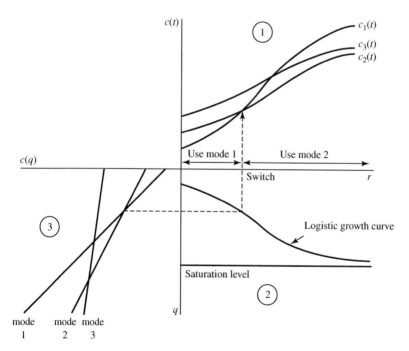

Figure 2.3 Optimal switching of modes.

at which switches of mode should occur. Transferring from market growth (quadrant 2) to the time dimension indicates the *times* at which the switches will occur (quadrant 1). If the market size is limited some switches may *never* occur as shown by the absence of a switch to mode 3 in quadrant 1.

Assumptions (iv) and (v) imply that 'reswitching' can occur only if the market, having expanded, were then to begin to contract.

2.3   An application of the simple model

Consider three possible modes of market servicing; exporting, licensing and FDI.

When exporting, the firm's fixed production cost is negligible so long as the exports are produced by increasing the utilisation of existing plant in the source country. On the other hand, some fixed costs will be incurred in establishing a distribution network in the host country. Variable costs are almost certain to be high under exporting, since they include not only variable production costs but international transport costs and tariff payments as well.

To analyse licensing, we assume that the firm's monopolistic advantage is auctioned competitively to indigenous producers. Assuming that the two highest bidders have identical cost structures, the highest bid will value the licence at the excess of the potential revenue over the minimum indigenous cost (Casson, 1979).

However, the licensor must also take account of the transaction costs borne by him, in particular the costs of monitoring the licence and insuring against default. These transaction costs are fixed costs which must be added to the licensee's fixed costs to arrive at an implicit measure of the licensor's fixed cost.

The firm most likely to become a licensee is one which possesses assets complementary to the monopolistic advantage, for example, it already possesses a distribution and retail network suitable for a product offered under licence. Thus the typical licensee will exploit his licence partly by hiring new fixed assets (for production) and partly by increasing the utilisation of existing fixed assets (in distribution).

When the fixed costs of policing the licence are added to the licensee's fixed production costs, then the total fixed costs associated with licensing are likely to exceed the fixed costs of exporting (which are associated with the exporter's investment in distribution). On the other hand, because licensing avoids international transport and tariff costs, the variable costs are likely to be correspondingly lower than for exporting.

With FDI fixed costs are likely to be higher than for licensing, since the investor normally has to hire new production equipment and establish an independent distribution system as well. Similar reasoning suggests that the variable costs of FDI are likely to be lower than for licensing.

Our analysis therefore suggests that exporting, licensing and FDI are in ascending order of fixed costs and descending order of variable costs.[2]

Suppose each mode of servicing is efficient over some range of output. In a market subject to autonomous growth the theory predicts that the firm will begin by exporting, switch to licensing as market size increases and then finally switch to FDI. By following such a policy the firm is in effect ensuring that existing fixed assets, wherever located, are utilised fully before new fixed assets are installed (cf. Robinson (1931), Penrose (1961)).

Suppose now that one or other of the modes is inefficient. For example, licensing may have a significantly higher fixed cost than exporting, and a significantly higher variable cost than FDI (see Figure 2.4). In this case, as the market grows, it may be efficient to switch directly from exporting to FDI and forego the use of licensing altogether. Another reason why the licensing stage may be omitted is discussed later.

It is quite possible that the market will become saturated before all of the modes have been used. If the potential size of the market is small then the firm may export indefinitely. If the potential market is only of moderate size, the firm may switch from exporting to licensing, but not from licensing to FDI. Alternatively, if the market is large to begin with,

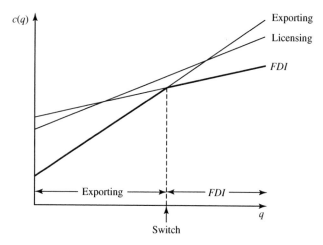

Figure 2.4   Direct switching from exporting to FDI.

the firm may omit the exporting stage and begin with licensing; if the market is very large it may even commence servicing with FDI.

Thus even in this simple model, with its very restrictive assumptions, there are many possible ways in which market servicing strategy can evolve, depending upon the cost structures of alternative modes and the pattern of market growth. The only firm prediction that can be made is that in an expanding market where two or more different modes of servicing are used, FDI will never precede licensing, licensing will never precede exporting and FDI will never precede exporting.

2.4   Extensions of the simple model

Possible extensions of the model are to include discounting over time and dynamic cost reductions arising from familiarisation with the market.

Suppose there is an efficient integrated capital market embracing both source and host economies in which the instantaneous cost of capital is $r(t) \geq 0$ at time t (writing r as a function of t enables us to consider non-trivial yield curves – see Samuelson (1937)). Let $\emptyset_i(t)$ be a multiplicative factor indicating how costs of the ith mode reduce with the length of time the firm has been servicing the host market $(\varphi_i(0) = 1, d\varphi_i / dt \leq 0)$. We may then define the adjusted cost $c_i^*(t)$ of servicing the market by mode i at time t to be the discounted value of cost, adjusted for familiarisation, that is,

$$c_i^*(t) = \varphi_i(t)c_i(t)\exp\left[-\int_0^t (T)dT\right] \qquad (2)$$

It is readily established that a wealth-maximising firm will select the mode with the lowest adjusted cost at any given time. It follows that the analysis of switching based on adjusted cost functions parallels exactly the analysis of section 2.2. The only difference is that the time-dependence of cost is more complex; the typical form of an adjusted cost function is illustrated by the graph BCF in Figure 2.5.

The introduction of discounting does not affect switching behaviour so long as all modes have the same cost of capital. In this case the timing of switching is invariant with respect to the yield curve, because all the cost functions are modified in exactly the same way and so the marginal conditions for a switch are unchanged. The timing of switching is exactly the same as that predicted by the analysis of unadjusted cost functions. A similar result applies if all modes experience the same cost reductions through familiarisation.

The analysis above depends crucially on two assumptions. The first is that familiarisation applies to the market in general, and not to each

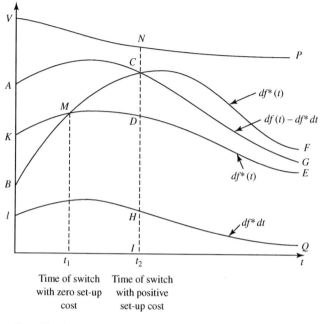

Note $CD = III$

Figure 2.5 Dynamics of switching.

specific mode. If costs reduce according to the time that the market has been serviced by a particular mode then φ_i becomes a function of t_i, the time elapsing since the ith mode was adopted. In this case the economics of switching becomes extremely complex. In practice, however, this case does not give too much cause for concern because the empirical evidence suggests that it is familiarisation with the market, rather than the mode of servicing which is of prime importance in reducing 'the costs of doing business abroad'.[3]

The second crucial assumption is that there are no set-up costs. If this assumption is relaxed then the yield curve can exert a significant influence on the choice of mode, and on the times at which switches are made. This case is examined in the following section.

2.5 Optimal market-servicing with set-up costs

Suppose that switching at time t from mode i to a mode $j > i$ with lower recurrent variable costs incurs a non-recoverable set-up cost $f_{ij}(t)$. The existence of set-up costs influences switching in two ways; it almost invariably induces postponement of a switch, and it may also result in a switch that would have been made never being made at all – in other words it may result in a switch being postponed indefinitely.

When set-up costs are present, a switch between modes represents an investment made by the firm. The 'initial outlay' is the set-up cost, while the subsequent 'net cash flow' is represented by the stream of savings due to the adoption of a mode with lower recurrent costs.

Investment decisions are often analysed as though they involved a once-for-all decision whether or not to invest. It is well known that with an efficient capital market the appropriate criterion for this decision is to invest if the net present value (NPV) is positive (cf. Levy and Sarnat, 1978). But this represents an essentially static analysis of a fundamentally dynamic problem. In many contexts, including the present one, the issue is not so much whether the investment should be undertaken at all, but rather *when* it should be undertaken. It may be profitable to undertake it today, but even more profitable to undertake it tomorrow. In this case the appropriate criterion is to time the investment to maximise its *NPV*. Only in very special cases is this equivalent to undertaking the investment as soon as the *NPV* becomes positive.

It is readily established that the *NPV* at time zero of a switch undertaken at time $t \geq 0$ is

$$NPV(t) = C_i^*(t) - C_j^*(t) - f_{ij}^*(t) \tag{3}$$

where

$$C_i^*(t) = \int_t^\infty c_i^*(T) dT \tag{4a}$$

$$C_j^*(t) = \int_t^\infty c_j^*(T) dT \tag{4b}$$

$$f_{ij}^*(t) = \exp\left[-\int_0^t r(T) dT\right] f_{ij}(t). \tag{4c}$$

Among the necessary conditions for a maximum of *NPV*, there are two of particular relevance in the present context.

The first is the marginal condition

$$c_i^*(t) - c_j^*(t) = -df_{ij}^* / dt \tag{5}$$

Eliminating the factor $\exp\left[\int_0^t r(T)dT\right]$ which is common to both sides of (5) gives

$$\varphi_i(t)c_i(t) - \varphi_j(t)c_j(t) = r(t)f_{ij}(t) - df_{ij}/dt \tag{6}$$

The marginal condition (6) states that the additional recurrent cost incurred by failing to switch to the new mode of servicing equals the saving due to a marginal postponement of the set-up costs; this saving has two components: the avoidance of interest charges on the capital outlay and the capital gain due to the net reduction over time in the outlay required.

The application of this marginal condition to the timing of a switch is illustrated graphically in Figure 2.5. The net saving in recurrent cost at any time is measured by the difference between the heights of the graphs *BCF* and *KDE*. The saving of interest and capital costs by postponing the switch is measured by the height of the graph *LHQ*. The optimal time of the switch is t_2; it is at this point that the saving of recurrent costs, measured by the distance *CD*, is equal to the saving of interest and capital costs, measured by *HI*. Geometrically, the easiest way to determine t_2 is to add the graph *LHQ* to the graph *KDE* and determine the point of intersection *C* of the resultant graph *ACG* with the graph *BCF*; the ordinate of *C* is t_2.

In the absence of set-up costs the optimal timing of the switch would have been t_1, corresponding to the intersection *M* of the graph *KDE* and the graph *BCF*. It can be seen that the effect of set-up costs is to postpone the switch from t_1 to t_2. That set-up costs always postpone the switch can be proved from the second order conditions for a maximum of *NPV*.

Another necessary condition for a maximum of *NPV* is that an indefinite postponement of the switch is uneconomic. Any switch which is postponed indefinitely has *NPV* = 0. Thus any switch which is undertaken should also satisfy the static criterion that at the optimal time of switch the *NPV* is positive, that is,

$$C_i^*(t) - C_j^*(t) > f_{ij}^*(t) \tag{7}$$

This condition is also illustrated in Figure 2.5. The present value of the total saving in recurrent costs after the switch (the left hand side of the inequality (7)) is measured by the area *CDEF*. The present value of the set-up cost (the right hand side of the inequality (7)) is measured by the height of the graph *NJP*, which is *IJ* at time t_2. The condition indicates that the switch is undertaken if the area *CDEF* exceeds the height *IJ*.

Both the static and dynamic conditions must normally be satisfied for the timing of the switch to be efficient. If the firm uses only the static condition then there will be a tendency for it to switch *as soon as* the NPV of the switch becomes positive. In this case it will normally invest too early. For at the optimal time of the switch the NPV may be quite high. As the time of the switch is brought forward the NPV will be reduced, but only gradually. Thus even some time before the optimum is reached the NPV may still be positive. Thus firms which switch using only the static criterion are liable to invest well before the optimal time.

The analysis above is confined to a single switch between two specific modes. It becomes much more complex when a sequence of switches between different modes is contemplated. The problem is that the choice of the initial mode is not independent of which subsequent modes it is planned to switch to, and when it is planned to make these switches. The solution of such problems calls for sophisticated techniques of dynamic programming, which are beyond the scope of this chapter.

2.6   An application: The set-up costs of transferring technology

In this section we apply the preceding analysis to the timing of the switch between exporting and *FDI*. Following Hirsh (1976) and others, we identify the set-up cost of *FDI* as the cost of transferring technology to the foreign subsidiary. The product cycle theory (Vernon, 1966) suggests that this cost will be related to the degree of standardisation of the product: the greater the standardisation, the lower the cost. The degree of standardisation reflects the stage the product has reached in its technical development; Hufbauer (1970) has suggested that a surrogate for this is the age of the product (see also Teece (1977)). We therefore postulate a time-dependent set-up cost which represents the dependence of the cost of technology transfer on the age of the product.

If we now invoke the marginal condition (6), it can be seen that there are two reasons why FDI will be deferred until after its recurrent costs are lower than those of exporting. The first is that deferring FDI delays the payment of interest on the capital tied up in the technology transfer. The second, and much more interesting, reason is that deferring FDI reduces the cost of technology transfer, by allowing the product to be transferred when it has become more standardised. Intuitively it seems that rapid standardisation ought to bring forward the date of technology transfer, but so long as the potential for further standardisation remains, transfer is liable to be postponed. This is the difference between the static and dynamic criteria outlined in the previous section.

2.7 Extensions

Three extensions of the theory are considered briefly below. They are concerned with the following possibilities:

(a) that the limit price may decline over the life cycle of the product due to increasing competitive threats;
(b) that the firm may have already gained some familiarity with the market by producing a substitute product, and
(c) that the firm has already invested abroad and so has a production and distribution infrastructure ready to receive the product.

So far it has been implicitly assumed that the limit price is constant over the life cycle of the product. In practice, however, the limit price is liable to decrease as information about the monopolistic advantage diffuses and potential imitators appear. Eventually the advantage may be lost altogether: limit price falls to minimum average cost and the firm's market share becomes indeterminate.

Before this point is reached, however, the falling limit price shows up in the investment decision only through its tendency to increase the rate of growth of the market. Let demand for the product be denoted $q(p, t)$, where p is the price, that is, the limit price and t represent the time-dependence of the demand curve. Taking the total derivative of q shows that the rate of growth of demand is

$$dq/dt = \partial q/\partial t + (\partial q/\partial p)(dp/dt) \tag{8}$$

where the first term on the right hand side is the growth of the market due to the outward shift in the demand curve and the second term is the growth due to a movement along the demand curve caused by a fall in the limit price. Insofar as the increasing threat of imitation is perceived by the firm and reflected in its pricing policy, there will be a tendency for demand to grow faster than it otherwise would. This will encourage the firm to accelerate the switch to licensing and also to accelerate the switch from licensing to *FDI*.

Hitherto it has also been assumed that the firm is a single-product firm. In this case it is reasonable to suppose that prior to the creation of the monopolistic advantage the firm has no familiarity with the market. However, if the firm has previously been manufacturing a close substitute for the product – perhaps a lower-quality version of it – then a reasonable degree of familiarity may have already been obtained. This may be easily incorporated into the analysis by setting $\varphi(0) < 1$. Under the assumption that familiarisation is independent of the mode of servicing this in itself has no effect on the firm's investment decision. However the fact that φ is low initially means that the scope for further familiarisation may well be small.

Finally, it is interesting to compare the decision of a firm investing abroad for the first time with the decision of a firm that has already invested abroad. If the firm is already operating in the host country, then it may well be able to produce the new product abroad by increasing the utilisation of existing assets (just as it does when exporting). In this case there is no longer any reason to suppose that the fixed costs of FDI will exceed those of exporting. However, variable costs will still be higher for the exporter than for the foreign investors: first, because the exporter incurs tariffs and transport costs, and secondly, because most monopolistic advantages are developed in high-income countries where labour costs are higher; since labour costs are a major component of variable costs, variable costs in the typical source country will exceed those in the typical host country. With FDI having no higher fixed costs, and lower variable costs than exporting, the firm is likely to invest abroad immediately, and so the exporting phase will be eliminated altogether.

This prediction is borne out well by the history of the product cycle in the post-war period. In the early years when many firms were investing abroad for the first time, exporting almost invariably preceded FDI. But as firms became increasingly multinational there was a tendency for the product cycle to shorten, and eventually for the exporting phase to be eliminated altogether. Obviously there are many factors that could explain this trend. The theory above suggests that a particular pattern will be associated with this trend, namely, that the exporting phase is shortest for products whose producers have already invested in the host country.

2.8   Conclusion

This chapter has analysed the foreign market servicing decision of firms in terms of the costs of servicing the foreign market, demand conditions in that market and host market growth. We are able to specify the optimal timing of a switch in modes of market servicing by reference to the above variables. Decisions on market servicing are more complex than is sometimes assumed, particularly where time-dependent set-up costs are involved. However, the model developed above is of sufficient generality for it to be applied to many different special cases. It therefore affords an opportunity for unifying the treatment of different aspects of the market servicing decision.

Notes

This chapter was stimulated by correspondence with Ian Giddy and Alan Rugman and in particular by Giddy and Rugman (1979). We are grateful to two anonymous referees for their constructive comments.

1. It is to be noted that Aliber here introduces elements of the monopolistic advantages (Hymer/Kindleberger) approach, for in a footnote (pp. 24–5) he assumes that the source country firm can appropriate greater rent from the patent when utilised internally than it can from selling the patent on the external market *after a certain market size*. See Hymer (1976), Kindleberger (1969) and also Buckley and Casson (1976).
2. This is, of course, not an invariable rule. It is most likely to apply when the firm is investing abroad for the first time. Other possibilities are considered in section 2.7.
3. Inter alia Newbould et al. (1978), Johanson and Vahlne (1977) and Robock, Simmonds and Zwick (1977), who refer to the process as 'creeping incrementalism'.

References

Alchian, A. A. 1959. Costs and outputs, in M. Abramovitz and A. A. Alchian (eds), *The Allocation of Economic Resources*, pp. 23–40. Stanford: Stanford University Press.

Aliber, R. Z. 1970. A Theory of Direct Foreign Investment, in *The International Firm* (ed. C. P. Kindleberger), pp. 17–34. Cambridge, MA: MIT Press.

Buckley, P. J. 1979a. The Modern Theory of the Multinational Firm. *Management Bibliographies and Reviews*, vol. 5, pp. 171–85.

——. (1979b). The Foreign Investment Decision. *Management Bibliographies and Reviews*, vol. 5, pp. 186–202.

——. and Casson, M. 1976. *The Future of the Multinational Enterprise*. London: Macmillan.

Casson, M. 1979. *Alternatives to the Multinational Enterprise*. London: Macmillan.

Giddy, I. and Rugman, A. M. 1979. A Model of Foreign Direct Investment, Trade and Licensing. Graduate School of Business, Columbia University, New York, mimeo.

Hirsh, S. 1976. An International Trade and Investment Theory of the Firm. *Oxford Economic Papers*, vol. 28, pp. 258–70.

Horst, T. O. 1971. The Theory of the Multinational Firm: Optimal Behaviour under Different Tariff and Tax Rates. *Journal of Political Economy*, vol. 79, pp. 1059–72.

Hufbauer, G. C. 1970. The Impact of National Characteristics and Technology on the Commodity Composition of Trade in Manufactured Goods, in *The Technology Factor on International Trade* (ed. R. Vernon), pp. 145–213. New York: Colombia University Press for National Bureau of Economic Research.

Hymer, S. H. 1976. *The International Operations of National Firms*, Lexington, MA: Lexington Books.

Johanson, J. and Vahlne, J. E. 1977. The Internationalisation Process of the Firm – a Model of Knowledge Development and Increasing Market Commitments. *Journal of International Business Studies*, vol. 8, pp. 22–32.

Kindleberger, C. P. 1969. *American Business Abroad*. Cambridge, MA: Yale University Press.

Levy, H. and Sarnat, M. 1978. *Capital Investment and Financial Decisions*. Englewood Cliffs: Prentice-Hall.

Newbould, G. D., Buckley, P. J. and Thurwell. J. 1978. *Going International: The Experience of Smaller Companies Overseas*. London: Associated Business Press.

Penrose, E. T. 1961. *The Theory of the Growth of the Firm*. Oxford: Blackwell.

Robinson, E. A. G. 1931. *The Structure of Competitive Industry*. London: Nisbet.

Robock, S. H., Simmonds, K. and Zwick, J. 1977. *International Business and Multinational Enterprises*, revised ed. Holmewood, IL: Irwin.

Samuelson, P. A. 1937. Some Aspects of the Pure Theory of Capital. *Quarterly Journal of Economics*, vol. 51, pp. 469–96.

Teece, D. J. 1977, Technology Transfer by Multinational Firms: The Resource Cost of Transferring Technology Know-How. *Economic Journal*, vol. 87, pp. 242–61.

Vernon, R. 1966. International Investment and International Trade in the Product Cycle. *Quarterly Journal of Economics*, vol. 80, pp. 190–207.

Viner, J. 1931. Cost Curves and Supply Curves. *Zeitschrift fur Nationalokonomie*, vol. 3, pp. 23–46, reprinted in *Readings in Price Theory* (American Economic Association) (1953), pp. 198–232. London: Allen and Unwin.

3
A Theory of Cooperation in International Business

3.1 The concept of cooperation

To what extent are cooperative ventures really cooperative? What exactly is meant by *cooperation* in this context? In international business the term *cooperative venture* is often used merely to signify some alternative to 100 per cent equity ownership of a foreign affiliate; it may indicate a joint venture (JV), an industrial collaboration agreement, licensing, franchising, subcontracting, or even a management contract or countertrade agreement. It is quite possible, of course, to regard such arrangements as cooperative by definition, but this fudges the substantive issue of just how cooperative these arrangements really are.

If not all cooperative ventures are truly cooperative, then what distinguishes the cooperative ones from the rest? To answer this question it is necessary to provide a rigorous definition of cooperation. This chapter attempts to distill, from the common-sense notion of cooperation, those aspects of the greatest economic relevance. It is not intended, however, to pre-empt the use of the word *cooperation* for one specific concept. There is a spectrum of concepts – concepts variously known as cooperation, collaboration, copartnership, and so on – and a diversity of fields of application – employee-ownership of firms, intergovernment collaboration in economic policy, and so on; several different concepts will be needed to do full justice to the complex issues raised by cooperative behaviour in the broadest meaning of that term.

Because the manifestations of cooperative behaviour are so wide-ranging, it is desirable, within the scope of a single chapter, to restrict attention to a single case. The 50:50 equity JV has been chosen. It is argued that while genuine cooperation is a feature of some JVs, adversarial elements can be present too and, in some cases, can dominate.

The factors that govern the degree of cooperation are delineated. The organisational structure of the venture and the extent and nature of the other ventures in which the participants are involved turn out to be crucial. It is potentially misleading to analyse a JV in isolation from other ventures, for the extent of cooperation in any one venture is strongly influenced by the overall configuration of the ventures in which the parties are involved.

3.1.1   Coordination

The definition *of cooperation* advocated here is 'coordination effected through mutual forbearance'. This identifies cooperation as a special type of coordination. *Coordination* is defined as effecting a Pareto-improvement in the allocation of resources, such that someone is made better off, and no one worse off, than they would otherwise be. Coordination is an appropriate basis upon which to build a concept of cooperation, for it articulates the idea that cooperation is of mutual benefit to the parties directly involved (Casson, 1982).

Coordination sounds as if it must always be a good thing, but the following points should be noted about the way that the concept is applied in practice.

The externality problem: Coordination is defined with respect to all parties who are in any way affected by a venture, and not just those who join in voluntarily. Those who join presumably expect to benefit, but others who do not join may lose as a result. Sometimes the losers have legal rights which can be used to block the venture, or they can organise themselves into a club to compensate the beneficiaries for not going ahead. But when there are many non-privileged losers who have difficulty organising themselves, it is quite possible that a venture may go ahead even though the losers, as a group, suffer more than the beneficiaries gain.

Coordination under duress: Coordination is defined with respect to an alternative position – namely, what would otherwise happen – so that what is assumed about this alternative position is crucial in determining whether coordination occurs. A voluntary participant may decide to join a venture simply because it is in such an adverse position that the alternative to joining would be absolute disaster.

In some cases the adversity may be deliberately contrived by others – in particular, by other participants anxious to increase their bargaining power. Even where the adversity has not been contrived, other participants may still seek to take advantage of the unattractive nature of the alternatives available to the party concerned. A related point is that where adversity stems from a recent setback, the party may expect coordination to return it to a position as good as its original one, and it may regard as exploitative any terms that fail to do this.

Empty threats and disappointments: It is a party's perception of the outcome of a venture, and of the alternative position, that governs its decision concerning whether to join. These perceptions are subjective, in the sense that they depend upon the information available to the participant, and can vary, within the same situation, between one person and another. Expectations can be erroneous, so that a venture that effects coordination ex ante may turn out not to do so ex post. Astute individuals or managements may be able to influence the expectations of others to their own advantage. One participant may threaten another participant that if it does not join on onerous terms, the first participant will act to make the other participant's alternative position considerably worse than it would otherwise be. It is quite possible, therefore, for a participant to join a venture under a threat that subsequently turns out to have been empty and, either for this reason or for some other, to later regret having joined at all.

Autonomy of preferences: In conventional applications of the concept of coordination it is assumed that a party's objectives are unchanged by involvement in a coordinating venture. This assumption is relaxed when introducing the concept of commitment later on. Many economists consider it methodologically unsound to introduce endogeneity of preferences in this way, but in the present context, there are good reasons for doing so. Not everyone is likely to be convinced of its necessity, however.

3.1.2 Interfirm coordination

Coordination applies first and foremost to people rather than to firms. In certain cases, however, a firm can be regarded as a person, as when it consists of a single individual who acts as owner, manager and worker. In large firms, of course, these various functions are specialised with different individuals. The firm then becomes an institutional framework for coordinating the efforts of different people working together. This exemplifies intrafirm coordination. The focus of this chapter, however, is on interfirm coordination, in which one firm coordinates with another. It is analytically useful to separate the intrafirm and interfirm aspects of coordination by assuming that interfirm coordination takes place between single-person firms of the kind just described. Subject to this qualification, interfirm coordination may be defined as an increase in the profits of some firms that is achieved without a reduction in the profits of others.

It is also important to distinguish interfirm coordination from extrafirm coordination, which is coordination effected between firms on the one hand and households on the other. Extrafirm coordination is exemplified by trade in final product markets and factor markets. Because of externalities of the kind just described, certain types of interfirm coordination can damage extrafirm coordination to the point where coordination within the economy as a whole is reduced. It is well known, for example, that when firms collude to raise the price within an industry to a monopolistic level, the additional profit accruing to the firms is less than the loss of consumer welfare caused by the higher prices and the associated curtailment of demand. Because the consumers are usually more numerous than the firms, it is difficult for them to organise effective opposition to this. Thus when interfirm coordination is motivated by collusion, even though the firms gain, the economy as a whole may be a loser.

3.2   Forbearance

All the parties involved in a venture have an inalienable de facto right to pursue their own interests at the expense of others. It is one of the hallmarks of institutional economics – and transaction cost economics in particular – that it recognises the widespread implications of this. It can manifest itself in two main ways: aggression and neutrality. An aggressive party perpetrates some act that damages another party's interests, while a neutral party behaves more passively; it simply refrains from some act that would benefit someone else. In either case, the party is deemed to cheat; if it refrains from cheating, it is said to *forbear*. Often, both options are available: the party can either *commit* a damaging act or merely *omit* to perform a beneficial one. Under such conditions, neutrality is regarded as *weak cheating* and aggression as *strong cheating*.

Forbearance and cheating can take place between parties that have no formal connection with each other. They also occur in the establishment of a venture. To fix ideas, this chapter focuses on the problem of sustaining a venture once operations have commenced. It is assumed that at this stage each participant has accepted certain specific obligations. Typically, a minimal set of obligations will have been codified in a formal agreement, while a fuller set of obligations has been made informally. Failure to honour minimal obligations represents strong cheating, honouring only minimal obligations represents weak cheating, while honouring the full obligations represents forbearance. In the special case where the obligations relate to the supply of effort, strong cheating involves disruption, weak cheating involves supplying a minimal amount of effort and forbearance involves providing maximum effort.

3.2.1   The incentive to forbear

When only the immediate consequences of an action are considered, it often seems best to cheat. But when the indirect effects are considered, forbearance may seem more desirable. This means, intuitively, that forbearance appeals most to those agents who take a long-term view of the situation.

A short-term view is likely to prevail when the agent expects the venture to fail because of cheating by others. The risk of prejudicing the venture through its *own* cheating is correspondingly low, and there may be considerable advantages in being the first to cheat because the richest pickings are available at this stage.

Knock-on effects arise principally because of the responses of others. Their perceived importance depends upon the *vulnerability* of the party. A party is vulnerable if some course of action that might be chosen by another party would significantly reduce its welfare. Vulnerability encourages a party to think through how its own actions affect the incentives facing others. The more vulnerable the party is, the more important it is to avoid stimulating an adverse response from other agents. Each party can, to some extent, induce long-term thinking in other parties by threats that emphasise their vulnerability to its own actions. Partly because of this, the likely pattern of response by others, in many cases, is to match forbearance with forbearance, but to punish cheating. Confronted with this pattern of response, the optimal strategy in most cases is to do the same. Specifically, it is to forbear at the outset and to continue forbearing as long as others do. The situation in which all parties forbear on a reciprocal basis is termed *mutual forbearance*. According to the earlier definition, coordination effected through this mechanism is the essence of cooperation.

If other parties cheat, the victim has a choice of punishment strategies. These strategies differ in both the nature of the evidence required and the severity of the punishment inflicted.

Recourse to the law: This method has very limited scope because many forms of cheating are perfectly legal. This is particularly true where weak cheating is concerned. Even where the law has been breached, the principle that the defendant is guilty until proven innocent, coupled with controls over what evidence is admissible in court, makes it costly, in many legal systems, for the victim to translate circumstantial information about cheating into convincing evidence.

Do-it-yourself punishment: This strategy is often much cheaper. The victim can rely upon its own assessment of the situation. It does not need to convince others of its case. There are two main problems with this strategy. First, the victim may have far more limited sanctions than the law and, indeed, in some cases (such as punishing theft), the victim may have lost, as a direct consequence of the crime, the very resources needed to inflict the punishment. Second, there may be a credibility problem. If the potential victim threatens to withhold promised bonuses, the threat will have little force if it is not trusted to pay them when they are deserved anyway. If it threatens to perform some seriously damaging action instead, it is possible that the victim may damage its own interests too – as when it threatens to undermine the entire venture – and this may create the belief that it will not actually do it. Despite these difficulties, do-it-yourself punishment is widely used. A common strategy is tit for tat, which matches acts of cheating with similar acts in kind. It has an appropriate incentive structure, is simple to implement, is not too costly, and is easily intelligible to other parties (Axelrod, 1981, 1984).

Residual risk sharing: In some cases, punishment is semiautomatic, as when each participant requires each of the others to hold a share in the residual risks of the venture. If anyone cheats, the venture as a whole suffers, and the value of their equity stake diminishes as a result. This device is particularly appropriate in ventures calling for teamwork, when it is difficult to pinpoint the individuals who are cheating. This means that incentives must be based not on the inputs (because they are difficult to observe) but upon the joint output instead. This principle works well for small teams, but not for large ones, where the link between individual performance and the share of the team rewards is relatively weak. It is also dependent on there being less likelihood of cheating in the sharing out of residual rewards than in the supply of inputs – which is a reasonable assumption in many cases.

Although these three methods are substitutes in dealing with any one type of cheating, most ventures provide opportunities for various types of cheating. In this respect the methods complement one another quite nicely. Formal agreements between participants are often drafted by professional lawyers to make them easy to enforce through the courts. The formalities typically refer to readily observable aspects of behaviour on which convincing evidence is easy to collect. The law provides an appropriate punishment mechanism in this case. But the formal aspect of a venture cannot usually guarantee much more than its survival. True success can only come if informal understandings between the parties are honoured as well (Williamson, 1985). In this context, legal processes are seriously deficient. A system of shared equity ownership provides a suitable incentive framework, but almost invariably needs to be supplemented by do-it-yourself rewards and punishments too.

3.2.2 Reputation effects

We have noted that do-it-yourself arrangements often suffer from a credibility problem. One way of resolving this problem is for the potential victim to gain a reputation for always carrying out threatened reprisals. Reputations can have other benefits too. A party with a reputation for never being first to abandon forbearance gives partners a greater incentive to forbear themselves, for it increases the likelihood that if they too forbear, then the venture as a whole will reach a successful conclusion. A reputation for forbearance also facilitates the formation of ventures in the first place; it makes it easier for the reputable party to find partners because prospective partners anticipate fewer problems in enforcing the arrangements (Blois, 1972; Richardson, 1972).

A reputation is an investment. It requires a party to forgo certain short-term gains in order to save on future transactions costs. The most valuable reputation appears to be a reputation for reciprocating forbearance: never being the first to abandon it, but always taking reprisals against others who do. The factors most conducive to investment in reputation are as follows:

1. *The prospect of many future ventures in which the party expects to have an opportunity to be involved.* The number of ventures will be larger, the greater the party's range of contacts, the longer its remaining life expectancy, and the higher its expectation of the frequency with which new economic opportunities occur.
2. *The conspicuous demonstration of forbearance in a public domain.* A high-profile venture with a large number of observers, and a dense network of contacts spreading information about it, facilitates reputation building. Conspicuous forbearance is favoured by a cultural environment that is open rather than secretive. A dense network of contacts is most likely within a stable social group, in which few parties enter or leave.
3. *A propensity for observers to predict the future behaviour of a party by extrapolating its past pattern of behaviour.* This governs the extent

to which a party can signal future intentions through current behaviour. If peoples' attitudes are governed by prejudice based on superficial appearance rather than upon actual behaviour, acquiring a reputation that is at variance with prejudice may prove very difficult.

3.3   Cooperation, commitment and trust

To what extent can it be said that one contractual arrangement is more cooperative than another? To answer this question, it is necessary to distinguish between cooperation as an input to a venture and cooperation as an output from it. An arrangement that gives all parties a strong incentive to cheat requires a great deal of mutual forbearance if it is to be successful. Loosely speaking, it requires a large input of cooperation. In one respect this is a weakness rather than a strength of the arrangement, since it means that in practice the arrangement is quite likely to fail. This is important when considering JVs later, for it does seem that JVs that begin by being hailed extravagantly as a symbol of cooperation have a high propensity to fail.

Cooperation may be regarded as an output when an arrangement leads to greater trust between the parties, which reduces the transaction costs of subsequent ventures in which they are involved. Focusing on cooperation as an output gives a perspective that is closest to the common sense view that cooperative ventures are a 'good thing'.

There is a connection, however, between input and output. This is because an arrangement that calls for a considerable input of cooperation and then turns out successfully enhances the reputations of the parties. First and foremost, it enhances their reputations with each other, but, if there are spectators to the arrangement, then it enhances their reputations with them too.

The connection between input and output suggests that some arrangements may be more efficient than others in transforming an input of cooperation into an output. More precisely, cooperation is efficient when a given amount of mutual forbearance generates the largest possible amount of mutual trust. Efficiency is achieved by devising the arrangement of the venture so as to speed up the acquisition of reputation. One reason why reputation building may be slow is that cheating is often a covert practice – it is more viable if it goes undetected – and so it may be a long time before parties can be certain whether or not an agent has cheated. The importance of this factor varies from one venture to another, depending upon how easy it is for agents to make their own contributions and monitor and supervise their partners at the same time.

3.3.1 Reputation building

To speed up reputation building it may be advantageous to create, within the arrangement itself, additional opportunities for agents to forbear reciprocally. Thus a venture may provide for a sequence of decisions to be taken by different parties, in each of which the individual agent faces a degree of conflict between its own interests and those of others. Each agent (except the first-mover) has an opportunity to respond to the earlier moves of others. The essence of this reputation-building mechanism is that, first, the decisions are open and overt, rather than secretive and covert, and second, there is some connection between the overt decisions made by agents and their covert ones. In other words, the mechanism rests on the view that what the agent does when observed is a reflection of the way it behaves when not observed. Because of bounded rationality and the persistence of habits, it is difficult for most agents to adjust their behaviour fully according to the conditions of observation. A sophisticated arrangement can set traps to catch agents off guard; provided agents do not face similar sequences of decisions too often, all but the cleverest and most alert are likely to unintentionally reveal something about the pattern of their unobserved behaviour as a result.

This device has certain dangers, however, not least of which is that it increases the amount of discretion accorded to each party. For it is the essence of the deferred decisions that agents have discretion over how they use the information at their disposal. If they were instructed to follow a decision rule prescribed at the outset, then their only discretionary decision would be whether to cheat on the rule. The situation would revert to one that encouraged covert rather than overt behaviour. To avoid creating excessive risks for the other parties, however, it is necessary to carefully control the amount of discretion by focusing the earliest decisions in the sequence upon issues that do not really matter. As the venture proceeds and trust grows, so the degree of real discretion can be increased. To start with, therefore, the situation may resemble a game in which only token gains and losses are made, and only as time passes does the game become fully integrated into the real world.

There are certain types of venture that naturally create game-playing situations. In long-term ventures in a volatile environment, for example, there is a very sound logic for deferring certain decisions until after the venture has begun – namely, that new information may subsequently become available that is relevant to how later parts of the venture are carried out. It may well be appropriate to delegate these decisions to the individuals who are most likely to have this information at hand. It then becomes possible to fine-tune the degree of discretion to the amount of trust already present. Thus it is quite common to observe that when a number of parties work together for the first time, a tight discipline is imposed to begin with, which is then progressively relaxed as the parties begin to trust each other more.

3.3.2 Commitment

Up to this point it has been assumed that cooperation is encouraged by appealing to the agents' enlightened self-interest – their incentive to cooperate is strengthened by reducing the cost of building up a reputation for reciprocity. It is also possible, however, to encourage cooperation by changing an agent's preferences so that the successful completion of the venture receives a higher priority than it did before. One way of doing this is to encourage the agent to perceive cooperation not as a means but as an end in itself. Cooperation then ceases to be based on strategic considerations – considerations that recommend cooperation as an appropriate means – and becomes based on commitment to cooperation in its own right.

It is worth noting, in this connection, that many everyday situations call for forbearance to be shown to people whom it is unlikely that one will ever meet again, and where there is, as a result, little incentive to forbear so far as self-interest alone is concerned. A typical situation arises in connection with unanticipated congestion in the use of a facility. When there is insufficient time to negotiate agreements between the users, and when there is either no system of priorities or the system in force is an inappropriate one, coordination may depend upon spontaneous forbearance. Examples include moving out of other people's way when shopping and giving way to traffic entering from byroads. The reason many people forbear in these situations, it seems, is that they derive welfare directly from their constructive role in the encounter.

It is likely that participation in certain types of venture can affect parties in a similar way. Indeed, participation in a venture may leave an individual far more oriented towards spontaneous cooperation than it was before. The main reason for this is the role of information sharing in a venture. It is characteristic of many ventures that agents are asked to agree to share certain types of information with their partners.

This is principally because the agents who possess certain types of information (or are in the best position to obtain it) are not necessarily those with the best judgement on how to use it. Another reason is that information provided by an agent may act as an early warning that, due to environmental changes, it (and perhaps others too) has a strong incentive to cheat, which can be reduced, in everyone's interests, by a limited renegotiation of their agreement.

In asking people to share information, however, it is likely that the response will divulge some of their more general beliefs and their moral values too. Thus the sharing of information provides those who stand to gain most from the successful completion of the venture with an opportunity to disseminate – whether deliberately or quite subconsciously – a set of values conducive to cooperation. In this case, a venture can promote cooperation simply by providing a forum for the preaching of the cooperative ethic.

The degree of commitment to a venture is likely to be conditional upon certain characteristics of the venture. The commitment of the partners is likely to be higher, for example, the more socially meritorious or strategically important the output is deemed to be. Commitment will also tend to be higher if the distribution of rewards from the venture, when it is successfully completed, is deemed equitable by all parties. Envy of the share of gains appropriated by another partner cannot only diminish motivation but can encourage cheating – which may be 'justified' as a means of generating a more equitable outcome. It is one of the characteristics of the JVs analysed in the next section that, superficially at least, the distribution of rewards seems fair because it is based on a 50:50 principle. As subsequent discussion indicates, however, such equity may be illusory, and once any such illusion is recognised, the degree of commitment may fall dramatically.

The psychology of commitment, if understood correctly, can be used by one party to manipulate another. But securing commitment through manipulation is a dangerous strategy for, once it is exposed, some form of reprisal or revenge is likely. The commitment previously channelled into the venture by the victim of manipulation may be transferred and channelled into punishing the manipulator instead.

From the standpoint of economic theory, these propositions are equivalent to a postulate that an agent's preferences depend not only upon material consumption (or profit) but also upon the characteristics of the ventures in which it is involved. These characteristics relate both to the nature of the venture itself and to the extent of mutual commitment shown by the parties concerned. This postulate provides the basis for further developments of the theory of cooperation, which lie beyond the scope of the present chapter.

3.4   The economic theory of joint ventures

Analysis of the cooperative content of cooperative ventures must be based upon a rigorous theory of non-equity arrangements. Because non-equity arrangements can take so many different forms, it is useful to focus upon one particular type. The 50:50 equity JV seems appropriate because it is very much symbolic of the cooperative ethos. The main focus is on arrangements involving two private firms, for, although arrangements involving state-owned firms and government agencies are very important in practice (particularly in developing countries), they raise issues lying beyond the scope of this chapter. To the extent, however, that the state sector is primarily profit-motivated, the following analysis will still apply.

It is assumed that each partner in the JV already owns other facilities. It is also assumed that the JV is preplanned, and that the equity stakes are not readily tradeable in divisible units. This means, in particular, that the joint ownership of the venture cannot be explained by a 'mutual fund' effect – in other words, it is not the chance outcome of independent portfolio diversification decisions undertaken by the two firms.

Working under these assumptions, theory must address the following three key issues.

Why does each partner wish to own part of the JV rather than simply trade with it on an arm's-length basis? The answer is that there must be some net benefit from internalising a market in one or more intermediate goods and/or services flowing between the JV and the parties' other operations. A *symmetrically motivated* JV is defined as one in which each firm has the same motive for internalising. This is the simplest form of JV to study, and it is the basis for the detailed discussion presented later. (See also Buckley and Casson, 1985, Chapters 2–4.)

Why does each firm own half of the JV rather than all of another facility? The force of this question rests on an implicit judgement that joint ownership poses managerial problems of accountability that outright ownership avoids. To the extent that this is true, there must be some compensating advantage in not splitting up the jointly owned facility into two (or possibly more) separate facilities. In other words, there must be an element of economic indivisibility in the facility. The way this indivisibility manifests itself will depend upon how the JV is linked into the firms' other operations.

1. If the JV generates a homogeneous output which is shared between the partners, or uses a homogeneous input which is sourced jointly by them, then the indivisibility is essentially an economy of scale.
2. If the JV generates two distinct outputs, one of which is used by one partner and the other by the other, then the indivisibility is essentially an economy of scope.
3. If the JV combines two different inputs, each of which is contributed by just one of the parties, then the indivisibility manifests itself simply as a technical complementarity between the inputs (a combination of a diminishing marginal rate of technical substitution and non-decreasing returns to scale).

Given that, in the light of the first two issues, each partner wishes to internalise the same indivisible facility, why do the partners not merge themselves, along with the JV, into a single corporate entity? The answer must be that there is some net disadvantage to such a merger. It may be managerial diseconomies arising from the scale and diversity of the resultant enterprise, legal obstacles stemming from antitrust policy or restrictions on foreign acquisitions, difficulties of financing because of stock market scepticism, and so on.

It is clear, therefore, that JV operation is to be explained in terms of a combination of three factors, namely internalisation economies, indivisibilities and obstacles to merger.

As noted in Chapter 1, there are many contractual alternatives to JV operation, but for policy purposes, particular interest centres on the question of when a JV will be preferred to outright ownership of a foreign subsidiary. Given that location factors, such as resource endowments, result in two interdependent facilities being located in different countries, the first of the three factors mentioned – internalisation economies – militates in favour of outright ownership. It is the extent to which it is constrained by the other two factors – indivisibilities and obstacles to merger – that governs the strength of preference for a JV. The larger the indivisibilities, the greater the obstacles to merger; the smaller the internalisation economies (relative to the other two factors), the more likely it is that the JV will be chosen (Casson, 1987, Chapter 5). The interplay between these factors in governing the choice of contractual arrangements is illustrated by the following examples.

3.4.1 The configuration of a JV operation

The configuration of a JV operation is determined by whether it stands upstream or downstream with respect to each partner's other operations, and by the nature of the intermediate products that flow between them. A JV arrangement is said to be *symmetrically positioned* if each partner stands in exactly the same (upstream or downstream) relation to the JV operation as does the other. Figure 3.1 illustrates symmetric forward integration and Figure 3.2 shows symmetric backward integration. Sometimes an operation may be integrated both backward and forward into the same partner's operations. Figure 3.3 illustrates a symmetric buy-back arrangement in which each partner effectively subcontracts the processing of a product to the same jointly owned facility.

Some writers seem to suggest that JVs are inherently symmetric – presumably because of the 50:50 symmetry in the pattern of ownership – but this is far from actually being the case. JVs may, for a start, be

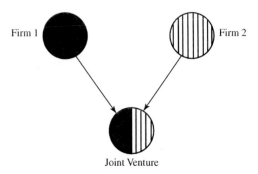

Figure 3.1   Forward integration into a JV.

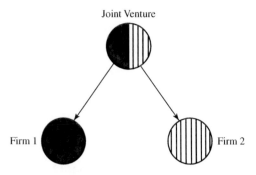

Figure 3.2   Backward integration into a JV.

asymmetrically positioned with respect to the partners' operations. Figure 3.4 illustrates a multistage arrangement in which one partner integrates forward into the JV and the other integrates backward; such an arrangement is quite common in JVs formed to transfer proprietary technology to a foreign environment.

Even if a JV is symmetrically positioned, it does not follow that it is symmetrically configured, for the intermediate products flowing to and from the respective partners may be different. It is only when both the positioning is symmetric and the products are identical that the configuration is fully symmetric in the sense we defined above.

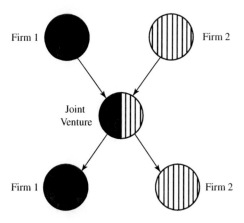

Figure 3.3 Buy-back arrangement.

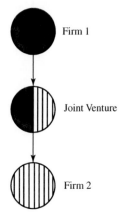

Figure 3.4 Multistage arrangement.

The fact that a configuration is symmetric does not guarantee that the motivation for internalisation is symmetric too. If each partner, for example, resells the JV output within a different market structure, then the motivation for internalisation may differ in spite of the fact that the configuration is symmetric.

The symmetry properties illustrated in Figures 3.1 through 3.3 refer only to the immediate connections between the JV and the rest of the partners' operations. Each partner's operations may be differently configured from the others. This means that while the activities directly connected with the JV are symmetrically configured, the operations when considered as a whole may be asymmetric. Thus the symmetry concept just used was essentially one of local symmetry, and not of global symmetry. While global symmetry implies local symmetry, the converse does not apply.

The distinction between local and global symmetry has an important bearing on the question of the distribution of economic power between the parties. It is important to appreciate that local symmetry does not guarantee that there is a balance of economic power between the parties to the JV. It is quite possible, for example, that one of the partners may own facilities that are potential substitutes for the jointly owned facility, while the other partner does not. This becomes important if the other partner could not easily gain access to an alternative facility should the first partner place some difficulty in its way. It may be, for example, that the first partner holds a monopoly of alternative facilities. This means that in bargaining over the use of the jointly owned facility, the first partner is likely to have the upper hand. It can use power either to secure priorities for itself through non-price rationing or to insist on trading with the JV at more favourable prices. The fact that the JV is 50:50 owned implies only that residual income is divided equally between the partners; it does not guarantee that total income is divided equally. And, as we have argued, a locally symmetric configuration does not guarantee that total income will be divided equally. It is the symmetry of substitution possibilities that is crucial in this respect. Symmetry of substitution is likely to occur only with global symmetry, and this is a much less common type of configuration. One important consequence of this is considered in section 3.5.2 below.

3.4.2   JV operations motivated by lack of confidence in long-term arm's-length contracts

The next four sections illustrate how different motives for internalisation manifest themselves in various contexts. Readers familiar with the most recent literature on internalisation theory may prefer to proceed directly to section 3.5, where the main line of argument is resumed.

This section presents three simple examples in which both the configuration of the JV and the motivations for it are symmetric. The examples are designed to illustrate a progression from internalisation involving no day-to-day operational integration between the JV and the partners' operations to internalisation involving very close operational integration indeed.

Hedging against intermediate product price movements in the absence of a long-term futures market: Consider the construction industry, in which main contractors have to quote fixed prices for long-term projects, some of which require a large input of cement, which is liable to vary in price over the life of the project. For obvious reasons, the cement cannot be stored, and there is no organised futures market either. Cement has to be purchased locally for each project, and because the sites are geographically dispersed, there is no one supplier that can economically supply all the projects. Nevertheless prices of cement at different sites tend to vary in line with each other, so that ownership of a cement making facility at any one location will still help to hedge against price fluctuations in the many different sources of supply that are used. There are two major contractors of equal size who specialise in cement-intensive projects. Because of economies of scale in cement production, however, a cement plant of efficient scale generates much more cement than either contractor uses. There is one plant whose output price varies most closely with the average price of cement paid by the contractors, and so they each acquire a half of the equity in this plant. This is the most efficient mechanism available for diversifying their risks relating to the price of cement. It involves no operational integration whatsoever between the cement facility and the site activities.

Avoiding recurrent negotiation under bilateral monopoly over the price of a differentiated intermediate product: Suppose there are two firms that are the only users of an intermediate product produced with economies of scale. It is difficult for either firm to switch away from the product, since it has no close substitutes. Upstream, therefore, there is natural monopoly, while downstream there is duopsony. Before any party incurs non-recoverable set-up costs through investment in specific capacity, it would be advantageous to negotiate once and for all long-term supply contracts for the product. Because of the difficulty of enforcing such contracts, however, the duopsonists may prefer to jointly acquire the upstream facility. This insures both of them against a strategic price rise initiated by an independent natural monopolist. The fact that both share in the residual risks also helps to discourage them from adversarial behaviour towards each other. A modest degree of operational integration is likely in this case.

Operational integration between upstream and downstream activities in the absence of efficient short-term forward markets: Extending the construction industry example, suppose that the two firms have long-term projects in hand at adjacent sites and require various types of form work to be supplied to mould the concrete foundations. The form work is customised and each piece has to be in place precisely on time. Both firms are sceptical about devising enforceable incentives for prompt supply by a subcontractor, as arms' length forward contracts are difficult to enforce in law. Because of the small scale of local demand relative to the capacity of a team of workers of efficient-size, the two contractors may decide to secure quality of service through backward integration into a JV. Unlike the previous arrangements, this involves close day-to-day management of an intermediate product flow between the owners and the JV.

3.4.3   Quality uncertainty

Quality uncertainty can manifest itself in different contexts. Four examples are given to demonstrate the ubiquity of this phenomenon.

Insuring against defective quality in components: This example relates to forward integration involving two distinct flows of materials. Consider two components which are assembled to make a product. The quality of the components is difficult to assess by inspection, while other methods of assessment, such as testing to destruction, are expensive – not least in terms of wasted product. Reliable performance of the final product is crucial to the customer; failure of the final product is often difficult to diagnose and attribute to one particular component. Because of legal impediments, it is impossible to comprehensively integrate the assembly with the production of both components, and an independent assembler would lack confidence in subcontracted component supplies. If two independent component producers form a JV, however, then each can enjoy a measure of confidence in the other, since each knows that the other bears half the penalty incurred by the venture if it supplies a defective product to it. This is the JV analogue of the 'buyer uncertainty' argument emphasised in the internalisation literature.

Adapting a product to an overseas market: This example involves the combination of two distinct but complementary types of know-how in the operation of an indivisible facility. The first type of know-how is technological and is typically embodied in the design of a sophisticated product developed in an industrialised country. The other is knowledge of an overseas market possessed by an indigenous foreign firm. The complementarity concerns their use in adapting the design and marketing strategy of the product to overseas conditions. The indivisible facility is the plant used to manufacture it overseas. Together, these elements make up the classic example of the use of a JV to commence overseas production of a maturing product.

Management training and the transfer of technology: In some cases, a JV may be chosen as a vehicle for training (Kojima, 1978). Employees of a technologically advanced firm are seconded to a JV to train other employees who will remain with the venture when it is later spun off to the currently technologically backward partner. Training involves two inputs, rather than just the one that is usually assumed. It requires not only the knowledge and teaching ability of the tutor but also the tutee's time, attention and willingness to learn. The tutee may be uncertain of the quality of the tutor's knowledge and ability, and may demand that the tutor bears all the commercial risks associated with the early stages of the venture. The tutor, on the other hand, may be uncertain of the effort supplied by the tutee, which could jeopardise the performance of the venture if it were poor, and so the tutor may require the tutee to bear some of the risks as well. These conflicting requirements are partially reconciled by a JV that requires both to bear some of the risks and thereby gives each an incentive to maintain a high quality of input. Those incentives can be further strengthened, in some cases, by a buy-back arrangement – or production-sharing arrangement as it is sometimes called – which encourages each party to use the output that the newly trained labour has produced and thereby gives an additional incentive to each party to get the training right.

Buy-back arrangements in collaborative R&D: Buy-back arrangements, which combine backward and forward integration, are particularly common in collaborative research. In the research context, both the inputs to and the outputs from the JV are services derived from heterogeneous intangible assets (that is, they are flows of knowledge).

Consider two firms, each with a particular area of corporate expertise, who licence their patents and personnel to a joint research project (the indivisible facility). The planned output – new knowledge – is a proprietary public good, which is licenced back to the two firms. Each firm may be suspicious of the quality of the input supplied by the other firm, but the fact that the other firm not only holds an equity stake in the project but also plans to use the product of the research for its own purposes serves to reassure the first firm that the quality will be good (though there still remains a risk that personnel and ideas of the very best quality will be held back). Likewise, the fact that the firm itself has partially contributed to the production of the new knowledge is a reassuring factor when it comes to implementing this knowledge in downstream production.

3.4.4   Collusion

The role of indivisible facilities in the previous discussion can, in fact, be taken over by any arrangement that either reduces the costs of two plants by coordinating their input procurement or enhances the value of their outputs by coordinating their marketing. The former is relevant to backward integration by firms into a JV, while the latter pertains to forward integration instead. The forward integration case, to be discussed shortly, shows the JV to be an alternative to a cartel.

Consider two firms that have identified an opportunity for colluding in their sales policy. They may have independently discovered a new technology, territory or mineral deposit and wish to avoid competition between them in its exploitation. They may, on the other hand, be established duopolists operating behind an entry barrier, who would benefit from fixing prices or quotas to maximise their joint profits from the industry. (The nature of the entry barrier is irrelevant to the argument; it may be based on technological advantage, brand names, statutory privilege, or exclusive access to inputs, and so on.)

The main problem with a sales cartel is the mutual incentive to cheat by undercutting the agreed price – for example, by selling heavily discounted items through unofficial outlets. This poses an acute monitoring problem for each party Channelling sales through a JV reduces the incentive to cheat, since the gains from cheating are partially outweighed by the reduction in profits earned from the JV. Economies in monitoring costs may also be achieved if both parties specialise this function with the JV.

3.4.5   Hostages: Internalising the implementation of counterthreats

In an atmosphere of mutual distrust, an imbalance in the vulnerability of two parties to a breakdown of the venture can further undermine confidence in it. This suggests the possibility that instead of collaborating on a single venture, they should collaborate on two ventures instead. The function of the second venture is to counteract the imbalance in the first venture by giving the least vulnerable party in the first venture the greatest vulnerability in the second venture. Suppose, for example, that the two firms wished to collude in a product market where one firm has a much larger market share, coupled with much higher fixed costs, than the other. This is the firm that is most vulnerable to cheating by the other. To redress the balance, it may be advantageous for the two firms to agree on some other venture – say, collaborative research – to run in parallel with a collusive JV to give the weaker firm an effective sanction against the stronger one. In such a case, the primary motive for the second JV concerns nothing intrinsic to the venture itself, but simply its ability to support the other venture.

It should be clear from the preceding examples that there are an enormous number of different forms that a JV operation can take. Each of the three main factors – the internalisation motive, the indivisibility and the obstacle to merger – can take several different forms. The internalisation motive may differ between the firms. Add to this the considerable diversity of global configurations, and it can be seen that the permutations to which these aspects lend themselves make any simple typology of JV operations out of the question. While the economic principles governing the logic of JV operation are intrinsically quite straightforward, the way that environmental influences select the dominant factors in any one case is extremely complex.

3.5 Building reputation and commitment

It was established in the first part of the chapter that almost all coordinating activity calls for some degree of mutual forbearance and that, therefore, most ventures – even simple trade or team activities – involve an element of cooperation. It was also established that extensive reliance on mutual forbearance was not necessarily a good thing. The essence of cooperative efficiency, it was suggested, is that as a result of a venture, a small amount of mutual forbearance is transformed into a large amount of trust. Cooperatively efficient ventures will tend to accord all parties an opportunity to reciprocate forbearance within a sequence of decisions, observable to the others, calling for increasing levels of commitment. Ventures of this kind are likely to be followed by a succession of other ventures involving the same parties – perhaps in the same grouping or perhaps in other groupings involving other parties with whom the original participants have established a reputation. (Propositions of this kind are certainly testable, even if the propositions regarding 'quantities' of forbearance and trust, from which they derived, are not.)

Some ventures lend themselves naturally to an internal organisational structure that encourages participation. These ventures call for widespread decentralisation of decision making, afford decisions of varying degrees of responsibility and call for the sharing of information. They provide ample opportunity for overt behaviour and only limited opportunity for covert behaviour. These considerations suggest that certain motives for JV operation are far more conducive to cooperation than are others. It is, in fact, the combination of the motive and the main activity performed by the JV that seems to be crucial in this respect.

In the production sector, JVs that involve very little operational integration with the partners' other activities provide little opportunity for the partners to meet and interact on a regular basis. The greater the degree of operational integration, the greater is the regularity with which forbearance may have to be exercised when short-term holdups occur in production, and the greater are the opportunities for sharing information in the planning of production. Quality uncertainty provides a motive for both parties to open up their wholly owned operations to their JV partner once a certain degree of trust has been established, and so provides a natural route through which cooperation could progress to a point where it embraces production, product development and basic research.

Joint R&D is naturally cooperative because it is based upon the sharing of information and, for reasons already noted, the sharing of information often leads to the emergence of shared values too. This may, perhaps, partly explain why collaborative R&D seems to enjoy a special mystique all of its own.

Of the various functional areas in which JV operations can occur, sales and procurement are the least promising so far as true cooperation is concerned. A dominant motive for JV operations in this area is collusion. Collusion affords large incentives to cheat and therefore requires a major input of cooperation. The maintenance of a high price in a static market environment – so characteristic of many collusive arrangements – does not, however, create much need for meetings at which open forbearance and reciprocity can be displayed. Collusion emphasises the covert rather than overt dimensions of behaviour. It therefore generates little output of trust. The most promising area for cooperation in marketing arises when a proprietary product is transferred to a new country, for then both the source firm and the recipient firm need to share information.

Since the demand is uncertain, but has considerable growth potential, the market environment is dynamic rather than static, and so, unlike the case of collusion, it provides opportunities for deferring key decisions and delegating in a way that allows both parties to demonstrate forbearance.

3.5.1   The international dimension

So far nothing has been said specifically about the international aspects of JV operation. To a certain extent, this is deliberate, since there are no reasons to believe that the familiar factors of international cost differentials, tariffs, transport costs and variations in the size of regional markets are any different for JVs than they are for other international operations. It can, however, be argued that the political risks of expropriation, the blocking of profit repatriation, and so on, are lower in the case of a JV than in the case of a wholly owned operation, though empirical support for this view is very limited, to say the least. Tax-minimising transfer pricing, though not impossible with JVs, is more difficult to administer because of the need to negotiate the prices with the partner and to find a subterfuge for paying any compensation involved.

So far as the general concept of cooperation is concerned, the international dimension is much less important than the intercultural dimension. In purely conventional analysis of transaction costs, the focus is on the legal enforcement of contracts, and so the role of the nation state is clearly paramount, in respect to both its legislation and its judicial procedures. The mechanism of cooperation, however, is trust rather than legal sanction, and trust depends much more on the unifying influence of the social group than on the coercive power of the state. Trust will normally be much stronger between members of the same extended family, ethnic group or religious group, even though it transcends national boundaries, than between members of different groups within the same country.

This means that in comparing the behaviour of large firms legally domiciled in different countries, differences in behaviour are just as likely to reflect cultural differences in the attitudes of senior management as the influence of the fiscal and regulatory environment of the home country. Cultural attitudes are certainly likely to dominate in respect of the disposition to cooperate with other firms. In this context it may be less important to know whether a corporation is British or Italian, say, than to know whether its senior management is predominantly Quaker or Jewish, Protestant or Catholic, Anglo-Saxon or Latin, and so on. National and cultural characteristics are correlated, but not perfectly so. In some instances, such as Japanese firms, it has proved extremely problematic to disentangle them.

In the light of these remarks, it is clear that JV operations involving firms with different cultural backgrounds are of particular long-term significance. Once established, they provide a mechanism for cultural exchange, particularly as regards attitudes to cooperation. The success of this mechanism will depend upon how receptive each firm is to ideas emanating from an alien culture. Where the firm is receptive, participation in international JVs may have lasting effects on its behaviour, not only in international operations but in many other areas too.

3.5.2   Networks of interlocking JVs

The recent proliferation of international JVs means that many firms are now involved in several JVs. Two JVs are said to interlock when the same firm is a partner in both. It is not always recognised as clearly as it should be that a set of interlocking JVs is an extremely effective way for a firm to develop monopoly power at minimal capital cost. By taking a part-interest in a number of parallel ventures, producing the same product with a different partner in each case, the firm can not only establish a strong market position against buyers of the product, but it can also create a strong bargaining position against each partner as well.

Once an individual partner is committed to a venture, it is vulnerable if the monopolist threatens to switch production to one of its other JVs instead. The partner has no similar option because the remaining facilities are all partly controlled by the monopolist. The vulnerable firm may be obliged to renegotiate terms under duress. Although the monopolist may stand to lose by withdrawing production from one JV, it will be able to recover most of these losses from enhanced profits arising from the JVs to which production is switched.

A situation of this kind is illustrated in Figure 3.5. Firm 2 has the ability to switch production between the two downstream plants, but neither firm 1 nor firm 3 has this option because the only other plant is partly controlled by firm 2. Although each JV is symmetrically configured in a local sense, the overall situation is globally asymmetric. Superficially, it may seem that firm 2 is a 'good cooperator' because it is involved in more JVs than either of the other firms, but in reality its claim to cooperate may simply be a subterfuge. Firm 2 can, in fact, not only exercise monopoly power against the buyers of downstream output, but also play off its partners against each other. In this case, it is conflict (not cooperation) and deception (not trust) that is the driving force in firm 2's choice of JV operation.

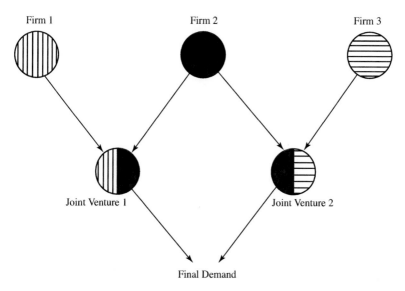

Firm 1   Firm 2   Firm 3

Joint Venture 1   Joint Venture 2

Final Demand

Figure 3.5   The dominant partner in networks.

3.6   Conclusion

JVs are, first and foremost, a device for mitigating the worst consequences of mistrust. In the language of internalisation theory, they represent a compromise contractual arrangement that minimises transaction costs under certain environmental constraints. But some types of JV also provide a suitable context in which the parties can demonstrate mutual forbearance and thereby build up trust. This may open up possibilities for coordination that could not otherwise be entertained. The prospect of this encourages partners to take an unusually open-ended view of JV partnerships and gives JVs their political and cultural mystique.

An important role of JVs, from the limited perspective of internalisation economics, is to minimise the impact of quality uncertainty on collaborative research and training. From the more open-ended perspective of long-term cooperation, however, JVs designed to cope with quality uncertainty are also well adapted to help partners to reciprocate and also to learn the values that inspire the other partner to unreserved commitment to a venture. Without doubt, JVs of this type offer a way forward to genuine cooperation in international economic relations in the future.

The analysis also suggests, however, that a degree of cynicism may be warranted in respect of the claims advanced for JVs of certain kinds. A JV may be merely a subterfuge, luring partners into making commitments that leave them exposed to the risk of renegotiation under duress. It may be a device for enhancing collusion – a practice that may be warranted if it is necessary to recover the costs of technological or product innovation, but not otherwise. It may represent a pragmatic response to regulatory distortion – as when a misguided national competition policy outlaws a merger between the partners that would afford considerable efficiency gains; the JV, in this case, is better than nothing at all, but is only second best to a policy of removing the distortion itself.

One of the most topical applications of the theory of the JV is to industrial cooperation and production-sharing arrangements involving Japanese firms. To what extent, for example, can quality uncertainty in the training process support the argument that the Japanese JV is an appropriate vehicle for tutoring partners in developing countries? Are Japanese JV networks in Southeast Asia merely agglomerations of independent JV operations, or are they part of a wider strategy to play off one partner against another in an effort to maintain low prices for Japanese imports and thereby assure the competitiveness of Japanese re-exports?

Other questions may be asked, for example, of Western corporations that seem anxious to cooperate with the Japanese. Are they really interested in long-term collaboration in the development of leading-edge technologies, or is it their hope that token research collaboration with the Japanese can open the door to short-term cartel-like restrictions on international trade? Do Western collaborators really hope to learn something of a cooperative ethic (and perhaps even a new system of values) from the Japanese, or are they merely interested in cooperation as a mask to disguise the replacement of competition by collusion?

There do not seem to be any easy answers to these questions. More empirical evidence is required. It is hoped that the analysis presented in this chapter affords a framework within which such evidence can be interpreted. So far it is only possible to clarify the questions, but eventually it should be possible to answer them.

Notes

A preliminary version of this chapter was presented to the joint seminar of the Swedish School of Business Administration, Helsinki, The Finnish School of Economics, and the University of Helsinki (kindly arranged by H. C. Blomqvist, T. Bergelund, and I. Menzler-Hokkanen) and to the staff workshop at the University of Reading. Steve Nicholas provided considerable encouragement, mixed with healthy scepticism. We are grateful to Farok Contractor, Peter Lorange, Peter Gray, Kathryn Harrigan, Ingo Walter, and others for their constructive comments.

References

Axelrod, R. 1981. The Evolution of Cooperation among Egoists. *American Political Science Review*, 75: 306–18.

Axelrod, R. 1984. *The Evolution of Cooperation*. New York: Basic Books.

Blois, K. J. 1972. Vertical Quasi-Integration. *Journal of Industrial Economics*, 20: 253–72.

Buckley, P. J. and Casson, M. C. 1985. *Economic Theory of the Multinational Enterprise: Selected Papers*. London: Macmillan.

Casson, M. C. 1982. *The Entrepreneur: An Economic Theory*. Oxford: Blackwell.

Casson, M. C. 1987. *The Firm and the Market*. Cambridge, MA: MIT Press.

Kojima, K. 1978. *Direct Foreign Investment*. London: Croom Helm.

Richardson, G. B. 1972. The Organisation of Industry. *Economic Journal*, 82: 883–96.

Williamson, O. E. 1985. *The Economic Institutions of Capitalism: Firms, Markets, Relational Contracting*. New York: Free Press.

4
Multinational Enterprises in Less Developed Countries: Cultural and Economic Interactions

4.1 Introduction

This chapter analyses the operations of multinational enterprises (MNEs) in less developed countries (LDCs) in terms of the interplay between two types of culture. The MNE, it is claimed, personifies the highly entrepreneurial culture of the source country, while the LDC personifies the less entrepreneurial culture of the typical social group in the host country. This view places MNE–LDC relations in an appropriate historical perspective. It is the entrepreneurial culture of the source country which explains why in the past that country had the economic dynamism to become a developed country (DC). Conversely, the limited entrepreneurial culture of the host country explains why it has been so economically static that it has remained an LDC. The current problems perceived by MNEs in operating in certain LDCs – and also the problems perceived by these LDCs with the operation of foreign MNEs – reflect the difficulties of attempting to bridge this cultural gap.

The concept of entrepreneurial culture is, of course, related to the concept of 'modernisation' which appears in the sociology of development (Eisenstadt, 1973; Herskovits, 1961; Inkeles and Smith, 1974). There are important differences, however. The concept of entrepreneurial culture derives from economic theories of the entrepreneur (Hayek, 1937; Kirzner, 1973; Knight, 1921; Schumpeter, 1934) which identify specific functions such as arbitrage, risk-bearing and innovation needed for economic development. It describes the cultural values which stimulate the emergence of individual personalities capable of performing these functions competently. Modernisation, on the other hand, typically begins with a wide range of attitudes associated with Western industrial societies, and examines how far these attitudes have permeated LDCs. Entrepreneurial theory suggests that not only are some 'modern' attitude's irrelevant to economic development, but others are actually inimical to it. Emphasis on entrepreneurial culture does not therefore imply a trite endorsement of 'modern' values. Entrepreneurial theory has been applied to development issues by a number of previous writers – Hagen (1962), Hoselitz (1961), Kilby (1971) and McClelland and Winter (1969), for example – but along rather different lines.

Countries classified as LDCs form an extremely heterogeneous group. Indeed, differences between the poorest and the wealthiest LDCs are in some respects greater than those between the wealthiest LDCs and many DCs. This chapter is concerned principally with the poorest and most persistently underdeveloped LDCs – such as some countries of sub-Saharan Africa. Since these countries are, generally speaking, the ones with the lowest MNE involvement, it may be asked why a focus on these countries is appropriate. One reason is that this low involvement itself merits explanation, since the continuing confinement of these countries to the periphery of the world economy is of considerable policy interest (Wallerstein, 1979). By examining the difficulties encountered by the small number of MNEs that actually invest in these countries, the lack of interest of the majority can be explained in terms of their rational perception of the size of the problem. The second reason is that the starker contrast between wealthy DCs and the poorest LDCs reveals cultural influences in a sharper relief.

Levels of development can vary not only across LDCs but also across regions within any one of them. This point is fully recognised by the analysis in this chapter, which emphasises that regional differences in development are endemic in DCs as well (Berger and Piore, 1980). The difference between urban (especially metropolitan) and rural areas is fundamental in this respect. Indeed the analysis below suggests that many international differences in levels of development can be ascribed to differences in the relative influence of urban as opposed to rural culture.

Multinationals differ too; in the present context, differences between source countries are likely to be most significant because these affect the national culture upon which the headquarters of the firm draws. There can also be differences between firms from the same country due, for example, to the religious affiliations of the founders, or the impact of the size of the firm on its organisation and leadership style. Due to limited space, however, this chapter abstracts from such considerations by working with the concept of a representative MNE.

Section 4.2 delineates the main areas in which conventional economic theory appears to be deficient in explaining MNE behaviour in LDCs. The 'residual' phenomena which remain unexplained by economic factors, it is suggested, may be explicable by cultural factors instead. The analytical core of the chapter comprises sections 4.3–4.7. These sections consider in detail the interaction between geographical and cultural factors in the process of development. Section 4.3 identifies three conditions for successful economic development; one is geographical – entrepôt potential – and two are cultural – a scientific outlook and a commitment to voluntary methods of social and economic coordination. Sections 4.4–4.6 elaborate on each of these factors in turn, generating a checklist of country characteristics relevant to economic development. Section 4.7 draws on the core analysis to expound an evolutionary model of world development, which focuses on the dynamics of the linkages between DCs and LDCs, as mediated by MNEs. Section 4.8 returns to the key issues identified in section 4.2. It explains how difficulties faced by some LDCs in learning new technologies originate in specific cultural factors and argues that these same cultural factors explain other phenomena too. Attention is drawn to the weaknesses as well as the strengths of contemporary entrepreneurial cultures, and it is suggested that some of the cultural values transmitted by MNEs to LDCs hinder rather than help the process of development. Section 4.9 concludes the chapter with suggestions for further research.

4.2   Key issues

Any analysis of multinational operations in LDCs must address a number of key stylised facts. Some of these facts are readily explained by conventional economic theory (see, for example, Casson and Pearce, 1987), but others are not. The facts that conventional theory can explain include:

(1) The limited scale and disappointing economic performance of import-substituting manufacturing investments in LDCs. This is partly attributable to inappropriate LDC trade policies. By protecting relatively small domestic markets for finished manufactures, LDC governments have encouraged the proliferation of downstream assembly-type operations of less than efficient scale. It is only the ability to charge monopoly prices well above world export prices that has encouraged MNEs to continue operating in these protected markets.

(2) The increase in foreign divestments since the oil price shocks of the mid-1970s is partly explained by the reduction in real consumer incomes in oil-exporting LDCs, which has reduced local demand for relatively sophisticated MNE-produced goods. The threat of blocked profit repatriations from countries with balance of payments difficulties has also encouraged a pre-emptive liquidation of foreign investments by MNEs.

(3) The recent poor performance of resource-based investments in Africa and Latin America is partly explained by another consequence of the oil price shocks – namely the recession in Western heavy industries – and by the continuing protection of domestic agriculture in industrial societies. It is also due partly to the development of new mineral deposits in the Asia-Pacific region. Finally, the emergence of synthetic substitutes has reduced the long-term demand for certain minerals (although the price advantage of oil-based substitutes has declined).

(4) The use of capital-intensive technologies by MNEs in labour-abundant LDCs can be explained partly by the cost of adapting to local conditions a technology originally developed for use in Western locations. It can also be explained by the importance of mechanisation in meeting quality standards in export markets – and in home markets dominated by wealthy consumers (in countries with a highly skewed distribution of income). The distortion of factor prices in LDC markets through minimum wage legislation, capital subsidies, and so on may also be significant.

Some of the salient points which existing theory cannot easily explain are:

(5) The failure of technology transfer to generate sustained innovative capability in LDC industries. The much slower rate at which foreign technologies are assimilated by the poorest LDCs compared to newly industrialising countries such as South Korea, or successfully industrialised countries such as Japan, suggests that cultural factors may inhibit the acquisition of scientific ideas and Western working practices.

(6) The confinement of modern industry to 'enclaves', and in particular the failure of foreign investors to develop backward linkages with indigenous suppliers. Where resource-based investments are concerned, there may be limited opportunities for backward linkages in any case. Even in developed countries, furthermore, large-scale investments often fail to develop a local supply base; the disciplined

routine of work in large plants seems to inhibit the 'incubation' of entrepreneurial skills in the local workforce. Nevertheless the frequent claim by MNE managers of medium-size manufacturing operations that the quality of local supplies is persistently deficient suggests that there may be a systematic failure in LDCs to appreciate the importance of component quality and of precision work in manufacturing industries.

(7) Poor internal relations, both between headquarters and subsidiary, and between management and labour within the foreign subsidiary. Conflicts between different groups within the firm over the distribution of profit, the level of investment, and so on are common in any business activity, and there may be special reasons – such as the high risks perceived by foreign investors and their consequently short-term perspective on cash flow – why these conflicts may be particularly acute in respect of LDC operations. Nevertheless it is also possible that the failure to resolve these conflicts effectively is due to frequent misunderstandings caused by cross-cultural barriers to communication.

(8) The tendency for industrialisation through foreign technology to precipitate the disintegration of traditional social groups within the host economy. All innovation does, of course, involve 'creative destruction', but the social groups of developing countries seem to be much more vulnerable in this respect than do equivalent social groups in the developed world.

It is worth noting that even the 'successful' explanations in (1)–(4) involve only the most proximate causes of the effects involved. Thus in respect of (1), for example, it is possible to ask the more fundamental question of why so many LDC governments opted for protectionism in the first place. Were they susceptible to economic analysis supporting import-substitution because they were predisposed to break economic as well as social and political ties with their colonial powers in order to bolster independence? It seems that – in this case at least – the more fundamental are the questions asked and the further back the quest for explanation goes, the more likely are cultural factors to become significant.

A good theory often has the capacity to explain more than was originally asked of it, and it is claimed that this is also true of the analysis presented here. The theory can explain not only contemporary differences between DCs and LDCs but also certain aspects of the historical process of industrialisation in countries which have become DCs.

Thus the vulnerability of traditional social groups, for example, noted above, applies also to the social groups which became extinct a century or more ago during the industrialisation of DCs. There is insufficient space in the present chapter, however, to document all the relevant facts, let alone substantiate the claim of the theory to explain them.

4.3   The process of development

A necessary condition for development in any locality is that there are resources with a potential for exploitation. Conventional economic theory tends to underestimate the obstacles that lie in the path of realising this potential, however. Working with traditional concepts of resource endowment – land, labour and capital – cross-section regressions using the total factor productivity approach have only limited success in explaining international differences in material economic performance (as measured by per capita GNP) (Pack, 1987). Some countries clearly underperform by failing to realise their potential, and the question is why this should be so (Leibenstein, 1968).

Differences in education and training are commonly cited as a possible explanation, and the analysis presented here is generally consistent with this view. It goes beyond it, however, in recognising that education takes place largely outside formal institutions. Early education, in particular, is effected through family influence, peer group pressure within the local community, and so on. To benefit fully from formal education it may be necessary for people to 'unlearn' beliefs from their informal education. But if the conflict between the two sets of beliefs is acute then psychological obstacles to unlearning may arise. Measures of educational input based on gross expenditure fail to capture these important factors. The analysis in this chapter helps to identify those aspects of the formal curriculum which are crucial in supporting economic development. It also identifies those elements of general culture which prepare people to benefit from such education.

Two main obstacles to the efficient use of national resources can be identified. The first is geographical: the inability to effect a division of labour due to obstacles to transportation. In this context, it is argued below that the presence of a potential entrepôt centre is crucial in facilitating the development of a region. The second is the absence of an entrepreneurial culture. An entrepreneurial culture provides an economy with flexibility – in particular, the structural flexibility to cope with changes in the division of labour. These changes may be progressive changes stemming from essentially autonomous technological innovations

Table 4.1   Factors in the long-run economic success of a nation

I. Geographical factors that influence entrepôt potential

A Location near major long-distance freight transport routes.

B Natural harbour with inland river system.

C Extensive coastline.

D Land and climate suitable for agriculture with potential for local downstream processing.

E Mineral deposits and energy resources.

II. Entrepreneurial culture

Technical aspects

A Scientific attitude, including a systems view.

B Judgemental skills, including

(i) ability to simplify

(ii) self-confidence

(iii) detached perception of risk

(iv) understanding of delegation.

Moral aspects

C Voluntarism and toleration.

D Association with trust, including

(i) general commitment to principles of honesty, stewardship, and the like

(ii) sense of corporate mission

(iii) versatile personal bonding (friendship not confined to kin)

(iv) weak attachments to specific locations, roles, and so on.

E High norms in respect of effort, quality of work, accumulation of wealth, social distinction, and so on.

or defensive changes made in response to resource depletion or various environmental disturbances.

An entrepreneurial culture has two main aspects: the technical and the moral (see Table 4.1). The technical aspect stimulates the study of natural laws through experimentation and the assimilation of technologies developed by other cultures too. It also develops judgemental skills in decision making – skills that are particularly important in simplifying complex situations without unduly distorting perceptions of them (Casson, 1988b).

Entrepreneurial opportunities are usually best exploited through contracts, organisation building, and other forms of association. The moral aspect involves a grasp of the principles involved in voluntary associations of this kind. These principles include commitments to honesty, stewardship and other values that underpin contractual arrangements of both a formal and informal nature. They also include a concept of group mission which is needed to mitigate agency problems in large organisations. A willingness to trust people other than kin is also important. Finally, there must be no rigid attachments to specific occupational roles or places of residence which can inhibit social or geographical mobility at times when structural adjustments are required.

It is worth stressing the diversity of the elements embraced by this moral aspect. Some of these elements have recently been eroded within Western industrial societies (Hirsch, 1977). These societies – notably the US – have developed an extreme competitive individualism, in which levels of trust are inefficiently low. The level of trust required for successful voluntary association is more likely to be present in countries with sophisticated traditional cultures that have recently been modernised – such as Japan.

It is useful to distinguish between high-level entrepreneurship, as exemplified by Schumpeter's heroic vision of system-wide innovation, and low-level entrepreneurship of the kind undertaken by petty traders in small market towns, which can be analysed using the Austrian concepts of arbitrage and market process. High-level entrepreneurship generally requires all the elements of entrepreneurial culture itemised in Table 4.1, while low-level entrepreneurship requires only some – it depends principally on good judgement, and to some extent on the absence of attachments that impede mobility. It is this contrast between high-level and low-level entrepreneurship – rather than the presence or absence of entrepreneurship – which seems to be important in explaining the difference between DCs and LDCs. In other words, it is a relative and not an absolute difference with which the analysis is concerned.

Geographical and cultural factors are linked because the geography of a territory can influence the kind of culture that emerges within it. This is because geographical impediments to communication reduce personal mobility and partition a country into small isolated social groups. Internal coordination within these groups tends to rely on primitive mechanisms of reciprocity and the like which depend crucially on stability of membership (Casson, 1988a, b). As explained below, the cultures of these groups are likely to emphasise conformity and coercion rather than individuality and choice, and so inhibit spontaneous entrepreneurial activity.

Good communications, on the other hand, provide opportunities for appropriating gains from interregional trade. Groups that inhabit areas with good communications will tend to prosper, provided their leaders adopt a tolerant attitude towards entrepreneurial middlemen who promote trade. Groups which develop an entrepreneurial culture will tend to expand the geographical scope of their operations (through commercially inspired voyages of discovery, and so on). Technological advances in transportation will be encouraged because their liberal policies permit the appropriations of material rewards by inventors and innovators. Geographical expansion eventually brings these groups into contact with isolated groups who occupy resource-rich locations. These locations would be inaccessible without the transportation technology and logistical skills of the entrepreneurial group. Equipped with superior technology, the entrepreneurial group can, if its leaders wish, subdue the isolated groups by military means. Different entrepreneurial groups may become rivals in pre-empting opportunities for the exploitations of overseas resources. This may lead to military conflict between the groups, or to a compromise solution where each group maintains its own economic empire and political sphere of influence.

The creation of a transport infrastructure within these hitherto isolated territories not only gives access to resources (and incidentally improves imperial defence); it also tends to undermine the viability of indigenous cultures. Ease of transportation promotes personal mobility and so destroys the stability of membership on which the local groups' methods of internal coordination depend. The confrontation between MNEs and LDCs can be understood as one aspect of this final phase in which the technologies of the entrepreneurial societies are transferred to the regions occupied by the hitherto isolated social groups. To fully understand the nature of this confrontation, however, it is necessary to study in detail the various aspects of the process of development outlined above.

4.4   Geographical determinants of entrepôt potential

A division of labour creates a system of functionally specialised elements. The elements which constitute the system have complementary roles. The division of labour is normally effected over space. Different activities are concentrated at different locations and are connected by intermediate product flows. A large system typically comprises interrelated subsystems, and usually the subsystems themselves can be further decomposed.

System operation over space depends on ease of transportation, and in this context the existence of low-cost facilities for the bulk movement of intermediate products is crucial.

Water transport has significant cost advantages for the bulk movement of freight, and this implies that a good river system and a long coastline (in relation to land area) is an advantage. These conditions are most likely to be satisfied by an island or peninsula with low-lying terrain. Water transport is, however, vulnerable through icing, flooding and the like, and so geological features that facilitate road and rail construction are also useful.

Good transportation expands the area of the market for the final output of each process. It permits a much finer division of labour because economies of scale in individual plants can be exploited more effectively. In general, steady expansion of the market permits the evolution of system structure. The horizontal division of labour expands to proliferate varieties of final product while the vertical division of labour extends to generate a larger number of increasingly simple (and hence more easily mechanised and automated) stages of production.

The development of a region depends not only on the progress of its internal division of labour but also on its ability to participate in a wider division of labour beyond its boundaries. The external division of labour (as traditional trade theory emphasises) allows the region to specialise in those activities which make the most intensive use of the resources with which it is relatively best endowed.

The interface between the internal and external division of labour is typically an entrepôt centre. Whether or not a region includes a location with entrepôt potential will exert a significant influence on its development (Hodges, 1988). The general advantages of water transport, noted earlier, are reflected in the fact that the cost of long-distance bulk transportation is normally lowest by sea. This means that port facilities are normally necessary for successful entrepôt operation. Since ships afford significant economies of scale in their construction and operation a successful port must be designed to handle large sea-going (and ocean-going) vessels.

A port located close to major international and intercontinental shipping routes may become an important node on a global network of trade. Port activities will comprise both the transshipment of bulk consignments on connecting trunk routes and also 'break bulk' and 'make bulk' operations geared to local feeder services. In this context, the location of the port on the estuary of an extensive river system is advantageous. A centre of transshipment and consolidation is, moreover, a natural place at which to carry out processing activities. Handling costs are reduced because goods can be unloaded directly into the processing facility from the feeder systems, and then later loaded directly from the processing facility onto the trunk system (or vice versa).

The need for processing exported goods depends upon the type of agricultural and mineral production undertaken in the hinterland of the port. In the pre-industrial phase of port development, agricultural processing is likely to be particularly significant. Now crops such as corn and barley offer relatively limited opportunities for downstream processing before consumption – baking and brewing being respectively the main activities concerned – while rice feeds into even fewer activities. Animal production, by contrast, generates dairy products, meat and hides, while hides, in turn, feed into the leather and clothing sequence. Sheep are particularly prolific in generating forward linkages, as their wool feeds into the textile sequence. The textile sequence is simple to mechanise and has the capacity to produce a wide range of differentiated fashion products. (Cotton feeds into a similar sequence, but unlike sheep does not generate meat and hides as well.) The potential for forward linkages varies dramatically, therefore, from rice growing at one extreme to sheep farming on the other.

The location of the processing at the port depends, of course, on it being cheaper to locate the processing in the exporting rather than the importing country. This requirement is generally satisfied by both agricultural and mineral products. The perishability of agricultural products means that processing is usually done as close to the source as possible. Mineral products, though durable, lose weight during processing, and so to minimise transport costs it is usually efficient to process close to the source as well.

Mineral processing is, however, energy-intensive, and energy sources, such as fossil fuels, are often even more expensive to transport than mineral ores themselves. The absence of local energy resources can therefore lead to the relocation of processing away from the exporting country. Mineral processing can also generate hazardous by-products. Access to a coastline near the port where such by-products can be dumped is important, therefore, if minerals are to be processed before export.

While the processing of imported products is likely to be of much less economic significance, for reasons implicit in the discussion above, there are a few exceptions. Imports from an LDC, for example, may well arrive in a raw state, because of the lack of suitable energy supplies or labour skills in the exporting country. Furthermore, the more sophisticated are consumer tastes in the importing country, the more extensive is the processing that is likely to be required. Thus the greater the gap in development between the exporting and importing country, the more likely it is that the amount of value added in import-processing will be significant.

The agglomeration of activities within a port provides an opportunity for exploiting economies of scale in the provision of defence, law and order, drainage and sewage systems, and so on. It also provides a large local market which promotes the development of highly specialised services – not only commercial services but also consumer services – of the kind that could never be provided in country areas with dispersed populations. (Such economies of urbanisation can, of course, be provided without a port, and many countries do, in fact, contain inland administrative capitals which support such services. The viability of such capitals often depends, however, on cross-subsidisation from tax revenues generated at an entrepôt centre, and the social benefits derived from them may therefore be imputed to entrepôt activity.)

It is sometimes claimed that, contrary to the argument above, entrepôts devoted to the bulk export of agricultural products and raw materials are inherently enclavistic. The crucial question here is how fast the linkages between the entrepôt and the village communities of the hinterland develop. In the history of Western DCs provincial agricultural marketing and light manufacturing have grown up in medium-sized towns whose merchants intermediated between the village and the entrepôt. Even in LDCs with limited rural transport infrastructure, the tentacles of trade can extend to the village in respect of livestock farming because livestock can be driven to market over distances that are prohibitive so far as the carriage of crops is concerned. It is, therefore, only if rural culture is strongly opposed to merchant activity that the entrepôt is likely to remain an enclave indefinitely.

The conditions most favourable to industrialisation, it may be concluded, are the existence of a natural harbour close to major shipping routes, good internal communications between the port and its hinterland, livestock farming in the hinterland, abundant endowments of both minerals and primary energy sources and a coastline suitable for the disposal of pollutants. These considerations alone go some way towards explaining both the early industrialisation of temperate-climate, mineral-rich island countries with coastal deposits of fossil fuels and good inland river systems, such as the UK, and their relative decline once their minerals and fossil fuels have been depleted and their comparative advantage in livestock farming has been undermined by the development of overseas territories.

4.5   Scientific outlook and systems thinking

A territory with entrepôt potential can find its development inhibited by an unsuitable culture. Cultural constraints inhibit entrepreneurship both directly, by discouraging individual initiative, and indirectly by encouraging political leaders to distort incentives and overregulate the economy.

In some societies the absence of a scientific outlook may well be a problem. Western analysts studying LDCs typically perceive this problem as resulting from the absence of any Renaissance or Enlightenment. The society has not gone through an intellectual revolution in which a mystical view of the world gives way to a more realistic one. The society still relies on anthropomorphic explanations of natural processes, interprets unusual but scientifically explicable events as omens and perceives its real-world environment as the centre of a metaphysical cosmos. This emphasis on things as symbols of something beyond inhibits recognition of things as they really are. It discourages the understanding of nature in terms of mechanism and system interdependency.

A realistic systems view of nature does, however, raise philosophical problems of its own, which can be resolved in various ways. A major difficulty is that if man himself, as a part of nature, is pure mechanism, then choice and moral responsibility become simply an illusion caused by lack of self-knowledge. Western liberal thought resolves this problem through Cartesian dualism, in which the moral world of intentional action coexists alongside the physical world of mechanism.

The scientific outlook does not imply, as is sometimes suggested, a completely secular view of the world. Western Christian thought has also embraced dualism by redefining the role of God as the creator and architect of a self-contained universe, rather than as a supernatural force intervening directly through everyday events. The view that man is fashioned in the image of God encourages the idea that man too has creative abilities. Rejection of the view that the earth is the centre of the universe diminishes man's stature and raises that of nature, encouraging the idea that nature is worthy of serious investigation. Man's contact with God can no longer reasonably be maintained through sacrifices offered in anticipation of favours, but it can be sustained in other ways, such as an appreciation of the elegance and simplicity of physical laws which express this design. Man's creative abilities can be used to explore this design through observation and experiment.

The systems view of nature translates readily into a systems view of production. Production involves a system created by man and superimposed on the system of nature, with which it interacts. A systems view of production involves awareness of the principle of the division of labour – in particular, the importance of decomposing complex tasks into simple ones and allocating resources between these tasks according to comparative advantage. The systems view also emphasises that the strong complementarities between different elements of the system make it vulnerable to the failure of any single element and so create a strong demand for quality control.

The close connection between religious beliefs and attitudes to nature means that in countries where mysticism or superstition prevail, a scientific outlook and systems thinking are unlikely to develop. The concept of harnessing nature to control the future is absolute folly to people who believe that the future is already preordained, or is in the personal hands of powerful and arbitrary gods. As a consequence, their ability to assimilate technological know-how will be very low. Awareness of how local operations fit into a global division of labour will be minimal. For example, the idea that system complementarities necessitate continuity of operation, rigorous punctuality, and so forth, will be quite alien to local operatives. Appreciation of the importance of quality control in the manufacture of components and intermediate products will be missing too.

4.6 Competitive individualism versus voluntary association

The development of a scientific attitude in the West was associated with the rise of individualism. The idea that people are intelligent and purposeful was applied democratically. Intelligence was not something confined to a traditional élite, but a feature of every mature adult. Emphasis on intelligence led to demands for reasoned argument rather than appeal to traditional authority or divine revelation for the legitimation of moral objectives.

Individualism asserts that each person is the best judge of how his own interests are served. He can deal with other individuals as equals and use his intelligence to safeguard his own interests in his dealings with them. Interference in other people's affairs on paternalistic grounds is unacceptable. Individualism claims that everyone is capable of forming judgements on wider issues too. Since different people have different experiences, no one can assume that their own opinion is necessarily correct, and so toleration of other people's views is required. Differences of opinion over collective activity need to be resolved peacefully, and so in political life commitment to the democratic process is regarded as more important than approval of the outcome of the process.

Four aspects of individualism are worthy of special mention. The first is the alienability of property, which helps to promote markets in both products and labour. The demystification of the world through the emergence of a scientific outlook undermines the view that people impart something of themselves to the things they produce. It breaks the anthropomorphic link between production and use. As the product of labour becomes depersonalised and objectified it becomes acceptable to alienate it for use by others. Conversely, it becomes acceptable to claim ownership over things one did not produce. So far as natural resources are concerned, they no longer need to be held in common by the territorial group. They can be privately appropriated, giving the owner an incentive to manage them properly and avoid excessive depletion.

The second aspect is freedom of entry (and of exit) which allows individuals to switch between trading partners and between markets without the permission of established authority. Such freedom also implies freedom from statutory regulation of entry.

Thirdly, respect for contract, and a right of recourse to an independent judiciary for the resolution of contractual disputes, are aspects of individualism which are important in reducing transaction costs.

Finally, an individualist appreciates that multilateral trade is most easily established through separately negotiated bilateral trades in which goods are bought and sold using a medium of exchange. He recognises that currency is useful as a specialised medium of exchange, and that the most convenient currency is the debt of a reputable debtor such as the sovereign or the state. Individualism is therefore tolerant of debt and of the personality cult that surrounds notes and coin that carry the head of the sovereign. It imposes obligations on the debtor, however, to live up to his reputation through self-restraint: in particular he must not debase the currency through overissue.

A major cultural weakness of LDCs seems to be a lack of individualistic thinking. In the extreme case of a primitive rural economy, the link between production and consumption remains unbroken: individuals consume what they themselves produce, and thereby forego the gains from trade. In so far as there is a division of labour, it is confined within a social group. Different activities are coordinated both by relations of reciprocity between individual members and by members' common sense of obligation to the leader. These mechanisms are most effective within small, stable and compact groups, such as the extended family or the village community. In such groups members regularly expect to encounter one another again, offenders quickly acquire a reputation for bad behaviour and can be easily punished by the leader and, indeed, by other members of the group.

A major defect of such coordination mechanisms is that they depend crucially on stability of membership. If it becomes easy for members to quit, then reputations become less valuable, and punishment is easier to evade. Moreover, conditions of geographical isolation, which tend to promote stability of membership, also mean that the threat of expulsion from the group can be very severe. This allows a leader to acquire enormous power over individual members, provided he can 'divide' the members against each other or otherwise prevent them joining forces to overthrow him. Thus while isolation may help to promote close emotional ties between the followers, the leader may be feared rather than respected or loved.

Individualism has its own problems, however, in coordinating the activities of groups. Because individualism promotes inter-group mobility, it not only undermines the 'despotic' solution to intra-group coordination but also the internal reputation mechanism too. A purely competitive form of individualism, which encourages individuals to join teams purely for the material benefits, offers no effective substitute for primitive reciprocity.

When followers' efforts can be easily monitored by the leader there is little problem for competitive individualism, because the material rewards of each member can be linked to his individual performance. When effort becomes difficult to monitor, however, material incentives have to be related to team output, and when the team is large a share of the team bonus may be insufficient to prevent team members slacking. Unless there is a share sense of corporate mission, individuals are likely to put too little effort into team activity. The leader cannot trust his followers not to slacken. If the leader cannot be trusted either then the followers may not respond to his incentives anyway, because they believe he will default on the agreement if he can get away with it.

Another problem of individualism is that the inealienability of the individual's right to quit may induce higher rates of inter-group mobility than are compatible with efficiency. Successful teamwork often requires members to accumulate on-the-job experience in learning to anticipate each other's action; unrestricted freedom to enter and exit can allow transitory members who lack this experience to profit at the expense of their colleagues.

Widening the range of an individual's legitimate commitments from mere respect for property and contract to generate trust by instilling a sense of corporate mission significantly modifies the moral basis of individualism. The resulting philosophy is essentially one of voluntary association. This philosophy retains many of the attributes of competitive individualism, but emphasises that the contract of group membership involves acceptance of discipline imposed by the leader. Freedom exists principally in choosing between alternative group commitments, rather than in maintaining full discretion within the chosen group. It also emphasises that commitment to a group is a source of emotional satisfaction, and that more commitment rather than less may make people better off. It does not attempt to repudiate the 'minimal commitment' of competitive individualism but rather to augment this commitment with others.

Widening the range of commitments creates the possibility of moral conflicts. To a heavily committed individual, indeed, it is the resolution of moral dilemmas that often appears to be the essence of choice. Experience in coping with moral dilemmas of this kind may well improve general decision-making skills.

The global organisation of production implemented by sophisticated MNEs depends crucially upon such commitments to mitigate what would otherwise be insuperable agency problems. However intense the competition between MNEs, within each MNE cooperation between the parent and each subsidiary needs to be maintained at a high level. A clear group mission, articulated by a charismatic business leader who makes an effective role model, can be crucial in this respect.

It is therefore worth noting that the kind of individualism harnessed by the successful MNE is very different from the culture of unrestrained self-assertion – or even exhibitionism – which can be found in many societies, including LDCs. The extrovert 'individualism' of adolescent males, for example, has little connection with the mature individualism of the successful entrepreneur. People who exhibit no self-restraint cannot normally be trusted, and so make poor business risks for financiers, and bad employees. The observation, often heard, that there is 'too much individualism' rather than too little in LDCs, confuses exhibitionism with the mature individualism described above. It is not too much individualism that is the problem, but too little individualism of the appropriate kind.

4.7 Geographical and cultural aspects of a global trading system

The preceding analysis suggests that the differences between DCs and LDCs lie not only in resource endowments but in the fact that the territories of the former embrace potential entrepôt centres, and that cultural obstacles to the realisation of this potential in these territories are relatively weak. An LDC is likely to be a country that has no entrepôt potential and poor internal communications which make it unlikely to develop an indigenous entrepreneurial culture. A DC, on the other hand, is a country with both entrepôt potential and an entrepreneurial culture.

A country that has entrepôt potential but lacks an indigenous entrepreneurial culture is likely to find that, in the course of time, entrepôt operations emerge under the ownership and control of foreign entrepreneurs based in DCs. These entrepreneurs have the system thinking needed to recognise the entrepôt potential, and are likely to control established international transport and distribution systems into which the new operations can be integrated. The external commercial relations of these countries may become heavily dependent upon an international trading system governed by the requirements of DC markets and controlled by DC interests, while profits generated by entrepôt operations may be repatriated too.

Within any given historical epoch, the process of development begins with the countries that later emerge as the DC investors in LDCs. These countries may subsequently go into decline, but this process of decline is not considered here – it is treated as a separate issue, involving the transition from one historical epoch to another (cf. Wiener, 1981).

In modelling the process of development in global terms, the advantages of water transport over land-based transport – emphasised earlier – play an important role. These advantages mean that maritime trade between entrepôt centres in different countries is likely to be of much greater significance for each country than inland trade between the entrepôt and its remoter hinterland. The fortunes of individual countries are therefore closely linked to their place within the world trading system. Another consequence of the dominance of maritime trade is that even DCs may experience a degree of dualism in their development, between the entrepôt centre on the one hand, and the remoter hinterland on the other. A somewhat ironic corollary of this is that the most unfortunate LDCs, which have no valuable resources and no entrepôt potential, may be the only countries not to experience dualism, purely because they have no development either.

A typical sequence of global development is shown in Figures 4.1 and 4.2. There are two phases. The first involves the rise of DCs prompted by the development of trade between them. The second involves the emergence of LDCs and their own subsequent development.

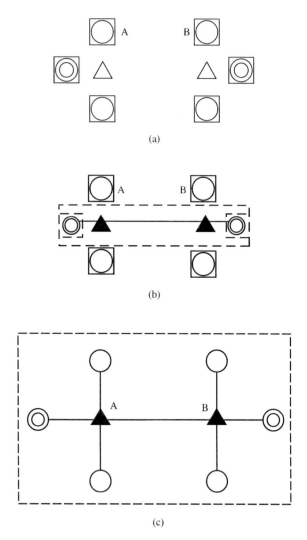

(a)

(b)

(c)

Figure 4.1   The development of international trade between developed countries.

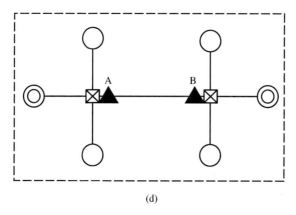

(d)

Figure 4.1   *(Continued)*

In the first phase (see Figure 4.1) it is assumed that there are two potential DCs, A and B, each of which is initially segmented into isolated social groups which control particular resources (see sector (a)). Resource endowments are denoted by circles, with large endowments that have foreign trade potential (because, for example, the output is non-perishable and has a high value per unit weight) being denoted by two concentric circles. Each square box encloses a group of people who share a common culture and reside close to a given resource endowment.

Both countries have a natural harbour which forms a potential entrepôt centre. The resources all lie in a hinterland which can be accessed given suitable investment in transport infrastructure. The harbour represents a potential entrepôt centre, and is denoted by a white triangle. It is assumed that in each country the indigenous culture around the major resource is reasonably progressive, so that this potential can be realised. A line of communication is established between the groups controlling the major resource of each country, and two-way trade develops through the entrepôt ports. Realisation of the entrepôt potential is indicated by the switch from the white triangle to the black one in sector (b).

The trade flow intensifies communications between the two countries, leading to cultural homogenisation. This is illustrated by the fact that the two countries now lie within the same box – at least so far as the entrepôt centres and the export-oriented hinterlands are concerned. This culture differs from the cultures of the isolated groups in the less promising hinterlands. The trading system strengthens the progressive element in the indigenous culture of the export-oriented hinterland by giving greater emphasis to the individual's right to hold property and his ability to fend for himself in the negotiation of trades. Competition between the port and the hinterland for employees also stimulates a friendlier and less autocratic style of leadership within social groups. This new commercial culture is distinguished from the culture of the isolated groups by the use of a dashed line in Figure 4.1.

As each entrepôt centre develops, the advantages of utilising more fully its indivisible facilities – notably the port – encourage the generation of additional feeder traffic by investment in transport links with the less-promising areas of hinterland (see sector (c)). The entrepôt now handles not only additional export traffic but also inter-regional traffic between different parts of the hinterland. In other words, the entrepôt becomes a hub for domestic freight transport too. Each country becomes homogenised around the commercial culture as a result. This stage of evolution may well be protracted. Many so-called developed countries still contain isolated rural areas where the commercial culture has made limited inroads.

Before this stage has been completed, the fourth stage may begin. This involves processing exports at the port, in order to reduce the bulk and increase the value of long-distance cargo. Downstream processing of this kind is illustrated in the figure by a cross within a square (see sector (d)). Industrialisation around the port will have further cultural consequences, but these are not considered here.

The second phase of the development sequence begins when one of the developed countries, say A, makes contact with an LDC, C. C is still in the situation that A was in at the beginning of the first phase, but with this difference – C remains undeveloped partly because it has a less progressive culture. Its initial state is illustrated in sector (a) of Figure 4.2. The figure has been simplified by omitting the domestic trade flows within countries A and B.

If A discovered C before B does, A may attempt to monopolise trade with C, so that all trade between B and C has to be routed via A (see sector (b)). Colonial occupation or control of international shipping lanes may be used to enforce the exclusion of B. So far as C is concerned, it is faced with the impact via A, of an established commercial culture which has evolved over a long time from roots which were, in any case, more progressive. This opens up a wide cultural gap within C between the highly commercial imported culture of the entrepôt centre on the one hand and the less-promising areas of hinterland on the other. This is illustrated in sector (c). Cultural dualism

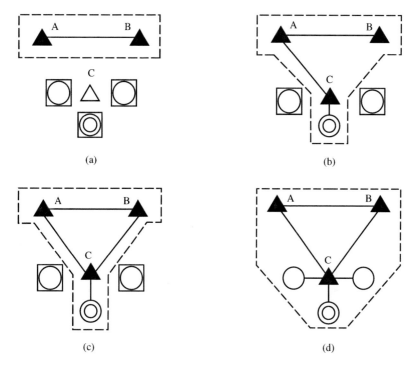

Figure 4.2 The role of developed countries in the development of LDCs.

impedes the final stage of development, shown in sector (d), where linkages are established with the remaining hinterland. Downstream processing around the entrepôt centre may also develop in this final stage, but this is not shown in the figure.

Two main social groups are available to bridge this cultural gap. One is the resident expatriates, who may have moved abroad originally as employees of the MNE or the DC government. The other is the group of indigenous individuals – merchants and other educated people drawn mainly from the middle and upper ranks of the host society – who are quick to take advantage of the profit opportunities from cultural brokerage. They are willing to learn the language and customs, and adopt the style of dress, of the DC – and perhaps send their children to be educated there as well – in order to consolidate their position. The size of these two groups, and their ability to combine forces where necessary, is crucial in determining the spread of entrepôt influence within the DC.

The analysis suggests that while the process of development in an LDC is similar in outline to that previously followed by an established DC, there are three important differences, which arise chiefly because the LDC is a latecomer to development.

First, the reason why it is a latecomer is partly that it has an unprogressive culture. There may be considerable resistance to the development of entrepôt activity, and indigenous entrepreneurs may be so slow off the mark that foreigners dominate the operations. There may even be political support for a policy of closing the harbour to foreign merchants.

Secondly, if the entrepôt centre is opened up under colonial rule, foreign merchants may enjoy significant market power. Thus few of the gains of trade that accrued to the developed country in the early stages of its own development may accrue to the LDC as it passes through a similar stage itself.

Thirdly, the LDC is confronted with a very sophisticated trading system designed to support developed country trade, and with a matching culture very much at variance with its own. Thus, although superficially it might seem that an LDC should be able to catch up quickly with developed countries, its vulnerability to the exercise of market power and the magnitude of the cultural gap may well cause discrepancies in the level of development to persist for a very long time.

4.8   Cultural aspects of MNE operations

The MNE is the major institution through which both the technology and the entrepreneurial culture of the DC is transferred to the LDC economy. The largest and most sophisticated MNEs are based in DCs; they utilise advanced technologies to operate internationally rationalised production systems. Systems thinking is highly developed in the headquarters of these firms. Strategic attitudes to competition are also well developed because of continuing oligopolistic rivalry between MNEs in major DC markets.

The analysis in this chapter shows that there are substantial cultural barriers to disseminating an outlook of this kind to indigenous managers, and to their subordinates, in LDCs. One obvious way of educating local employees is to send out managers from headquarters on short-term overseas appointments. This may encounter difficulties if the location is sufficiently unattractive to Western eyes that managers resist reassignment to the extent that they prefer to resign instead. In any case, these managers may have difficulties communicating with their subordinates, so while headquarters-subsidiary relations may be good, internal relations within the subsidiary may be poor. In some cases resident expatriates may be employed instead, though there is a risk that they will be out of touch with the more sophisticated ideas developed at headquarters.

An alternative is to hire locally and send recruits to headquarters for extensive training before they return to the subsidiary. Training is, however, likely to be difficult – even at headquarters – unless the local recruits already have some Western-style education, which may well mean that indigenous recruitment is confined to a small social elite. This strategy is inappropriate, moreover, when establishing a new subsidiary; managers will normally have to be sent out from headquarters to organise recruitment, and they can only be replaced when the flow of trained recruits has come on-stream.

Cross-cultural barriers also explain why spillovers from MNE operations in LDCs are so limited. The capacity of indigenous competitors to imitate – let alone adapt or improve upon – imported technologies is limited by their lack of scientific outlook. Similarly, the inability of local firms to emerge as subcontractors competing against imported component supplies stems from their failure to appreciate the importance of precision and punctuality – an importance that is so transparent once a systems view of production is adopted.

This is not to deny that profit-oriented indigenous innovation will occur. It will proceed slowly, however – because, for example, the nature of the innovation may have to be explained with the aid of an expensive foreign-run 'demonstration' plant, as the basic scientific logic cannot be assimilated. Cautious indigenous businessmen may wait for an indigenous innovator to operate successfully before committing themselves. Unfortunately, if the indigenous innovator does not understand the logic of the situation, he may be unable to improvise solutions to unforeseen difficulties, and so the innovation may gain an undeserved reputation for being unworkable.

When significant spillovers do occur, and agglomerations of local industries begin to develop, the effect on the cultural life of the indigenous communities can be devastating. The development of urban areas in which MNE activities are concentrated draws labour away from the rural areas. The migration of rural labour is a selective process. Younger and more entrepreneurial workers are attracted to the towns, leaving the least entrepreneurial workers, and the immigrants' aged dependents, behind. Although rural incomes may be partially sustained by intra-family remittances from the towns, the loss of the more productive and entrepreneurial individuals may well harden the conservative and inward-looking attitudes of those who are left behind. Faced with rising out-migration, the reputation mechanisms that coordinate the activities of rural communities are undermined. Rural economic performance declines, and the dualistic structure of the economy is reinforced.

Meanwhile, cut off from their traditional lifestyle, new urban workers tend to consume a higher proportion of the convenience products and sophisticated durables marketed by the MNEs. Some of these products are promoted using advertising strongly influenced by Western-style competitive individualism. Instead of creating an urban culture based upon voluntary association, which could lead in the long run to a lively entrepreneurial society, commercial media tend to promote attitudes of unrestrained self-assertion which are inimical both to industrial discipline and to honest business practices.

The social disruption caused by MNE activities does not end here, however. The tradition of subservience to despotic authority, sustained in isolated communities, can sometimes be usefully exploited by MNEs searching for cheap unskilled labour that is easily disciplined by intimidation. Women and children accustomed to absolute paternal authority may become useful factory or plantation employees, for example. Once the women acquire a measure of economic independence, however, the economic basis for paternal authority is undermined, and attempts to sustain it through religious teaching may only be able to slow the trend rather than reverse it. As a result, the whole fabric of traditional family organisation may be thrown into disarray.

Another form of disruption is to encourage mass immigration of refugees or landless peasants from other areas in order to depress wages in the locality of the subsidiary. Besides redistributing income away from labour, this strategy carries major problems of cultural integration within the local community, which may spill over into violence, particularly where the immigrants are readily recognised by their language, style of dress or physical characteristics.

Finally, there is the political disruption which may result from the fragmentation of political alliances which occurs when some local leaders opt for cooperation with foreign interests while others oppose it. Both groups may be forced into extreme positions – one as 'lackeys' of the foreign power and the other as intransigent fundamentalists favouring isolation. This fragmentation of the polity may enable the foreign power to 'divide and rule' the country.

This rather negative view of the social consequences of the MNE may be countered by many instances in which MNEs have attempted to become good corporate citizens of the host country. The difficulty here is that many LDCs – particularly former colonies – are in fact agglomerations of different tribes and castes, and that the concept of a good citizen with which the MNE conforms is merely the view held by the social group that is currently in power. Thus in a country with a long history of internal divisions being officially recognised as a good citizen may require covert discrimination against rival indigenous groups.

Situations of this kind pose various dilemmas for the MNE. In a country, for example, where the religion of the dominant group stresses paternal authority, should contracts for the employment of married women be negotiated through their husbands, so that women in effect become wage-slaves? Is obstructing the economic liberation of women a satisfactory price to pay for being a good corporate citizen and maintaining the economic basis of traditional family life?

In many recently independent LDCs political power changes frequently, often in response to military initiatives. Should the MNE favour political stability and, if so, use its economic influence on the military to secure the kind of stable regime most acceptable to the liberal Western conscience? If the MNE remains aloof, and instability continues, it is likely to be confronted with a series of corrupt demands for payments to government officials, as the holders of influential offices attempt to make their fortunes before they are deposed in the next change of government. Should the MNE jeopardise the interests, not only of its shareholders, but also of its indigenous employees by refusing to make payments, or should it respect 'local culture' and support the bribery endorsed by the 'unofficial constitution'?

The way managers resolve these moral issues will be determined by the MNE's own corporate culture which will in turn reflect, at least in part, the national culture of the DC in which it is headquartered. In this respect the balance between the philosophies of competitive individualism and voluntary association in the source country culture will be a critical factor in determining how far broad moral concerns dominate the pursuit of shareholders' short-term interests.

4.9   Conclusion

Previous economic literature on MNEs in LDCs has tended to concentrate on issues of market power and the choice of contractual arrangements (for example, Lall and Streeten, 1977; Calvet and Naim, 1981) The integration of cultural issues into an economic analysis of the subject reflects the authors' belief that economic factors such as these cannot entirely explain the relevant phenomena. This chapter has not proved that cultural factors must be taken into account. It is always possible that some new and more sophisticated economic explanation of these phenomena could be contrived instead. Putting this unlikely possibility to one side, however, this chapter has taken a step towards analysing the way that cultural factors in economic development impact upon, and are modified by, the MNE.

A great deal of further work needs to be done before the hypotheses advanced in this chapter can be properly tested. The full extent of the cultural differences among LDCs, and among the DC countries in which MNEs are based, needs to be recognised. The performance of a given MNE in a given LDC is likely to be governed by (a) the degree of entrepreneur-ship in the culture of the firm, (b) the degree of entrepreneurship in the culture of the host country and (c) an 'interaction' or 'coupling' term which captures the overall degree of similarity between the cultures, recognising that culture is a multifaceted phenomenon.

To apply this method it is necessary to profile the cultures of both the entities involved. It may require in-depth interviews with many people to establish profiles which can make any claim to objectivity. Complete objectivity can never be achieved, of course, in any study of cultural phenomena because of the distortion created by the culture-specific prejudices of the observer. Nevertheless it is unnecessary to go to the other extreme and adopt an entirely relativistic view. Different observ-ers may still be able to agree on some things, even if they cannot agree on everything.

Cultures contain a certain amount of inertia because of the way they are transmitted between generations through family upbringing. Nevertheless the advent of public education and mass media com-munications has the potential to accelerate cultural change. The trend towards greater rapidity of cultural change does, indeed, give a sense of urgency to understanding the mechanisms, and the economic effects, involved.

Economic changes can themselves precipitate cultural change, because they affect the shared experiences of members of a society. The increasing interdependence within the world economy is, in fact, another reason why the process of cultural change may have speeded up. This chapter has, unfortunately, treated culture as though it were an exogenous parameter rather than an endogenous variable. A full study of cultural factors would, however, involve a dynamic analysis containing feedback loops of a kind far too complex to be considered here.

Even in its present state, though, the theory provides some simple predictions about comparative economic development. It suggests, for example, that small island economies which enjoy a sophisticated cultural legacy may be better equipped to develop than mainly landlocked countries whose cultural traditions are derived almost exclusively from small isolated rural communities. The entrepôt potential and cultural legacy of Hong Kong, Singapore and Taiwan, say, may therefore explain why they have been able to industrialise and develop indigenous business services so much faster than many sub-Saharan African economies. This is quite consistent with the view that outward-looking trade policies have also promoted their development. It underlines, however, the earlier suggestion that trade policy itself may, in the long run, be culturally specific. Imposing outward-looking trade policies on a less entrepreneurial country in Africa is unlikely to have the same dramatic result as has the voluntary adoption of such policies in South East Asian NICs.

Finally, it should be noted that recognition of cultural factors has significant welfare implications. The emotional benefits that individuals derive from group affiliation are commonly omitted from the preference structures assumed in conventional social cost-benefit analysis of foreign investment. The cultural specificity of the policymaker's own attitudes are also ignored, although these attitudes are crucial in validating the highly materialistic individual preferences assumed in conventional policy analysis. On a more specific level, the failure of conventional analysis to recognise the important economic function of culture in reducing transaction costs means that conventional analysis has overlooked the significant material as well as emotional costs that cultural disintegration poses on many sectors of the economy. A number of judgements about the net benefits of foreign investment derived from conventional analysis will have to be carefully reconsidered in the light of this cultural analysis.

Notes

Previous versions of this chapter were given at the EIBA Conference, Antwerp, December 1987, to the Department of Economics seminar at the University of Surrey, October 1988 and to the First Japan AIB Meeting, Waseda University, Tokyo, November 1988. The authors would like to thank the contributors for their comments, and Geoffrey Jones, Matthew McQueen and Hafiz Mirza for comments on an earlier version.

5
Organising for Innovation: The Multinational Enterprise in the Twenty-First Century

5.1 Introduction

During the last half-century significant changes have occurred in international business operations – notably the internationalisation of production by US firms and the subsequent expansion of Japanese international operations. This chapter looks forward to consider the further changes that are likely to occur. It argues that the key factor governing the long-run success of multinational enterprises (MNEs) will be their managerial ability to cope with the accelerating pace of innovation.

The quickening pace of innovation has already placed MNE managements under enormous stress. Conventional management techniques rely heavily on chains of supervisory control. The system of supervision is predicated on the view that subordinates are inexperienced and potentially deceitful, and so cannot be fully trusted. The resulting atmosphere of distrust further complicates already complex management problems. Furthermore, the precautionary measure of requiring subordinates to gain their supervisor's permission delays action in an environment which increasingly calls for rapid response.

Existing management practices – even in quite sophisticated MNEs – seem to be geared too little to the management of innovation and too much to the management of routine. Historically, many organisations have evolved in order to coordinate routine activities within a fixed division of labour. Thus the origins of modern management practice have been traced back to the railways where rigid adherence to the timetable is the hallmark of efficiency (Chandler, 1977). Similarly, the essence of Fordist management is the precise synchronisation of operations within a continuous flow process. It is hardly surprising that the

96

structures which have evolved with such purposes in mind are unable to cope with the elements of chance and surprise in the innovation process.

The successful management of innovation, it is argued below, requires a high-trust corporate culture. This culture reduces the complexity of internal management by reducing the burden of the supervisory function. It frees management time to concentrate instead on responses to the external environment. High trust also makes it possible to empower more employees to innovate, and so it effectively decentralises the management of innovation too. Culture takes over the coordinating role previously played by organised supervision. The combination of high trust and decentralised innovation is the essence of an entrepreneurial corporate culture.

In ethnocentric firms, corporate culture is tied very much to the national culture of the parent firm. Corporate cultures in large MNEs are, however, becoming less ethnocentric over time. As they become less ethnocentric, MNEs in a given country may adopt very different cultures from domestic firms. As the ties between national and corporate culture weaken, the source countries for MNE operations may be much more diversified in the future than they have been in the past.

Corporate value systems in MNEs will increasingly reflect the functional requirements of coordination in particular industries. National cultures which by chance are well adapted to promoting coordination in certain industries will favour the selective internationalisation of domestic firms in those industries. In industries where no suitable national culture is available, successful firms will have to modify their ethnocentric cultures. There will be a tendency for firms in a given industry to converge on common values from different directions. Nations which incubate the most effective corporate leaders will be in the best position to effect this transformation quickly.

Section 5.2 demonstrates that the managerial pressures under which innovative MNEs are currently operating cannot be withstood using conventional methods. Adoption of matrix management and reorganisation into strategic business units have created almost as many problems as they have solved. Section 5.3 explains how recent innovations such as networking and interlocking joint ventures – although a step in the right direction – raise new problems of their own.

Section 5.4 analyses the requirements of an innovative system using the theory of entrepreneurship. Three requirements are identified; and the ways in which these requirements can be met using internal markets are examined in section 5.5.

Sections 5.6 and 5.7 examine the managerial implications of internal entrepreneurship within the MNE. It is shown that internal entrepreneurship requires much more than just the stimulation of adventurous behaviour by managerial employees. Rather it requires drastic changes to internal incentives which break traditional views of how managerial status is acquired. Managers need to be given responsibility to see projects through from initiation to completion. This in turn means that jobs must *evolve* rather than rotate. Managers' responsibilities need to change according to the fortunes of the projects for which they carry long-term responsibility.

Section 5.8 considers the role of world product mandates within the innovating firm. Section 5.9 examines existing national and corporate cultures to assess how closely they are already adapted to management of innovation in particular industries. It predicts that in innovation-intensive industries there will be steady cultural convergence among the dominant MNEs.

5.2   Increasing pressures on multinational management

It is a truism that the professionalisation and institutionalisation of scientific research within universities, corporate R&D departments and the military establishment has led to an historically unprecedented rate of technological advance in the post-war period. The increased supply of inventions has led to greater opportunities for sustained innovation, and a consequent shortening of product life cycles through rapid obsolescence (Ferdows, 1989; Jaikumar, 1986). But more significantly, it has provided increasing opportunities to synthesise different types of technology to produce radically new processes and products. This is particularly important because innovations that require a synthesis of different kinds of expertise are more difficult to manage than those which rely on just a single source of ideas.

The increasing opportunities for really fundamental innovations – as, for example, in the field of flexible manufacturing systems – mean that it is now much more difficult than it was to reduce the management of innovation itself to a purely routine activity. In the motor industry, for example, it was fairly straightforward to manage innovation so long as the planning of regular but superficial styling changes was the major issue. But when new technology began to affect the whole issue of the size of the model range, and to involve substantial capital-labour substitution in production, the management of change ceased to be a routine affair. The later Schumpeterian view (1942) that the process of innovation could be made routine just like the process of production, became demonstrably invalid. If innovation cannot be routine in the same sense that production is routine, then a management philosophy predicated on routine cannot be successfully applied to innovation.

So far as market structure is concerned, reductions in tariff barriers and transport costs have opened up national markets to greater import competition, while improvements in international travel and communications have opened up these markets to foreign direct investments too. Firms now have more sources of potential competition to monitor. To match foreign competitors they need to tap foreign as well as domestic sources of technical expertise, so that the synthesis of information becomes a globalised activity (Cantwell, 1989).

International economic integration also affects innovation through its impact on marketing strategies. To achieve price competitiveness based on economies of scale it is necessary to develop globally standardised products. But because economic integration precedes cultural integration, standardisation must somehow be reconciled with national and regional idiosyncracies in taste. Reconciliation is often achieved through the multi-component good, which combines standardised components in different ways to generate a family of differentiated products (Casson and associates, 1986). Multi-component design requires firms to innovate an entire system of interdependent components, rather than just a single product.

These marketing problems have been exacerbated by the growing demand for hyper-differentiation (Yasamuro, 1991). Status-conscious consumers, and those desiring 'lifestyle products', are prepared to pay a premium for uniqueness achieved by a combination of colour, texture and customised packaging. (Uniqueness also improves security by making it difficult to resell stolen products.) A technically successful product may not find a market unless it can meet these additional requirements.

Another stimulus to hyper-differentiation is the increasing subtlety of the division of labour among the users of products, and the increasing emphasis on quality of performance. A sophisticated division of labour among business customers generates a demand for a wide variety of specific products, whereas a crude division of labour only requires a small number of more general products. A wide range of specific requirements can often be satisfied using a versatile good – for example, durable goods often contain switching devices which adapt them for different uses. But versatility usually involves some sacrifice of performance in any given use because the specification of each component is a compromise between different requirements. A growing emphasis on quality therefore means that product versatility is not always a satisfactory alternative to the pro-liferation of product varieties.

Once the engineering of a hyper-differentiated range of products has been accomplished, it remains to match each variant to the needs of the individual segments. These segments represent not only different con-cepts of lifestyle but also different operating conditions in different climates and terrains. The matching process involves the assimilation of a huge amount of information. It is at this point that new information technology (IT) comes into its own.

The difficulty is that at present the full implications of new IT are not fully understood, and so the question of how far to exploit IT is still unclear – not only in the context of marketing hyper-differentiated products but in the field of management information systems as a whole. One of the key unresolved issues is the human–computer inter-face – a crucial issue for globally oriented firms for whom the costs of the personal mobility needed to sustain face to face contact is enormous, but where the potential effects on emotional bonding of removing it are not fully understood. Thus besides the problems of accessing different technologies and profiling proliferating segments of a global market, MNE managers also face the problem of gaining a proper understanding of the full implications of new IT.

Finally, the opportunities and threats of changing political alliances and alterations in regulatory environments must be taken into account. Although such changes occur regularly throughout the course of history, the 1980s have been particularly turbulent from this point of view. Perhaps the key factor from the standpoint of technological innova-tion has been the changing thrust of governmental regulation away from market intervention and towards more rigorous standard-setting on product safety, employee health, animal welfare, environmental pollution, and so on. This has made the interaction between technology choice and public affairs closer, probably, than at any time since the Industrial Revolution.

5.3   Weaknesses of existing strategy literature

Managers have not been short of prescriptions for handling the grow-ing complexity of their task. Many of these prescriptions are promoted by US-based consultants and business schools. Until the late 1970s US management still appeared to be strong, and so the provenance of these prescriptions gave them great authority. But implementation has revealed a number of flaws.

Matrix management, for example, has never adequately resolved the problem that 'no man can serve two masters'. The problems of matrix management are particularly acute for R&D vice-presidents operating in national subsidiaries, who have to report both to the CEO of the national subsidiary and the main-board R&D vice-president at group headquarters. Since tensions between parents and subsidiaries can often be high – particularly where foreign governments are attempting to 'tame' large US subsidiaries – R&D vice-presidents often need to make 'political' rather than 'business' decisions.

Matrix management also makes it difficult for both outsiders and insiders to understand the internal distribution of power. Outsiders do not know exactly whom they should be negotiating with inside the firm. Insiders face problems when they move jobs, as they have to learn each time the terms on which division of responsibilities between their bosses has been negotiated.

Compared to matrix management, the use of strategic business units has the advantage of transparency – it is easy to see how operations have been split into different units. The difficulty is that the separation between the units is often misleading. The organisational structure tends to make competitors of units whose activities are technologically complementary. Projects involving cooperation between different units become difficult to develop from 'the bottom up' because the heads of units are suspicious of them. On the other hand, top-down initiatives are often based on relatively superficial technical information.

This superficiality is a reflection of the dichotomy between the 'scientific' and 'managerial' promotion tracks in many firms, which means that senior managers in high-technology activities, even if they hold a science or engineering degree, have lost touch with the 'laboratory bench' many years ago. Practitioners with the detailed knowledge to formulate really good projects are either too junior within the management track, or are still on the 'scientific track' and so can be dismissed as 'boffins' lacking in business acumen. The recent acceleration in the pace of technical change has exaggerated this problem by causing the technical knowledge of senior managers to obsolesce even more quickly than it did before.

The growing opportunities for synthesising different technologies have made many senior managers aware that, in general terms, their firms lack comprehensive competence in core areas. To retain core business, newly relevant technologies need to be combined with the technologies in which the firm already has expertise. Various contractual arrangements are available for the acquisition of technology, including licensing, joint ventures, mergers and acquisitions and internal organic growth.

There has been a tendency among both managers and academic consultants to assume that the success of technology acquisition depends crucially on the form of the contractual arrangement used. Some writers have argued for the creation of a network of interlocking joint ventures (Bartlett and Ghoshal, 1990; Chesnais, 1988; Hedlund, 1986) on the grounds that this decentralises authority and promotes the free flow of information within the firm.

Joint ventures, it is true, often make a suitable compromise between licensing on the one hand and outright acquisition on the other, but the viability of the compromise varies from case to case (Buckley and Casson, 1988). Acquisition of technology through a joint venture is particularly useful where there is some need to influence the partner's direction of research, where the partner's technical lead is a medium rather than a long-term one and where their technology is neither fully 'core' nor entirely peripheral to the acquirer's business. Joint ventures are also particularly appropriate for capital-constrained high-growth firms since joint venturing requires less equity investment than outright acquisition.

In practice, however, joint ventures are often short-lived (Kogut, 1988), and awareness of this often reduces trust between the partners. This impairs the effectiveness with which information is shared, and can thereby make the expectation of a short lifetime a self-fulfilling prophecy. Experience suggests that successful technology acquisition often depends not so much on the form of the contractual arrangement as upon whether the contract has elicited a spirit of goodwill between the parties involved. It is not clear, for example, that a joint venture between mutually suspicious partners is systematically either better or worse than acquisition through hostile takeover. Any contract capable of engineering trust between the partners is better than one that does not. Trust encourages the partners to share their technology freely, and thereby promotes the synthesis of information on which successful innovation depends. Distrust encourages the withholding of information and frustrates the synthesis that needs to be attained (Casson, 1991).

Distrust between partners mirrors the distrust between superior and subordinate which characterises the large hierarchical firm. The problem with building innovation strategies around organisational structures and contractual arrangements is that the vital element of trust is too often left out. The converse is that the engineering of trust through corporate culture is one of the key strategies in the management of innovation.

5.4   The process of innovation

Innovation can be usefully analysed as a three-stage process involving the formulation, selection and implementation of projects.

Formulation requires a synthesis of information. Two main types of information are involved: technical and marketing. As noted above, several different types of technical information need to be brought together. It is not always clear at the outset exactly what types of information are required. Thus some sort of 'technology market' is needed, in which individuals seeking to formulate projects can browse around before deciding which technologies to take 'off the shelf'. The browsers need to have considerable imagination to visualise what results various combinations might produce. They also need a sufficiently broad scientific background so that they can understand what the research specialists have to say to them. The imaginative scientific generalist is thus a key individual in the formulation process.

Selection determines which project proposals go forward for implementation and which do not. Typically the costs and benefits of implementation are estimated for each project, and then a selection is made on financial criteria. The selection represents a 'venture capital' function. The venture capitalist needs to know the availability of funds (the risk-free cost of capital) and investor's attitude to risk (the degree of risk aversion). Given this information, the quality of the selection decision will mainly reflect the accuracy with which the costs and benefits have been assessed. This depends on the quality of communication between the formulator and the selector and the quality of background information and the skill in cross-examination which the selector uses to check the formulator's claims.

The final stage is *implementation*. Once selected, the project is developed to a 'ready for market' state, at which point it is integrated into the production system and the distribution channel. It joins other projects of various vintages which are at different stages of their life cycles.

The success with which a new project can be introduced into an existing system depends very much on the flexibility of the resources utilised in the system. In a very rigid system resources may have to be freed en bloc by closing down one project in order to start another. Thus the introduction of a new product may be held up until the production of some obsolescing product has ceased. In a flexible system, on the other hand, resources can be diverted incrementally from a wide range of alternative uses and brought together to support the new project. While marginal adjustments will have to be made elsewhere in the system, very discrete adjustments can be avoided. This prevents marketing problems caused by the premature withdrawal of a successful product to make way for an untried newcomer, or the too-late introduction of a product because existing products are still retaining market share.

Inherently rigid systems can, of course, achieve a measure of flexibility by regularly operating with excessive product inventory or idle capacity. But such measures can significantly increase overall production cost and so reduce the price-competitiveness of the product range as a whole.

The innovation process is summarised schematically in Figure 5.1. It is shown as a cycle which begins and ends with project formulation. It is cyclical because the implementation of a project generates a feedback of production and marketing experience which may stimulate a further project proposal – either to capitalise on unexpected success or to react to unexpected failure. The boxes on the periphery of the diagram illustrate the key external inputs at each stage.

Figure 5.1 highlights the fact that there are three basic requirements for successful innovation:

1. a rich and varied supply of specialist knowledge which can be imaginatively synthesised in different ways to formulate interesting project proposals;
2. a high quality of judgement that can be brought to bear on the selection process; and
3. resource flexibility that allows new projects to be integrated with existing ones without delay or disruption.

It is possible to go even further than this, however, and argue that behind the scenes are two fundamental factors which govern whether or not all of these requirements are met. These factors are social rather than economic. They are personal competence and the degree of trust.

Competence is important in several respects. In research and development it provides assurance that the claims of the technological specialists are well founded, so that practical problems caused by scientific misunderstandings are avoided. In selection, competence ensures that judgements are soundly taken on the basis of all the available relevant information. Where implementation is concerned, competence is likely to promote flexibility since competent people have the confidence to switch between projects which less competent people do not.

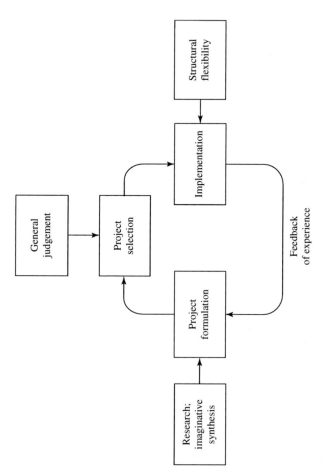

Figure 5.1   Schematic summary of the innovation process.

Specialist competence is most important in carrying out the research used at the formulation stage, whereas more general competence is of greater value in exercising judgement in project selection and in promoting flexibility between projects at the implementation stage.

As emphasised in section 5.3, trust is important in promoting effective communication. Because of the intensity of information used in the innovation process, confidence in other people's integrity is crucial. The technical issues are sufficiently complicated that innovators cannot easily cope with anxieties about the strategic withholding or misrepresentation of information as well.

In the context of Figure 5.1, competence refers to how well the activities of formulation, selection and implementation are performed, while trust is important mainly (though not exclusively) in maintaining a free flow of information between them.

5.5   Internalisation

The preceding discussion has established that the successful formulation of a project requires an efficient 'knowledge market', effective selection depends on an efficient 'venture capital market', and that effective implementation requires factor markets with high elasticities of substitution between different factor uses.

In conventional models of the entrepreneur it is assumed that these markets are mainly external to the firm, whereas when analysing the MNE it is more usual to assume that they are internal. This difference is fairly natural, since models of entrepreneurship tend to focus on small start-up firms, while models of MNEs focus on large, established firms. Thus the difference in internalisation strategies translates fairly easily into differences in the size and scope of the firm, and differences in the extent to which activities have been 'routinized' by the firm as it has accumulated experience.

Small firms enjoy a reputation (which is occasionally deserved) of being more flexible than large firms and more willing to contemplate radical as opposed to merely incremental innovation (Acs and Audretsch, 1990). This has encouraged the view that large firms need to become more like a coalition of small firms instead. The disadvantage of this approach, however, is that some of the advantages of internalisation may be lost at the same time. An important question is therefore whether internal markets can be retained but operated more flexibly in order to achieve some of the benefits of small-firm operation.

It is well known that one of the main advantages of internalising the market in knowledge is that incentive problems concerned with quality control (namely buyer uncertainty about the value of the technology) and appropriability (namely seller uncertainty about buyer integrity) are more readily overcome. In the absence of internal markets knowledge production often has to be publicly subsidised out of taxes because the only simple way to resolve the incentive problems is to set a zero price. One of the disadvantages of the small firm, therefore, is that it is generally restricted to synthesising information from the public domain whereas the large MNE can supplement public information with private internal sources.

An advantage of internalising the venture capital function is that the formulator of a project faces less risk that the financier will reject his project but pirate his idea (Casson, 1982c). Consequently he is more willing to divulge information fully, and the internal financier, knowing this, can place more confidence in what he is told. Only an enterprise with a strong reputation in the capital market can internalise this function, however, because individual investors will normally lack confidence in the ability of someone without a reputation to take such decisions on their behalf. The advantage of internalising the capital market is thus normally confined to large, established firms. There are disadvantages too, of course. One is that approval of large projects is a unitary function within the firm, so that the diversity of opinions available from different financiers in the external capital market is missing in the internal one. Thus the probability of wrongly rejecting a good project in an internal market may be relatively high (although the probability of a bad project being wrongly accepted may be lower as well).

The implementation of a project does not necessarily require that the production facilities and the distribution channel are under the innovator's control. There are, however, a number of well-rehearsed reasons why internalisation of implementation may be advantageous. In the present context, reasons connected with information flow are paramount. In particular, the feedback of information from production and marketing often plays a crucial role in suggesting new projects (as noted earlier), and this information will flow most freely in internal markets.

In some cases, however, the advantages of internalisation may be offset by the gains from access to external production facilities. A firm which is operating plant and equipment at full capacity, and where new investment involves significant installation lags, may find that a new project can be implemented internally only by either discontinuing a viable existing project or deferring implementation until either a new plant has been built or a firm with similar plant has been acquired. When similar firms are difficult to acquire, or where the pressure on capacity is expected to be only a temporary phenomenon, subcontracting may be preferable. It is probably for this reason that many highly innovative firms – particularly in cyclically sensitive durable-good industries – prefer subcontracting to internalised production. A compromise strategy is to own core capacity to internalise the production of most output but to use subcontractors to accommodate fluctuations.

Where distribution is concerned, however, it is often quite important that all the products share the same channel. Where the new product is a close substitute for an existing one the use of the same distribution channel permits closer control of the price differential. It is also convenient for the customer because if the products are sold through the same outlets, then price comparisons can be more easily made. Similarly, where the new product is complementary to existing products it benefits the customer if they can take delivery of all the products from the same outlet.

Finally, there may be an advantage in partially internalising certain factor markets – for example, by bringing education and training in-house. There are three main reasons for internalising education. First, the quality of external education – for example, public education – may be poor, or tailored to rather different needs. Secondly, some of the education may involve communicating the firm's secrets. Finally, education has an important moral dimension, as well as a technical dimension, and control over the moral dimension may be important in engineering corporate culture.

5.6   Continuity of personal responsibility

When small firms innovate using external markets there is one particular feature of project organisation which is often missing in large firms, namely that the entrepreneur who formulates the project also controls its implementation. In some cases the entrepreneur may remain committed to the implementation for the rest of their working life. In other cases they may sell-out later as the project becomes a large-scale routine operation which requires rather different kinds of management skill.

A major defect with organisation structures in MNEs is that they often divorce the formulation of a project from its implementation. The entrepreneurial employee who formulates the project loses responsibility for it once it has been selected for implementation. While those who gain responsibility may be more expert in implementation, they may lack the same commitment to make the project work in the way that the formulator would have done. They may therefore work less intensively to make it a success. Furthermore, with a division of responsibility between formulation and implementation the attribution of blame for failure becomes more ambiguous, and this further impairs incentives at the implementation stage. In an organisation where responsibilities are very narrowly defined and rigid demarcation is enforced, this problem may be exacerbated because responsibility for implementation may itself change several times as the project continues to evolve.

Given that there is no rigid division of responsibility between formulation and implementation, there is no real reason to confine formulation to any one subgroup of individuals either (Peters and Waterman, 1982). Since all projects have to be screened by the selector, allowing free entry into formulation need not reduce the quality of the projects implemented and should, on balance, increase it. Of course, some restriction must be placed on the amount of the firm's time that employees with specific responsibilities devote to formulation, but there is no good reason why most people should, on principle, have this time restricted to zero.

The best way of organising innovation within a large firm may therefore be to decentralise the responsibility to internal entrepreneurs who, like their external counterparts, retain responsibility throughout the early life of the project – at least until the process of implementation has become relatively routine. The reason why more firms have not already adopted this approach would appear to be two-fold. First, the pace of technological change has only fairly recently quickened to the point where such radical organisational changes are indispensable. Secondly, organisational behaviour is, as yet, much less of a science than the physical sciences, because the issues are much more complex and experimentation is more difficult, so that it takes longer for the best-practice strategy to reveal itself.

It does not follow, however, that the best of all responses to accelerating technical change involves the restructuring of large firm operations. The disintegration of large firms into sets of smaller ones (either by liquidation, divestment, or management buyout) may be more appropriate – indeed, hostile takeovers sometimes may be launched with such a programme in mind. In other cases the large firm may simply go into decline because internal entrepreneurs switch to the external market instead. The external financial market is always available to entrepreneurs who have been turned down in the internal market, and the 'second opinions' available in the external market may be more favourable. In other cases, proposals, though internally acceptable, may be exploited externally because the entrepreneur is dissatisfied with their prospective internal rewards. In some cases employees may join the firm simply to gain access to its internal knowledge market and have little or no intention of using the internal capital market to finance their projects because of the poor prospective rewards. A firm which suffers from incentive problems of this kind will gradually lose market share as it fails to renew or update its product portfolio.

5.7   Job rotation versus job evolution

Modern MNEs have, of course, made some attempt to respond to the requirements identified above. For example, in order to improve the efficiency of the internal market for knowledge they have encouraged job rotation. The idea is that the synthesis of specialist knowledge will be improved if managers have a more varied background. The difficulties are two-fold.

First, because learning a new job takes time, only people with high learning ability can be offered extensive rotation. If everyone is rotated, then at any one time only a few people will have mastery of the jobs they are doing. A preliminary decision has to be taken, therefore, about who is to enter the 'fast track' to gain the job rotation experience; and there may be very little to go on, except candidates' educational and social background, at the time this decision is made. Moreover the fast-track people have to learn their jobs from slow-track people, who may deliberately withhold information in order to maintain their own power base within the firm.

Secondly, by the time the 'rotator' has learnt their job they have only a short time to make an impact before they are reassigned elsewhere. They need to do something dramatic to sustain their fast-track image – simply making a success of a project initiated by their predecessor is likely to advance their predecessor's career rather than their own. Finding an excuse to kill off their predecessor's project and start up their own is more likely to impress. And since their own successor is likely to kill off this project anyway (for the same reason) they are unlikely to be blamed for any failure due to hasty conception of the project.

The entrepreneurial model of innovation set out above replaces job rotation with job evolution. Any manager who has successfully formulated a project that has won the backing of the selector relinquishes their normal duties and stays with the project until either they or the selector believes that their comparative advantage lies elsewhere and the project should be placed in other hands. On this scheme managers are not preassigned to a fast track – the fast track is simply the path taken by those who are sticking with a successful project that they have initiated. Problems of short-termism are attenuated because the manager's rewards are closely linked to the financial returns from the project over a long period of time. Even though the actual sales receipts may be deferred, the manager can be paid a salary indexed to the estimated capital value of the project (which can be reassessed each year).

Once the concept of job evolution is accepted, other factors fall into place. Because the job specification evolves with the project, it can be made flexible from the outset. Thus managers may decide to partner one another in project management and share the rewards. Managers may bid to take over projects from other managers, who may then return to their original roles, with the hope of formulating another winning project. The organisational structure of the firm can therefore evolve by negotiation, instead of through intermittent revolutionary changes to formal lines of authority announced by the board.

Such flexibility sustains coordination, of course, only so long as the changes take place in accordance with the principles of entrepreneurial organisation outlined above. Individual compliance with these principles must be assured through a moral discipline imposed by corporate culture. This discipline checks opportunism by encouraging individuals to be self-monitoring, and by making them responsive to peer-group pressure. Without such discipline the hierarchy will have to be reinvented, for every individual will need a supervisor who regularly monitors and appraises them.

Promotion of internal entrepreneurship within a firm naturally challenges existing vested interests. But many MNEs have already gone through a major revolution during the 1980s in which the R&D headquarters has been transformed from a powerful autonomous cost centre into a profit centre oriented to supporting divisional initiatives (Casson, Pearce and Singh, 1991a). The power of the centre has already been weakened. So far as the centre is concerned, the new arrangements will merely replace divisional customers with individual entrepreneurial customers. The entrepreneurs will still need central services to provide backup to their projects – the centre can be useful in carrying out additional research as a subcontractor, and acting as a broker between the entrepreneur and the rest of the enterprise.

The main challenge to vested interests may not be so much at headquarters as at the divisional level, where the heads of powerful divisions or strategic business units may find that their right to 'own' and manage projects initiated by their subordinates is called into question. Thus the managerial revolution will continue, but at one level down the hierarchy. In terms of corporate politics, division heads seeking to defend their power base may find that they have fewer friends than they thought at headquarters, as headquarters personnel have already been through the chastening experience of surrendering power to the divisions. Headquarters staff may, indeed, find it much easier to deal with individual entrepreneurs, whose commitment is to their projects rather than to their power base, and so welcome the demise of the powerful divisional head.

5.8   World product mandates

A world product mandate (WPM) confers on a national subsidiary of an MNE an overall responsibility for seeing an innovative project through, from formulation to implementation (Etemad, 1986; Pearce, 1988). WPMs are often seen as a constraint imposed upon MNEs by nationalistic host governments. There is a sense, however, in which a WPM can be interpreted as a manifestation of the policy of decentralised innovation outlined previously. As a result an entrepreneurial firm may have less difficulty accommodating WPMs than a more conventional hierarchical firm.

The analogy between product mandating and the empowerment of entrepreneurs is not exact, however. There are three important differences. First, the WPM adheres to the subsidiary rather than to an individual or team within it. If the manager of the subsidiary is able and willing to delegate, then this distinction may be of little consequence, provided that the individual or team is happy to remain in the subsidiary. If the individual prefers to move the project to another location, however, then the link with the subsidiary will be broken. This highlights the second difference, namely that WPMs are inherently location-specific, while the empowerment of individual entrepreneurs is not. If the entrepreneur prefers immobility, and is given discretion by local management, then a WPM may be a perfect substitute for personal empowerment, so far as the entrepreneur is concerned. But if the entrepreneur is mobile, and believes that their project will benefit from relocation at the implementation stage, then it is not.

Finally, the granting of a mandate in response to government pressure is not the same thing as the award of a mandate in response to competitive bidding for funds by entrepreneurs. The competitive process is likely to lead to a more efficient allocation of mandates than does political pressure. If it were the case that the most nationalistic countries were also the most entrepreneurial, then the difference would not be particularly significant, but this is not, in general, the case. Indeed there may be a tendency for the opposite to be true. Governments which favour political leverage are often seeking to compensate for economic weaknesses caused by poor indigenous entrepreneurship. Their resort to political pressure indicates their preference for exploiting short-run bargaining power rather than tackling their long-term economic problems.

WPMs are, therefore, less efficient on the whole than the policy of empowering individual entrepreneurs. The fact that WPMs are not very widely used probably reflects a combination of their inefficiency compared to individual empowerment and the fact that many firms have so far been unwilling to envisage any sort of empowerment of subsidiaries as far-reaching as the WPM. The accelerating pace of technical change means, however, that firms may become more sympathetic to WPMs in cases where the national subsidiary contains suitable entrepreneurs. The countries which are best placed to benefit from WPMs are therefore not the more nationalistic countries but those which possess the most entrepreneurial indigenous culture.

5.9 The influence of source-country institutions on multinational performance

The promotion of innovation is, of course, the concern of governments as well as firms (Porter, 1990). At the national level there are significant differences in the institutional framework through which innovation is sustained.

In most Western countries, entrepreneurs rely upon their own personal network of social contacts in order to synthesise information. Project formulation is thus a heavily decentralised process. The most intense exchange of relevant information goes on within the business elite. The US business elite has the reputation of being open to newcomers, whereas in the UK the business elite appears to be more secretive and closed. If true, this means that opportunities for the synthesis of information are more restricted in the UK. In Japan the synthesis of information is promoted by large firms, some of which originated as general trading companies. The sorting of information within these companies provides plenty of opportunities for employees to make con-nections between seemingly unrelated information. While the West is forced to rely on individual initiative because the networks of informa-tion flow are not systematically planned, Japan has less need of such initiative because the social system provides a ready-made communica-tions infrastructure. Where special initiative is required, the Japanese entrepreneur is likely to be self-effacing and to attribute the initiative to their group rather than to themselves.

Further differences are apparent at the project selection stage – though here a crude distinction between Japan and the West will not do. Japan, in common with Germany, and to a lesser extent France, has large industrial banks, many of which were originally founded specifically to assist their country in catching up technologically with the US and UK. The close links between these banks and large domestically owned enterprises constitute an informal element of internalisation within the capital market. This facilitates a relatively free flow of information between the bank on the one hand and the champions of new projects on the other – provided the champions are large-firm employees. Links with small firms still exist, however, because of the key role of large firms within national cartels, or as hubs of subcontracting networks.

In the US and UK, by contrast, the financing of industry is split between the merchant banks, or investment banks, which intermediate between the firms and the new-issue markets, and the clearing banks, which provide short-term advances and routine financial services. Information on corporate short-term cash flows is available to the clear-ing bank but not to the merchant bank, while confidential information on corporate long-term strategy is available to the merchant bank but not to the clearing bank. This partitioning of information may well reduce the degree of trust between the parties concerned. Under such circumstances, a great deal depends on the personal effectiveness of bank-nominated non-executive board members to make coordination between bank and firm work well.

Project implementation is distinguished from project formulation by the fact that teamwork is relatively more important and individual flair correspondingly less important. This is one fairly obvious reason why Japan, with its cultural tradition of group-centred work, has a major advantage at the later stages of product and process development, while the West enjoys a culture-specific advantage at the early research stage.

These cultural differences are also reflected in the education system, where there is a much stronger emphasis on conformity and social obliga-tion in Japan. The degree of specialisation within the education system also has important implications for innovation. A highly specialised education system, as in the UK, generates a wide variety of reliable technical knowledge, but relatively few individuals who have sufficient general knowledge to synthesise the work of the specialists. Some of the most successful UK synthesisers are, in fact, people who dropped out of the education system fairly early before they became excessively specialised. One disadvantage of this is that they lack the social contacts and the 'fast track' management experience that is needed to commercialise their ideas effectively.

In the US and Japan, by contrast, a more general education is provided. Where specialist training is offered, it tends to be combined with relevant supplementary material. Thus while engineering specialists are widely used in Japanese management, the engineer will have relevant knowledge of cost accounting and is quite likely to begin their business career with experience on the shop floor. In the UK, on the other hand, an engineering specialist will often be recruited into the R&D department at the outset, so that engineering and management skills are never effectively combined.

Cultural differences between countries will tend to be reflected in cultural differences between their firms. But as firms multinationalise, this link is likely to become weaker, as indicated earlier. The successful MNE, while capitalising on the strengths of its home-country culture, must also transcend that culture in order to do business overseas. In evolving a corporate culture the successful firm will strategically combine those elements of different national cultures which support internal entrepreneurship of the kind outlined above. This process of cultural evolution may also involve combining elements of the relevant institutional traditions. Although institutional arrangements at the national level cannot be directly copied at the corporate level, these national institutions may be a useful source of inspiration when redesigning the corporate organisation to facilitate entrepreneurship.

Thus the routine collection and sorting of marketing information by the Japanese trading company and it successors provides a useful model for the provision of market intelligence within an entrepreneurial MNE. Similarly, the UK tradition of employing highly specialised scientific individuals in basic research (now partially lapsed) provides a useful model for generating the technical information that a successful synthesis requires. The culture of the individual entrepreneur, who responds to the opportunities that the new managerial freedom affords, could well be based on the traditional US model. The US entrepreneur has a good general education which allows them to combine both technical and marketing knowledge.

So far as project selection is concerned the industrial bank provides a suitable model for the internal capital market of an innovative firm, although many multidivisional firms already have a market of this kind in place (Williamson, 1975). The use of project teams for implementation, based on the Japanese model, is similarly an established practice with many non-Japanese MNEs as well. However, non-Japanese firms have had limited success in instilling the group-centred ethos exploited by Japanese firms.

Those firms which are the quickest to learn from others, and to make the necessary adjustments, will succeed in the long run. As a result, international convergence on best-practice corporate culture is likely to occur. Indeed Ouchi (1981) has pointed out that there are many successful US firms which already have what might be described as a 'Japanese' management philosophy, and some Japanese MNEs have evolved a distinctly Western approach – at least to some specific functional areas like basic R&D. Thus the key performance-enhancing elements of a national culture are no longer the absolute prerogative of firms headquartered in that country. It may be more expensive for foreign firms to adopt them, but not prohibitively so. The crucial factor appears to be the alertness of managers to the possibilities of cultural innovation and adaptation in building up an entrepreneurial firm.

The growing dominance of entrepreneurial MNEs which exploit corporate culture to decentralise innovation is the main prediction of this chapter. The advocacy of an entrepreneurial culture, which is also implicit in this chapter, may be viewed as part of the historical process by which this process occurs. For by encouraging firms to change, the manifestation of the predicted benefits of entrepreneurial culture is accelerated and the process of imitation is speeded up. Faster imitation of a successful strategy poses greater problems for the slow-learning firms and precipitates their decline. The domination of the entrepreneurial firm is realised more quickly – reflecting the fact that the dissemination of relevant information expedites adjustment to a new equilibrium.

Should the analysis be flawed, then the recommendations may, of course, be invalid, and as a result the predicted dominance will not occur. Even if the analysis is correct, it still applies only to firms operating in the most innovation-intensive sectors, and only so long as the climate of radical uncertainty persists. Should academic writing have no influence on practitioners (which seems unlikely, given the alertness of consulting firms to business-related research) the domination of the entrepreneurial firms will still be achieved eventually. The predictions are therefore contingent, but quite unambiguous regarding the direction of change.

References

Bartlett, C. A. and Ghoshal, S. 1990. Managing Innovation in the Transnational Corporation, in C. A. Bartlett, Y. Doz and G. Hedlund (eds), *Managing the Global Firm*, 215–55. London: Routledge.

Buckley, P. J. and Casson, M. C. 1988. A Theory of Cooperation in International Business, in F. J. Contractor and P. Lorange (eds), *Cooperative Strategies in International Business: Joint Ventures and Technology Partnerships between Firms*, 31–53. New York: Lexington Books.

Cantwell, J. A. 1989. *Technological Innovation and Multinational Corporations*. Oxford: Blackwell.

Casson, M. C. 1982. *The Entrepreneur: An Economic Theory*. Oxford: Blackwell.

Casson, M. C. 1991. *Economics of Business Culture, Game Theory, Transaction Costs and Economic Performance*. Oxford: Clarendon Press.

Casson and associates. 1986. *Multinationals and World Trade: Vertical Integration and the Division of Labour in World Industries*. London: Allen & Unwin.

Casson, M. C., Pearce, R. D. and Singh, S. 1991. A Review of Recent Ends, in M. C. Casson (ed.) *Global Research Strategy and International Competitiveness*, 250–71. Oxford: Blackwell.

Chandler, A. D. Jr. 1977. *The Visible Hand: The Managerial Revolution in American Business*. Cambridge, MA: Belknap Press of Harvard University Press.

Chesnais, F. 1988. Technical Cooperation Agreements between Firms, *STI, Review No. 4*, 51–119. Paris: OECD.

Etemad, H. 1986. Industrial Policy Orientation, Choice of Technology, World Product Mandates and International Trading Companies, in H. Etemad and L. S. Dulude (eds), *Managing the Multinational Subsidiary*, London: Croom Helm.

Ferdows, K. (ed.) 1989. *Managing International Manufacturing*. Amsterdam: North Holland.

Hedlund, G. 1986. The Hypermodern MNC – a Heterachy?, *Human Resource Management*, 25(1), 9–35.

Jaikumar, R. 1986. Postindustrial manufacturing, *Harvard Business Review*, Nov.–Dec., 69–76.

Kogut, B. 1988. A Study of the Life Cycle of Joint Ventures, in F. J. Contractors, and P. Lorange (eds), *Cooperative Strategies in International Business: Joint Ventures and Technology Partnerships between Firms*, 169–85. New York: Lexington Books.

Ouchi, W. 1981. *Theory Z: How American Business Can Meet the Japanese Challenge*. Reading, MA: Addison-Wesley.

Pearce, R. D. 1988. World Product Mandates and MNE Specialisation, *University of Reading Discussion Papers in International Investment and Business Studies*, No. 121, August.

Peters, T. and Waterman, R. H. Jr. 1982. *In Search of Excellence*. New York: Harper & Row.

Porter, M. E. 1990. *The Competitive Advantage of Nations*. New York: Free Press.

Schumpeter, J. A. 1942. *Capitalism, Socialism and Democracy*. London: Allen & Unwin.

Williamson, O. E. 1975. *Markets and Hierarchies, Analysis and Anti-trust Implications*. New York: Free Press.

Yasamuro, K. 1991. Conceptualising an Adaptable Marketing System: The End of Mass Marketing, paper presented to the Conference on the Rise and Fall of Mass Marketing, University of Reading, May.

6
An Economic Model of International Joint Venture Strategy

6.1 Economic methodology

Over the last 20 years the application of economic theory to international business studies has sharpened the analysis of key issues. Economists aim to ask the right questions and to answer these questions in a rigorous way. This means making their assumptions explicit, for a start. The set of strategies available to the firms that they are studying is clearly specified, and the details of each strategy are spelt out.

In a global environment, participation in an international joint venture (IJV) is an important strategic option (Beamish and Banks, 1987). Explicit assumptions are particularly crucial when studying IJVs. No IJV, however configured, performs perfectly, and so to understand why an IJV is chosen, it is also necessary to understand the shortcomings of the alternatives. Moreover, IJVs are configured in many different ways, and different configurations are associated with different kinds of behaviour (Tallman, 1992).

Economists invoke the principle of rational action to predict the circumstances (if any) under which a firm will choose a given strategy. When the firm's objective is profit-maximisation, the choice of any strategy, such as an IJV, is driven by the structure of revenues and costs. This structure is determined by the firm's environment. By identifying the key characteristics of this environment, the firm's behaviour can be modelled in a very parsimonious way. The predictions of the model emerge jointly from the profit maximisation hypothesis and the restrictions imposed by the modeller on the structure of revenues and costs. Predictive failure of the model is addressed by reexamining these restrictions and not by discarding the maximisation principle that is at the core of the theory (Buckley, 1988).

This methodology may be contrasted with the more usual approach in international business studies of leaving the assumptions implicit and deriving propositions from a discursive literature review (Parkhe, 1993). This dispenses with formal analysis and relies instead on synthesis. But a synthesis is no better than the analytical components from which it is built. This point is particularly salient to the study of IJVs. For the more complex the synthesis, the more important it is that each component is sound. The economic logic of rational action provides just the kind of check on analytical consistency that is required.

A further implication of this method is that the variables entering into the theory do not have to be of a strictly economic nature. The criterion for inclusion is that they are analysed from a rational action point of view. The modelling of IJVs illustrates this very well. A wide range of factors impact upon IJVs (Geringer and Hébert, 1989): not just traditional economic factors, such as market size, but also technological, legal, cultural and psychological factors. Variables of all these kinds appear in the model developed in this chapter.

A final point about economic models is that they permit judgements about efficiency to be made. While IJVs may be commended on social and political grounds, they could be criticised as inefficient for, say, large firms that are leaders in their industries. An economic model can address this issue head on. Since no firm, however large, can be completely self-sufficient, it is readily shown that participation in IJVs is efficient provided the conditions are right. The main objective of this chapter is to set out these conditions in full. It is because these conditions are now more widely satisfied than they were in the past that IJVs have become such an important aspect of international business.

6.2 The typology of IJVs

IJVs can take many forms. This chapter focuses on a representative equity-based joint venture between two private firms. Its rationale is to combine complementary resources. These resources comprise firm-specific knowledge, and the combination is effected by each firm sharing its knowledge with the other. The knowledge provided by a firm may relate to technology, or to market conditions, or both. The firm does not normally share all its knowledge through an IJV, but only a subset of it.

The geographical scope with which technology is exploited is normally wider than that of marketing expertise, which tends to be of a more localised nature. This has important implications for the structure of the IJV, and for the degree of symmetry between the partner firms (Harrigan, 1988).

It means that the combination of two technologies through R&D collaboration is normally geared from the outset to global market exploitation. The partner firms are in a symmetric situation in the sense that the assets that they each contribute to the IJV are of global application.

By contrast, the combination of a new technology with marketing expertise usually involves market access of a more local nature. There is an asymmetry between the globally oriented asset contributed by the high-technology firm and the locally oriented asset contributed by its partner. In the course of globalising the exploitation of its technology, the high-technology firm may make a series of market-access alliances with firms in different localities. This gives the high-technology firm more experience of joint ventures, and may also allow it to play off one partner against another later.

A final possibility is that each of the firms contributes marketing expertise in a different locality. This restores the symmetry of the first case, but does not restore the global dimension unless the partners' skills, when combined, span the whole of the global market place. The principal motive for such collaboration is the coordination of prices in different geographical segments of the world market. Such collusion is potentially significant when the product is easily traded and there are barriers to entry or overcapacity in the industry (for example, the steel industry).

These possibilities are summarised in the first two rows and columns of Table 6.1 and are illustrated schematically in Figure 6.1. The two firms are indexed 1 and 2, with Firm 1 based in Country A and Firm 2 in Country B. The figure employs the conventions introduced in Buckley and Casson (1988), refined in Casson (1995) and extended in Casson (1996). Two physical activities are identified – production, represented by a square, and distribution, represented by a diamond. Physical activities are linked by product flow, which is indicated by a double line; the direction of flow is shown by an arrow. Two knowledge-based activities are distinguished – R&D, indicated by a triangle, and marketing, indicated by a circle. Knowledge flow is represented by a single line; to differentiate technology from marketing expertise, an asterisk is applied to lines that represent technology flow. It is assumed that technology flows from R&D to production, while marketing expertise coordinates production and distribution, and therefore flows to both. In practice, of course, R&D and marketing are linked as well, but this is not directly relevant to the analysis in this chapter, and so in the interests of simplicity is omitted from the figure.

Ownership of an activity by Firm 1 is indicated by horizontal shading, while ownership by Firm 2 is indicated by an unshaded area. Jointly owned facilities are partly shaded and partly not, the proportion that is shaded

Table 6.1   Typology of IJVs according to the kind of knowledge shared

Firm 1	Firm 2		
	Technology	**Marketing**	**Both**
Technology	1. R&D collaboration	2. Market access by Firm 1 to Country B	7. R&D collaboration with access to market B firm 2 'buys back')
Marketing Expertise	3. Market access by Firm 2 to Country A	4. Collusion in markets of A and B	9. Firm 2 supplies technology for use in both markets (Firm 2 'buys back')
Both	6. R&D collaboration with access to market A (Firm 1 'buys back')	8. Firm 1 supplies technology for use in both markets (Firm 1 'buys back')	5. R&D collaboration with access to both markets (both firms 'buy back'}

indicating the share of the equity held by Firm 1. Unless otherwise stated it is assumed that the equity is owned 50:50, as reflected in Figure 6.1, where exactly half the area is shaded and half is not. The IJV facilities are the laboratory R0 and the marketing headquarters M0. These can be based in either A or B, or in a third country, C, as circumstances warrant.

Table 6.1 identifies nine types of IJV configuration altogether. Four of them, shown in the top left-hand block of the table, combine one type of knowledge from each firm, while the other five involve at least one of the firms contributing both types of knowledge. The four simple types are distinguished by the numerical labelling of the linkages in Figure 6.1. Pure research collaboration (type 1) is represented by the links from the partners' own laboratories $R1$ and $R2$ to the IJV laboratory $R0$ and the feedback of new technology to the partners' production plants $P1$ and $P2$. Market access by Firm 1 to Country B (type 2) is represented by the flow of exports from the production plant $P1$ to the IJV distribution facility $D2$. Technology from laboratory $R1$ is embodied in the product, and marketing expertise from $M2$ is used to coordinate the export flow. Conversely, market access by Firm 2 to Country A (type 3) is represented by the flow of exports from the plant $P2$ to the distribution facility $D1$. This combines technology from the laboratory $R2$ with marketing expertise from $M1$. Finally, collusion in the distribution of the products (type 4) is represented by the synthesis of marketing expertise from $M1$ and $M2$ effected by the jointly owned facility $M0$, which coordinates the jointly owned distribution facilities $D1$ and $D2$.

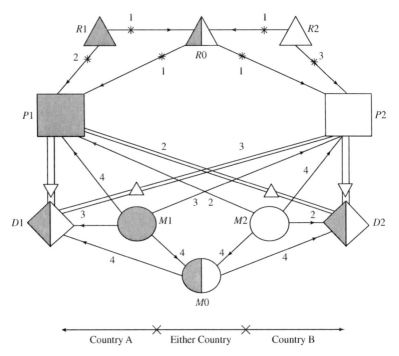

Figure 6.1 Schematic illustration of four IJV configurations generated by the sharing of technology and marketing expertise contributed by two firms.

The simplest case to analyse, and the one that has therefore attracted most attention from economists, is pure R&D collaboration (type 1) (Veugelers and Kersteloot, 1994). The practical difficulty with this case is that when the results of R&D are shared, competition between products exploiting the same technology can dissipate partner's rents. This encourages collusion in the marketing of the final product, and such collusion is likely to be most effective if the partners share their marketing expertise as well. This combination of R&D collaboration (type 1) and shared marketing expertise (type 4) generates type 5 in the figure. Because of its practical significance, this case forms the main focus of this chapter. Other cases are possible too, however. Studying the third row and third column of Table 6.1 reveals cases where both firms contribute technology, but only one contributes marketing expertise (types 6 and 7). Such cases can arise where a new technology controlled by one firm has to be adapted to local production conditions and local customer requirements in an idiosyncratic market controlled by another firm. Alternatively, both firms may contribute marketing expertise but only one of them may contribute technology (types 8 and 9). This can occur where a new technology generates a new product that requires a distinctive approach to retailing, which is familiar to the innovating firm, but where a knowledge of the local customer base is possessed only by the partner firm.

So far nothing has been said about joint ownership of production. This issue is highly relevant to globalisation. It is well known that many new products are nowadays developed with global markets in mind. The lower are transport costs and tariffs, the greater is the opportunity for exploiting economies of scale in production. If the existing plants of the partner firms exhibit economies of scope – for example, they have flexible equipment with unused capacity – then it may be possible to achieve economies of scale without investing in a production facility dedicated to the new product. But even if such plants exist, they may not be in an ideal location, given the specific input requirements of the product and the geographical distribution of its demand. If a new dedicated facility is indeed required, then it is natural that it should be jointly owned, particularly in a type 5 IJV where each firm is contributing both technology and marketing expertise. In fact, globalisation affords a particular stimulus to joint ventures of type 5: the development of a product with global appeal usually requires a synthesis of technical expertise, while the realisation of sales potential requires a synthesis of marketing expertise as well. The greater the fixed costs of R&D, and the greater the economies of scale in production, the more important is the marketing synthesis in achieving the critical level of global sales.

A joint-owned production facility $P0$ is illustrated in Figure 6.2. While the wholly owned facilities $P1$ and $P2$ continue to be used for other products, the product developed and marketed by the IJV is now produced in $P0$. The distribution facilities, $D1$, $D2$ may be jointly owned as well, but to avoid too many complications it is assumed instead that when production is jointly owned, the distribution facilities are not. This assumption can easily be relaxed if required. The figure is used to illustrate the types 5–9 which appear in the third row and third column of Table 6.1. The only symmetric type is number 5, in which both firms combine their technologies in the research laboratory $R0$ and coordinate their distribution using the marketing headquarters $M0$. A useful feature of this configuration is that each of the firms 'buys back' some of the output to which it has contributed a technological input. This gives each firm a strong incentive to ensure that its input is of high quality. It also gives it a strong incentive to ensure that the production facility $P0$ is

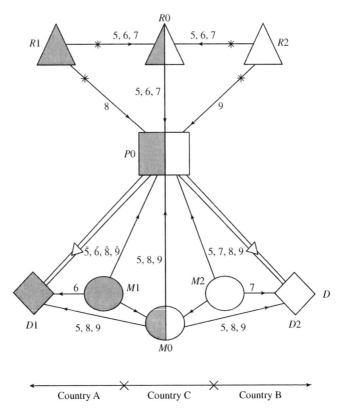

Figure 6.2 Schematic illustration of IJV configurations 5–9 based on a single shared production facility.

operated in an efficient way. Buy-back from a joint facility occurs with types 6–9 as well (as Table 6.1 makes clear) but the incentives are not as strong because only one of the firms is involved.

6.3   The alternative strategies

Not only are there many different configurations of IJV but there are many contractual alternatives to each particular configuration. It is impossible to discuss IJV strategy rigorously unless both the particular IJV configuration and the alternatives to it are clearly specified. The alternatives considered here are those suggested by internalisation theory (Buckley and Casson 1976), namely a merger and a licensing agreement. All three of these strategic options involve combining both the technology and the marketing expertise of the two firms, but they combine them in different ways.

The focus is on a type 5 IJV configuration, i.e., a symmetric globally oriented kind of IJV. It is assumed that production takes place in a dedicated plant owned by the IJV. Location factors are not explicitly considered: it is simply assumed that production is based in a country that has ready access for its exports (through free trade and low transport costs) to the major centres of global demand. To preserve the symmetry of the configuration, this location is assumed to be a third country, C, as indicated in Figure 6.2.

All three options require the consent of both the firms. If no consent is achieved then no collaboration occurs (this is the null option, strategy 0). To simplify the analysis it is assumed that Firm 1 takes the initiative in promoting inter-firm collaboration and that Firm 2 plays an entirely passive role. The consequences of relaxing this assumption are considered later. It is Firm 1 that evaluates the profits from merger, IJV and licensing and compares them to each other. Firm 2 agrees to any proposed arrangement, provided that the terms leave it no worse off than before (i.e., than under the null strategy). Under these conditions the private gains to Firm 1 coincide with the overall gains from each strategy, and so in economic terms Firm 1's decision is Pareto-efficient even though to an outsider the distribution of rewards may seem unfair.

A merger could in principle be effected either by Firm 1 acquiring Firm 2, or by Firm 2 acquiring Firm 1, or by a third firm acquiring them both. It is assumed that because Firm 1 takes the initiative, it is Firm 1 that acquires Firm 2. Note, however, that even though Firm 1 may be better at spotting opportunities, Firm 2 may be better at managing a large organisation, and so it might, in fact, be more profitable for Firm 1 to arrange a reverse takeover instead. Likewise with licensing: it is possible for Firm 1 to licence in Firm 2's technology (and the associated marketing expertise) or for Firm 1 to licence its own technology out to Firm 2. It is assumed that Firm 1 licences in Firm 2's technology, so that it retains its full independence, as in the case of acquisition. If, however, Firm 1's technology was much easier to value than Firm 2's then it might be easier for it to licence out its own technology instead. This is another complication that will not be considered here.

It is assumed that Firm 1 extracts its rewards from collaboration through the terms on which its deals with Firm 2 are made, and not through the proportion of equity which it holds. If the equity stake were the sole consideration, then acquisition of Firm 2 would always be more profitable than a joint venture, which in turn would be more profitable than licensing, which is clearly absurd. In the context of an acquisition, it is the price at which Firm 2'suity is valued which is crucial; in the case of an IJV, it is the management fees that the IJV must pay to Firm 1, while in the case of licensing it is the royalty rate offered to Firm 2.

The configuration of the merger is illustrated in Figure 6.3. The horizontal shading throughout indicates that Firm 1 has acquired all the facilities previously owned by Firm 2. R&D and marketing have been rationalised too: the laboratories $R1$ and $R2$ have been eliminated and all research concentrated on $R0$. Similarly, the local marketing activities $M1$ and $M2$ have been eliminated in favour of global marketing through $M0$. Such rationalisation is not an inevitable consequence of merger, but it is undoubtedly one of the advantages of merger that it is easier to do.

To illustrate the relationship between the new activity centred on $P0$ and the established activities centred on $P1$ and $P2$, all the activities of the firm are shown in the figure. Flows of established goods that were

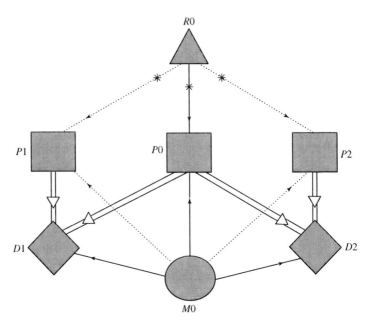

Figure 6.3 Configuration after Firm 2 has been acquired and rationalised by Firm 1.

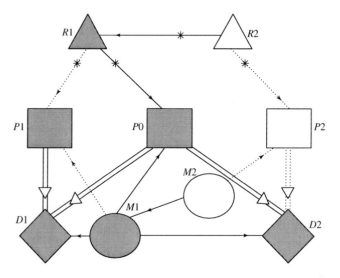

Figure 6.4   Configuration when Firm 1 licences in technology from Firm 2.

previously internal to the partner firms are indicated by broken double lines, while the flows of information that support them are indicated by broken single lines. The solid lines refer to flows involving the product that was previously generated in the IJV.

The same conventions are used in Figure 6.4 to illustrate the licensing option. Under licensing, Firm 2's laboratory $R2$ supplies technology directly to its 'opposite number' R1, which combines it with its own technology and transfers the resulting package internally to plant $P0$. The resulting product is supplied internally to $D1$, and externally to $D2$, both flows being coordinated by $M1$ using information supplied to it under the licensing agreement by $M2$. This particular configuration of licensing has been chosen because it affords the most direct comparison with the configurations assumed for the other options discussed above.

6.4   Internalisation factors in strategic choice

The rationale of the joint venture is that it allows both of the partner firms to acquire some of the benefits of internalising knowledge flow without incurring the full set-up costs of a merger. By contrast, licensing affords no benefits of internalisation, but it avoids the more modest set-up costs of an IJV.

There are many internalisation factors that potentially impact on IJVs (Buckley and Casson 1988). Some of the most important ones are listed on the left-hand side of Table 6.2, together with their notation, which is used in section 6.6. The column entries indicate the impact of each factor on the costs of each strategy.

The best-known factor is the general security of property rights and, in particular, the existence of patent rights on technology. It is far easier to sell access to a technology at arm's length when it is patented than when it is not. Thus patent coverage encourages licensing at the expense of both mergers and IJVs.

A more subtle point concerns the uncertainty that firms experience about their own degree of technological competence. A key feature of a joint venture contract, in contrast to a licensing agreement, is that it does not specify in detail exactly what technological expertise each partner will contribute to the venture. While neither partner normally commits itself to supplying all it knows, it does not attempt to restrict what it supplies under an IJV as explicitly as it would under a licensing agreement. Each firm generally agrees to contribute, within reason, whatever is necessary to achieve the agreed objective, such as the solution to a technical problem or the development of a new product. This arrangement provides mutual insurance to the partners under conditions where they are unsure, not only about their partner's technological competence, but about their own as well. If each partner firm knew exactly what it was capable of, and understood fully the requirements of the project, then it would be able to specify exactly what it required from its partner. At the same time, it would be perfectly clear as to what it was able to supply itself. Licensing would therefore involve no risk that either firm would lack the competence to fulfil its specific commitments. The more uncertain the partners are about their competence relative to the technical goal, however, the greater are the risks of specifying exactly what is required from their partner to complement their own skills, and conversely the greater are the risks of accepting an obligation to supply specific skills themselves.

This is evidently related to the tacitness of the knowledge involved (Polanyi, 1966). Although tacitness is normally discussed in terms of the costs of communicating knowledge to other people, a related, and indeed more fundamental, issue is whether people can actually communicate what they know to themselves. In other words, do managers understand where their competencies really lie before they get to put them into practice? It would seem that the concept of uncertainty about own competence is a useful way of conceptualising this difficult issue.

Table 6.2 Key determinants of the costs of alternative strategies

Determinant	Notation	Strategy		
		1. Licensing	2. IJV	3. Merger
Obstacles to licensing				
Lack of patent rights	*p*	+	0	0
Uncertainty about technological competence	*t*		0	0
Obstacles to IJV				
Cultural distance leading to misunderstanding and distrust	*d*	0	+	+
Obstacles to merger				
Protection of firm's independence	*n*	0	0	+
Scope economies in technology unrelated to other technologies of acquiring firm	*s*	0	0	+

Note: A positive sign indicates that costs increase while a zero sign indicates that costs are unaffected.

The lack of specificity of the joint venture agreement therefore provides each firm with the flexibility to modify what it requires of its partner in the light of what it discovers about its own expertise. The same flexibility of response can be achieved by merger, as the top line of Table 6.2 makes clear. The greater the firm's uncertainty about its own technological competence, therefore, the stronger the preference for a merger or an IJV is likely to be.

It is possible to construct a number of variations on this theme – for example, where the partners discover one another's shortcomings rather than discovering their own – but the basic principle remains the same. The lack of specificity in the IJV arrangement affords a degree of mutual insurance through flexible response that is missing in an ordinary licensing agreement.

Mutual insurance only works, however, if the other partner can be trusted to make the appropriate response (Casson, 1991; Ring and Van de Ven, 1994). Insuring people against their own incompetence creates a 'moral hazard' problem. They may plead incompetence merely to demand support from the other party, while claiming to be unable to deliver support themselves. Licensing requires less trust than an IJV because the contract, being more explicit in detail, is easier to enforce in law. This advantage of licensing depends, however, on the effectiveness of international law, which in turn depends upon the sanctions available, the rules of evidence, access to an impartial judiciary, and so on.

While IJVs are less dependent upon the law for their success, they are more dependent upon culture. From an economic perspective, culture may be defined as shared values and beliefs. Cultural homogeneity, acting through shared beliefs, reduces transactions costs by avoiding misunderstandings, while shared values – notably integrity and loyalty – underpin the willingness to share knowledge which is crucial to an IJV. Prudence requires that knowledge is shared only with those who can be trusted to reciprocate, which favours partnership with members of the same cultural group. This is reflected in the third line of Table 6.2, where cultural distance is identified as an obstacle to an IJV. Cultural distance may also be an obstacle to merger, though, contrary to popular opinion, the obstacle may not be as great as in the case of an IJV. This is because a merger permits hierarchical monitoring to be substituted for socially mediated trust, and in the long run allows corporate leadership to engineer a high-trust culture internal to the firm itself.

The last two factors in the table are classified as obstacles to merger. There is the well-known problem that some 'national champions' are protected from foreign takeover by their governments, while others are family firms whose shareholders value independence more than they value their profit stream. Such constraints can raise the cost of merger to a prohibitive level. Competition policy and antitrust policy can also protect firms from takeover, and in some cases antitrust policy may inhibit IJVs as well.

Then there is the nature of the acquired technology. If the acquired technology has many applications besides the particular application for which it is required, then the acquiring firm may need to diversify into these applications, or to licence such applications out to other firms. In either case, it may be more advantageous for the acquiring firm to leave the original owner to do this, rather than to attempt this in addition to all the other things it has to do. The disadvantages of acquisition are greater when the acquired technology is unrelated to the other technologies (if any) possessed by the acquiring firm.

6.5 The dynamics of innovation in a global economy

The choice of strategy can be analysed either as a one-off decision made afresh every time an opportunity for collaboration arises, or in terms of a commitment to handling a succession of opportunities of a given type using the same strategy. When technological innovation is spasmodic, then the first approach is the most appropriate, but in industries where innovation is a regular occurrence the second has more to recommend it. It is the second approach that is followed here.

Suppose that each firm is committed to combining one of its technologies with those of another firm, but that the firm it partners with keeps changing as new innovations continually occur. This is because innovative ability is dispersed across a number of potential partners in the industry, and indeed some major innovations may originate with entirely new entrants. When subsequent innovation renders an existing partner's technology obsolete, a change of partner is required. At any one time the firm has only one partner, but the identity of the partner changes with a frequency that reflects the rate of innovation in the industry.

Switching partners incurs considerable costs where merger is concerned, because of the expense of the legal reconstruction of the firms and their subsequent rationalisation (as indicated in Figure 6.3). While commitment to merger affords significant internalisation benefits, its costs are large as well. Thus rapid innovation which leads to frequent partner switching considerably increases the average recurrent cost of the merger strategy. The formation of an IJV also incurs significant set-up costs, though not as large as those of a merger. Correspondingly, the internalisation gains are lower too. At the opposite extreme to a merger is the licensing option, which involves low set-up costs but offers no internalisation economies at all. Licensing is therefore much cheaper than merger, and somewhat cheaper than an IJV, when technological change is rapid.

The costs of switching to a new partner are normally incurred at the outset of an arrangement, while the benefits are deferred: they are distributed continuously over time. There is, therefore, an element of interest cost in switching, and this must be allowed for when calculating the costs and benefits of alternative strategies.

Unlike the costs of internalisation, the benefits of internalisation are continuing ones. Moreover they normally vary directly with the size of the market in a way that set-up costs do not. The greater the value of the market for the product that the partner firms produce, the greater the gains from internalisation. One reason for this is that internalisation enhances the proportion of the rents from the marketing of the product that the firms can appropriate for themselves.

6.6   A formal model of IJV selection

There is a subtle interplay between the different factors mentioned above that requires a formal model for its elucidation. Let the three strategies be indexed in ascending order of internalisation: $k = 1$ for licensing, $k = 2$ for an IJV and $k = 3$ for a merger. In addition there is a null strategy ($k = 0$) which involves no collaboration between firms. As indicated at the outset, the firms maximise profit, subject to the constraints imposed by family ownership or national champion's status. It is assumed that these constraints do not apply to Firm 1, the decision maker, although they may well apply to its partner, Firm 2. The strategy is chosen by Firm 1 to maximise its overall profit, π.

Profit has three components: the basic gains from collaboration, which are independent of the chosen strategy but vary with the size of the market; the benefits of internalisation, which vary according to the strategy and according to market size; and the costs of internalisation, which are independent of market size but vary according to the chosen strategy, the frequency of partner change and a number of other factors described below.

Let π_k be the profit per period generated by the consistent pursuit of strategy k through a succession of collaborations with innovative partner firms. Let c_k be the set-up costs incurred by strategy k when switching to a new partner firm. All of the costs identified in Table 6.2 may be construed as costs of this kind. Reading down the right-hand columns of the table shows that the set-up cost of a licensing arrangement, c_1, is an increasing function of missing patent rights, p, and uncertainty about the firm's technological competence, t. The set-up cost of an IJV, c_2, is an increasing function of cultural distance, d, while the set-up cost of a merger, c_3, is an increasing function of cultural distance, d, the degree of protection of the independence of the partner firm, n, and the scope economies of the technology, s:

$$c_1 = c_1(p, f) \tag{1.1}$$

$$c_2 = c_2(d) \tag{1.2}$$

$$c_3 = c_3(d, n, s) \tag{1.3}$$

Let $f \leq 1$ be the frequency with which a change of partner occurs. This frequency may be interpreted as the probability that a change will occur in any given period. The value of f reflects the pace of innovation in the global economy. Let $r \geq 0$ be the rate of interest in the international capital market. When interest charges associated with the set-up costs are allowed for by summing the relevant geometric series, the average recurrent expense equivalent to a unit set-up cost turns out to be

$$v = (r/(1+r)) \sum_{n=0}^{z} (1/(1+r)n/f) = (f+r)/(1+r) \tag{2}$$

provided that r is suitably small. It is readily established that v is an increasing function of the frequency f and the rate of interest r,

$$\partial v / \partial f = 1/(1+r) > 0 \tag{3.1}$$

$$\partial v / \partial f = (1-f)/(1+r)^2 > 0 \tag{3.2}$$

Let b_k be the benefit from internalisation accruing when strategy k is applied to a market of unit size. It is assumed that the total benefit is directly proportional to the market size, x. As indicated above, the internalisation benefit of merger exceeds that of an IJV, which in turn exceeds that of licensing – which is, of course, zero; thus

$$b_3 > b_2 > b_1 = 0 \tag{4}$$

Since profit is by definition the excess of benefit over cost,

$$\pi_0 = 0$$

$$\pi_k = (a + b_k)x - c_k v \quad (k = 1, 2, 3) \tag{5}$$

where $a > 0$ is the basic gain from collaboration per unit market size. The chosen strategy k satisfies the inequality constraint

$$\pi_k \geq \pi_i \quad (i \neq k) \tag{6}$$

The choice of k is unique when the inequality (6) is strictly satisfied.

All of the factors shown in equation (5) affect the choice of k, as do the factors which in turn determine them; thus

$$k = (a, b_2, b_3, d, p, n, s, t, f, r, x)$$

Not all of these factors impact on IJV strategy all of the time. They only affect the choice when it is marginal, and there are three different margins that are involved. The marginal choice between an IJV and licensing depends on all of these factors except b_3, n and s, which are specific to a merger, and a, which is common to both. The marginal choice between an IJV and a merger depends on all of these factors except p and t, which are specific to licensing, and a, which is again common to both. The marginal choice between an IJV and the null strategy depends on all the factors except b_3, n and s, which are specific to mergers, and t, which is specific to licensing. In principle, all of these margins can be relevant, though only in exceptional circumstances will two or more of them be relevant at the same time.

6.7   The interaction of market size and volatility

Discrete choice models of this kind have many applications in international business. Indeed, Buckley and Casson (1981) use a variant of the present model to analyse entry through Foreign Direct Investment (FDI) to a foreign market. Their model excludes IJVs, but includes exporting as an alternative to FDI and licensing. Exporting is already included in the present model, as a component of all three strategies, and so does not need to be treated separately as in the previous model. The previous model also excludes volatility; it takes only a short-run view of technological change compared to the present chapter. The formal similarities can be seen by examining the influence of market size on strategic choice, as illustrated in Figure 6.5.

The figure measures profit vertically and market size horizontally. The zero-profit axis is A_0A_0', corresponding to the null strategy; the bottom axis is used purely to clarify the labelling of the figure. The variation of profitability with market size under licensing is indicated by the line A_1A_1'; since licensing affords low set-up costs but no internalisation

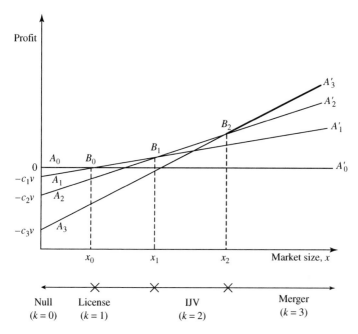

Figure 6.5 Influence of market size on strategic choice.

benefits, the intercept is only slightly below that of $A_0 A_0'$, while the slope (measured by a) is fairly modest. The situation under an IJV is indicated by $A_2 A_2'$; the intercept is lower, because the set-up costs are higher, but the slope (measured by $a + b_2$) is steeper because internalisation benefits are available. Finally the schedule $A_3 A_3'$ shows the situation under merger; the intercept is very low because the set-up costs are very high, but the slope (measured by $a + b_3$) is the steepest of all because the full benefit of internalisation is being obtained.

The envelope $A_0 B_0 B_1 B_2 A_3'$ indicates the maximum profit generated at each market size. The strategy that generates this profit is determined by the schedules that form the envelope at the appropriate point. The corresponding strategy can be read off along the horizontal axis, as indicated in Figure 6.5. The figure has been drawn so that all of the strategies have a role to play – no one strategy is dominated by the others. Under these conditions there is a steady progression, as market size increases, from no collaboration, to licensing, to an IJV and finally to a merger. This is because as the size of the market grows the set-up costs of internalisation, which are fixed costs independent of market size, can be spread more thinly and so greater investment in internalisation becomes worthwhile.

This is a very partial picture of the situation, however. While it is the size of the market that governs the benefits of internalisation, it is the factor v that governs costs. The factor v may be termed the volatility factor; it reflects the impact of both the pace of technological progress and the cost of capital.

A complementary view to Figure 6.5 is presented in Figure 6.6, which shows how the profitability of the different strategies varies with volatility for a given market size. The profits of licensing, IJV and merger are indicated by the respective schedules D_1D_1', D_2D_2' and D_3D_3'. The envelope of maximum profit is $D_3E_1E_2E_3D_0'$. It can be seen that as volatility increases so internalisation becomes less attractive. There is first a switch from merger to IJV, then from IJV to licensing, and finally collaboration is abandoned altogether.

This diagram provides a simple explanation of joint venture instability. Compared to a merger, the advantage of an IJV stems from the

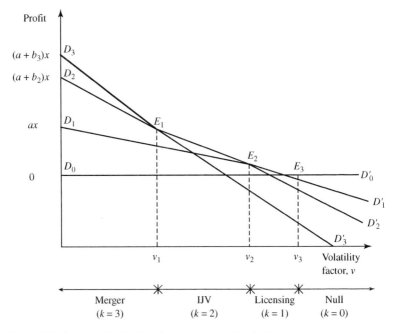

Figure 6.6 Impact of volatility factor on strategic choice.

ability to switch partners as technology evolves. It is intrinsic to an IJV that the arrangement is not as long lasting as a merger would be. Indeed, if an IJV turned out to be very long lasting it would suggest that management had made a strategic error, and that a merger would have been better instead. For example, a merger would have allowed for a more thorough rationalisation of activities than an IJV. The fact that many IJVs lead to a subsequent merger confirms this view, as it shows that such strategic errors can be corrected later. It also confirms the recent view that short-lived IJVs are not necessarily a failure. Indeed, it goes further than this, and shows that a firm that participates in a succession of short-lived IJVs, far from being a poor performer, may be sticking consistently to a successful strategy that affords flexibility under conditions of rapid technological change.

It seems natural to combine these two partial analyses by studying the interaction between volatility and the size of the market. An exercise of this kind is illustrated in Figure 6.7. Market size is plotted horizontally and volatility vertically. Once again it is assumed that no strategy is completely dominated by the others. Applying this condition to the inequalities (6), and invoking (4), shows that

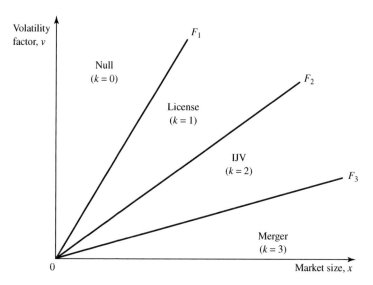

Figure 6.7 Combined impact of market size and volatility on strategic choice.

$$k = \begin{cases} 0 & \text{if } v > a/c_1 \\ 1 & \text{if } b_2(c_2 - c_1) < v \le a/c_1 \\ 2 & \text{if } (b_3 - b_2)/(c_2 - c_1) < v \le b_2/(c_2 - c_1) \\ 3 & \text{if } v < b_2/(c_2 - c_1). \end{cases}$$

These conditions indicate how the boundaries OF_1, OF_2 and OF_3 between the regimes shown in the figure vary in response to the costs and benefits of internalisation.

There are four regimes in the figure, each corresponding to one of the strategies. If the market size is very small and volatility very high, then the null strategy is chosen. As the market size increases and/or volatility falls, licensing is preferred instead. The IJV is preferred when either market size and volatility are both low – i.e., the market, though small, is subject to little innovation, or both high – i.e., there is a large market with considerable innovation. Finally, merger is selected when the market is very large but volatility is very low.

The major implications of these results are summarised in Table 6.3. IJVs are favoured in the symmetric situations where market size and volatility are either both low or both high. Licensing is favoured in the asymmetric situation where the market is small but volatile, and merger in the opposite situation where the market is large but stable.

Given the dependence of volatility on both the pace of technological change and the rate of interest, the results can also be summarised by saying that IJVs are favoured under the following conditions:

(a) limited innovation, low rate of interest and small market;
(b) moderate innovation, moderate rate of interest and moderate size of market; and
(c) rapid innovation, high rate of interest and large market.
(d) limited innovation, high rate of interest and moderate size of market; and
(e) rapid innovation, low rate of interest and moderate size of market.

Table 6.3   Impact of market size and volatility on strategic choice

Market size	Volatility	
	Low	High
High	Merger	IJV
Low	IJV	Licensing

It is suggested below that it is scenario (c) that is most relevant to the increase of IJV activity in the 1980s. Scenario (b) is also interesting, though, because it shows that IJVs can also occur under conditions of 'moderation in all things'. Other variants of this moderation theme can be generated by allowing one factor to increase while there is a compensating decrease in another factor; for example, 'size of market'.

The impact of the other factors can be analysed by examining their effects on each of the four regimes. Figure 6.8 illustrates how the effects described in Table 6.2 are reflected in the directions in which the various boundaries rotate in response to changes in cultural distance, d, the degree of protection of the independence of the partner firm n, missing patent rights, p, the scope economies of the technology, s, and the uncertainty about technological competence, t. It can be seen that in addition to the results reported above, IJVs are favoured by a high degree of protection of the independence of the partner firm (which inhibits merger), n, and by major uncertainty about technological competence, t. The effect of cultural distance d is ambiguous: although it may encourage IJVs at the expense of mergers, it also encourages licensing instead of IJVs. IJVs are definitely encouraged by economies of scope in technology, s, because such economies are difficult to exploit through a merger.

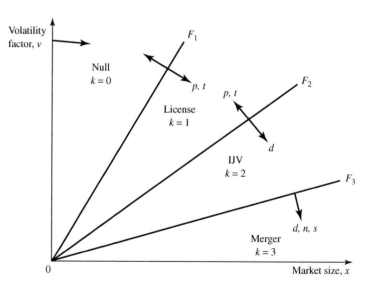

Figure 6.8 Impact of cultural heterogeneity, protection of independence, economies of scope and technological uncertainty on strategic choice.

Finally, IJVs are favoured by uncertainty about technological competence, t, because this makes licensing a relatively inflexible arrangement.

6.8   Application of the model – IJVs in the global economy

The model can be used to explain the increasing use of IJVs in international business during the 1980s (Dunning 1993, pp. 250–5) in terms of:

- reductions in trade barriers and improvements in freight transportation, which have 'globalised' markets and so increased market size;
- rapid increases in national income, particularly in the Asia-Pacific region, which have also increased market size, particularly for consumer durables;
- accelerated technological innovation which has increased volatility;
- the emergence of new technologies, combining ideas from different scientific traditions, which has increased firms' uncertainties about their own technological competences, and
- new technologies such as information technology, biotechnology and genetic engineering which seem to exhibit greater economies of scope than the dominant engineering technologies of the 1960s.

In terms of Figure 6.9, factors (a)–(c) represent a shift from area Z_0 - moderate market size and low volatility, in the 1960s, to Z_1 - large market size and high volatility, in the 1980s. Factor (d) corresponds to the anti-clockwise rotation of the boundary OF_2 to OF_2', while factor (e) corresponds to the clockwise rotation of the boundary OF_3 to OF_3'. As a result, some collaborations that would have been effected by merger are now effected by IJVs. Moreover, some collaborations that would have been effected by IJVs and might now be effected by licensing because of greater volatility are still effected by IJVs because technological uncertainty has increased as well.

IJVs have not had matters entirely their own way, however. Barriers to merger caused by the existence of 'national champions' have tended to diminish, allowing more foreign acquisitions to take place in high-technology industries. The speculative boom in the 1980s reduced the effective cost of capital to large firms and so reduced the interest burden of financing mergers and acquisitions. Moreover, the combination of expanding market size and a degree of 'technological protectionism' in the European Union has produced a combination of large market size and more moderate volatility which is conducive to mergers between 'protected' firms. Indeed, such mergers have sometimes been favoured

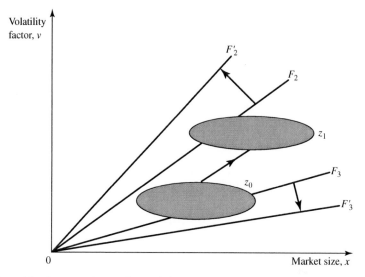

Figure 6.9 Comparative analysis of the international business environment in the 1960s and 1980s.

by the industrial policymakers on the grounds that they will help to create not national but 'European' champions.

6.9 Extensions of the model

The scope of every economic model is restricted by the nature of the assumptions that the modeller is required to make, and the present case is no exception. Because it is such a simple model, however, it is a straightforward matter to extend it. Greater relevance can be obtained at little cost in terms of analytical complexity.

It is not difficult, for example, to augment the set of strategies. One possibility worth considering is that the firm could 'go it alone' and attempt to replicate its partner's expertise for itself. Another is that the firm could licence out its own technology rather than licence in its rival's technology. Economies of scope and technological uncertainties introduce some complications here, though. Suppose that both firms have other technologies besides the ones that they plan to combine in the IJV. If the other technologies of Firm 2 have greater complementarity (or 'synergy') with the technology offered by Firm 1 than have the technologies of Firm 1 with the technology offered by Firm 2, then it is appropriate for Firm 1 to licence out to Firm 2 instead of the other way round.

This ensures the complementaries between the different technologies within the firms' portfolios are used to greatest effect.

Firm 2 will be willing to licence in the technology, though, only if it is sure that the technology will match its own competence. If Firm 2 is more uncertain of its own competence than is Firm 1, then it may be reluctant to licence in, so that Firm 2 may still finish up licensing out as a response to this difficulty. It is only when Firm 2 is reasonably certain of its competence that it will be willing to act on the basis that the greatest complementarities lie between its own technologies and the technology on offer from Firm 1. This leads to a further point, concerning the passive role that has been imputed to Firm 2 up till now. The possibility that Firm 2 will licence Firm 1's technology suggests a more active role for Firm 2. In particular, it suggests that Firm 2 may attempt to bargain with Firm 1 over the distribution of the rewards from collaboration. It will no longer be the case, therefore, that all the gains from collaboration accrue to Firm 1. If the two firms have similar information about the total gains to be generated by the different strategies then they may as well dispense with negotiations and agree right away upon the strategy that maximises their total gain. They can then divide this gain among themselves in some equitable way, such as a 50:50 split.

When the gains are always divided in some fixed proportion then the choice of strategy will be the same as when only one of the firms takes an active role. This is because the ordering of the strategies by the active firm in any given situation is unchanged when the profits of all the strategies are reduced by the same fixed proportion. Unfortunately, however, this condtion is not always satisfied in practice.

It is also possible to augment the list of exogenous variables both by addressing wholly new issues, such as the impact of tax incentives, and by refining the treatment of existing ones. Consider, for example, the impact of the pace of technological change on switching costs. When established firms are good at 'learning by doing' (Nelson and Winter, 1982), future technological improvements are likely to accrue to existing partners. It is mainly when established partners are poor at learning by doing that improvements are more likely to originate with entrants to the industry. The capability of established firms to maintain their leadership is, in turn, likely to be stronger when technological change is incremental, within an existing paradigm, rather than radical, involving the emergence of a new paradigm. This suggests that it is not just the overall pace of technological change that needs to be incorporated into the model but, more specifically, the pace of incremental change and the pace of radical change. Rapid incremental change may be perfectly compatible with the merger strategy because the enduring value of the other firms' competence is reasonably assured; but rapid radical change is likely to subvert the merger strategy and favour the IJV, or licensing, instead.

6.10 Generalisation of the results

The application of the model has focused on the growth of innovation-driven and rationalisation-driven IJVs of the kind that predominate in high-technology industries. The emergence of such IJVs has been associated with the downsizing and delayering of some large multinationals. These firms have been restructured in a more entrepreneurial and flexible form as a network of alliances. At the same time, however, a more traditional kind of IJV, concerned with market access, has continued to flourish. Such IJVs are favoured by Japanese firms seeking to consolidate their share in the European market. How far do the results derived above apply to these type 2 and type 3 IJVs, and indeed to other types of IJV as well?

The short answer is that many of the results remain unchanged, but some do not. Factors such as missing patent rights, government protection against foreign acquisition and cultural distance continue to affect IJV decisions in the same way as before. This reflects the generality of the internalisation theory from which they derive. The rate of interest and market size are basic economic variables that remain important too. Other factors, though, are more specific to the type 5 IJV.

Where other types of IJV are concerned, the interplay of technological expertise and marketing expertise takes a slightly different form. For example, where market access is concerned, the speed of learning becomes more important than the pace of technological change. The faster the high-technology firm can acquire the local expertise of the market-oriented firm, and the slower the market-oriented firm is to acquire technology, the more beneficial is the IJV as a transitional method of market entry to the high-technology firm. Uncertainty about the quality of marketing expertise becomes more important too.

6.11 Conclusions

The development of an economic model is often stimulated by the desire to explain certain 'stylised facts'. In the present case the stylised fact has been the increasing number of IJVs in high-technology global industries. Economic models offer a simple yet rigorous explanation of facts which other disciplines sometimes explain in more complicated and more heuristic terms. If economic models did no more than rationalise what everyone already knows, however, then their value would be rather limited. Fortunately, the way that economic models are constructed means that they do not merely explain the facts they were designed to explain but provide new predictions as well. It is their ability to draw attention to phenomena that have not been noticed, and to integrate the explanation of these phenomena with the explanations of already known phenomena, that is the true measure of their success.

The model developed in this chapter explains the formation of IJVs in terms of eight distinct but related factors. These factors are listed on the left-hand side of Table 6.4. They govern the margins of strategic interaction between IJVs and licensing on the one hand, and IJVs and mergers on the other. The impact of each factor on each of these strategies is indicated by the entries in the table.

The model shows that the impact of any given factor can only be understood by controlling for the seven other factors in the analysis. It is also necessary, in addition, to control for the levels of some of the factors; in particular, the effects of market size, the pace of innovation and the rate of interest reverse direction as their level increases.

The gist of the results can be summarised by saying that IJVs represent a strategy of moderation. Just as the equity participation in an IJV is intermediate between that in a licensing agreement and that in a full-scale merger, so the IJV emerges as intermediate in strategic terms as well. This may help to explain why the empirical evidence on IJVs is so difficult to interpret in terms of models that seek to relate IJV activities to extreme values of particular factors, such as the sunk costs of R&D.

Table 6.4   Impact of key explanatory factor on strategic choice

Explanatory factor	Strategy			
	Notation	Licensing	IJV	Merger
Market size	x	−	X	+
Pace of technological change	f	+	X	−
Rate of interest	r	+	X	−
Cultural distance	d	+	?	?
Protection of independence	n	+	+	−
Missing patent rights	p	−	+	+
Economies of scope	s	+	−	−
Technological uncertainty	t	−	+	+

Note: X indicates positive at a low value and negative at a high value.

The results summarised in Table 6.4 generate detailed predictions about how IJV formation will vary within industries, between industries, across countries and over time. Factors such as technological uncertainty are firm-specific and can therefore explain why firms in the same industry adopt different strategies. The pace of technological change is industry-specific and can therefore explain differences in the frequency with which IJVs are encountered in various industries. Cultural distance is specific to pairwise combinations of countries and can therefore account for differences in the international distribution of IJVs within an industry. With globally integrated capital markets, the rate of interest tends to be uniform across industries and countries and is therefore mainly a time-specific factor.

The other factors mentioned also vary with time, of course, though some (such as the pace of technological innovation) may vary more than others (such as cultural differences). Despite the apparently restrictive nature of the assumption of profit-maximisation applied to a representative pair of firms, therefore, a wide variety of relevant results can be obtained.

References

Beamish, P. W. and Banks, J. C. 1987. Equity Joint Ventures and the Theory of the Multinational Enterprise. *Journal of International Business Studies*, 19(2): 1–16.

Buckley, P. J. 1988. The Limits of Explanation: Testing the Internalization Theory of the Multinational Enterprise. *Journal of International Business Studies*, 19(2): 181–93.

——. and Casson, M. C. 1976. *The Future of the Multinational Enterprise*. London: Macmillan.

——. 1981. The Optimal Timing of a Foreign Direct Investment. *Economic Journal*, 91: 75–87.

——. 1988. A Theory of Cooperation in International Business, in F. J. Contractor and P. Loratige (eds). *Cooperative Strategies in International Business*, 31–53. Lexington, MA: Lexington Books.

Casson, M. C. 1991. *The Economics of Business Culture: Game Theory, Transaction Costs and Economic Performance*. Oxford, UK: Clarendon Press.

——. 1995. *The Organisation of Internal Tonal Business*. Aldershot, UK: Edward Elgar.

——. 1996. *Information and Organisation: A New Perspective on the Theory of the Firm*. Oxford, UK: Clarendon Press.

Dunning, J. H. 1993. *Multinational Enterprises and the Global Economy*. Wokingham, Berkshire, UK: Addison-Wesley.

Geringer, J. M. and Hébert, L. 1989. Control and Performance of International Joint Ventures. *Journal of International Business Studies*, 20(2): 235–54.

Harrigan, K. 1988. Strategic Alliances and Partner Asymmetries, in F. J. Contractor and P. Lorange (eds), *Cooperative Strategies in International Business*. 205–26. Lexington, MA: Lexington Books.

Nelson, R. R. and Winter, S. G. 1982. *An Evolutionary Theory of Economic Change*. Cambridge, MA: Belknap Press of Harvard University Press.

Parkhe, A. 1993. 'Messy' Research, Methodological Predispositions, and Theory Development in International Joint Ventures. *Academy of Management Review*, 38: 227–68.

Polanyi, M. 1966. *The Tacit Dimension*. New York: Anchor Day.

Ring, P. S. and Van der Ven, A. H. 1994. Developmental Processes of Cooperative Interorganisational Relationships. *Academy of Management Review*, 19: 90–118.

Tallman, S. B. 1992. A Strategic Management Perspective on Host Country Structure of Multinational Enterprise. *Journal of Management*, 18: 455–71.

Veugelers, R. and Kesteloot, K. 1994. On the Design of Stable Joint Ventures. *European Economic Review*, 38: 1799–815.

7
Models of the Multinational Enterprise

7.1 Introduction

The appearance of a major work of survey and synthesis, which goes into successive editions (Caves, 1996), is a clear sign that a subject has reached maturity. Maturity can sometimes indicate stagnation, however, and so the question naturally arises as to whether stagnation has set in to international business research. Caves' second edition is an encyclopaedic work, but it is very much like the first edition in its general structure. Only the details have been modified in the light of recent research.

This article argues that any impression of stagnation is misleading. Rather than quibble over a number of minor details of Caves' exposition, this article makes a single substantive point. It identifies a new research agenda for modelling multinational enterprises (MNEs) which is not fully reflected in Caves' work. This agenda has emerged over the last ten years. It is difficult to recognise because its various components have not yet coalesced. It is nevertheless unfortunate that Caves has failed to emphasise its significance in his recent revision of his book.

7.2 Models of multinational enterprises

The new agenda emphasises dynamic issues. It highlights the uncertainty that is generated by volatility in the international business environment. To cope with volatility, corporate strategies have to be flexible, and flexibility can be achieved by several means. New dimensions of corporate strategy therefore have to be recognised. Efficient information processing is crucial to cope with the resultant increase in the complexity of decision making. This has important implications for the organisational structure of the MNE and for the motivation of its managerial employees. The new agenda spells out these implications in a rigorous fashion.

The traditional agenda of Caves takes a more static view of international business. It focuses on:

- the nature of firm-specific competitive advantage;
- the choice of location of production; and
- the determination of the boundaries of the firm.

The classic application of the traditional agenda is to the foreign market entry decision. This agenda recognises change, but interprets it as a sequence of independent one-off events, rather than as a continuous systemic process. Thus entry into any given market is analysed independently of entry into others, and each entry strategy tends to be evaluated in terms of its immediate effects rather than in terms of the new opportunities to which it may ultimately lead. The market entry issue will remain important; it has, indeed, received new impetus from the recent wave of FDI into Central and Eastern European markets (Hood and Young, 1994). But the models of market entry developed in the 1970s remain too static to address the crucial issues of the 1990s, because they fail to take proper account of volatility.

This does not mean that static analysis is obsolete. Static analysis is much simpler than dynamic analysis, and for this reason the traditional static approach is a natural preliminary to the new dynamic one. A dynamic model always contains a static model as a special case, and the properties of this special case provide important clues as to whether the dynamic model is logically sound. The new dynamic agenda focuses on:

- uncertainty and market volatility
- flexibility and the value of real options;
- cooperation through joint ventures and business networks;
- entrepreneurship, managerial competence and corporate culture; and
- organisational change, including the mandating of subsidiaries and the 'empowerment' of employees.

The stimulus for the new agenda was the end of the 'golden age' of Western economic growth, which came abruptly with the oil price shock of 1973–4 (Marglin and Schor, 1990). Lags in recognising and interpreting the symptoms of this change caused its impact on academic literature to be delayed. The event marks a watershed in the post-war growth of Western MNEs. The intensification of international competition in the late 1970s had dramatic adverse effects on corporate profitability in the West. The focus of corporate strategy switched from entering new foreign markets to defending existing ones. International operations were restructured to drive down costs and improve supply responsiveness. Flexibility became the key to international competitiveness in the turbulent 1980s.

Flexibility is the leitmotif of the new agenda. It may be defined as the ability to reallocate resources quickly and smoothly in response to change. The significance of flexibility is greater with greater amplitude and frequency of change in the environment. As far as MNEs are concerned, the impact of change is captured by the volatility induced in the profit stream. The volatility of profit that would occur if the firm made no response to change summarises the impact on the firm of volatility in its environment.

Low volatility characterised the economic environment during most of the 'golden age.' The economic literature reviewed by Caves remains dominated by the experiences of this age. Selecting the most appropriate mode of entry into a foreign market remains the focus of attention. The international rationalisation of production receives surprisingly little attention. While flexibility has been the focus of some of the most original research of the last decade, there is little sense of this in Caves' work.

Following a brief review of economic methodology, the article examines the factors underlying the end of the 'golden age'. With the aid of theory and the benefit of hindsight, it is shown how international business factors stimulated productivity growth in Asia and eventually undermined the competitiveness of the West. It is argued that the entry of new multinational producers, and a general commitment to continuous innovation, has increased volatility in global markets. It is shown that survival and prosperity in a volatile environment depend upon flexible response. This applies to nation states, to industrial regions and to individual firms. Flexible firms need to locate in flexible regions of nation states with flexible economic policies. In this way the forces of flexibility are continuously restructuring the world economy. To understand these forces properly, the traditional 'tool kit' of international business theory, as deployed in Caves, needs to be supplemented with new techniques. The article concludes by setting out the kind of economic modelling that is appropriate for building a new dynamic theory with flexibility at its core.

7.3   Methodology: Models versus frameworks

The economic theory of international business attempts to answer practical questions in a rigorous way. This means making assumptions explicit – in particular, specifying the strategies available to each firm and spelling out their details. Strict assumptions are used in order to simplify the analysis as much as possible. Simplicity provides logical transparency and ensures that the results can be easily understood. This is the methodology employed by Caves and adopted in this chapter.

Economists invoke the principle of rational action to predict the circumstances under which firms will choose a given strategy. The assumption of rationality is not a piece of misguided psychology but a response to the practical need for simplicity (Buckley and Casson, 1993). When the firm's objective is profit maximisation, the choice of strategy is driven by the firm's structure of revenues and costs. This is determined by the firm's environment. The identification of the key characteristics of this environment enables the firm's behaviour to be modelled in a very parsimonious way. The predictions of the model emerge jointly from the profit maximisation hypothesis and the restrictions imposed by the modeller on the structure of revenues and costs. Predictive failure of the model is addressed by re-examining these restrictions and not by discarding the maximisation principle that is at the core of the theory (Buckley, 1988).

This method can be contrasted with an alternative approach in international business which leaves the assumptions implicit and derives propositions from a discursive literature review. This dispenses with formal analysis and relies on synthesis. Unfortunately, a synthesis is no better than the analytical components from which it is built. The more complex the synthesis, the more important it is that each component is sound. The logic of rational action provides just the check on analytical consistency which is required.

The variables entering into the theory do not have to be of a strictly economic nature. The criterion for inclusion is that they are analysed from a rational action point of view (Buckley and Chapman, 1996). A good illustration here is the analysis of international joint ventures (IJVs), where economic factors, such as market size, are supplemented by technological, legal, cultural and psychological factors to generate a satisfactory model (Geringer and Hebert, 1989).

The development of an economic model is often stimulated by the desire to explain certain 'stylized facts'. The traditional agenda, for example, sought to explain the predominance of US MNEs in high-technology manufacturing industries during the 'golden age'. The new agenda seeks to explain the rise of IJVs after the end of the 'golden age'. Economic models offer a simple, yet rigorous, explanation of facts which other approaches explain in more complicated and more heuristic terms. If economic models did no more than rationalise what everyone already knows, then their value would be limited, however. Fortunately, the way in which economic models are constructed means that they do not merely explain the facts which they were designed to deal with, but they also provide new predictions. It is their ability to draw attention to phenomena that have not been noticed and to integrate the explanation of these phenomena with explanations of already known phenomena which is a true measure of their success.

It is instructive to contrast the methods of economics with those of strategic management (Porter, 1991) and development studies (Lall and Streeten, 1977). Porter contrasts 'models' and 'frameworks'. He sees the traditional method of economics as model building which 'abstracts the complexity of competition to isolate a few key variables whose interactions are examined in depth' (Porter, 1991, p. 97). The applicability of any model's findings are almost inevitably restricted to a small subgroup of firms or industries whose characteristics fit the model's assumptions (p. 98). Porter identifies the progress of strategic management with its ability to construct frameworks. 'Instead of models, however, the approach was to build frameworks. A framework, such as the competitive forces approach to analysing industry structure, encompasses many variables and seeks to capture much of the complexity of actual competition' (p. 98). Frameworks are analogous to expert systems which are tailored to particular industries or companies. 'My own frameworks embody the notion of optimization, but no equilibrium in the normal sense of the word. Instead, there is a continually evolving environment in which a perpetual competitive interaction between rivals takes place. In addition, all the interactions among the many variables in the frameworks cannot be rigorously drawn.'

In contrast to Porter's support for frameworks rather than models, Krugman attributes the failure of development studies precisely to its rejection of rigorous models. Despite having identified important themes which are key to successful modelling of development issues – 'emphasis on strategic complementarity in investment decisions and on the problem of coordination failure' – development economists failed to explain them to academic colleagues and policymakers in a coherent way (Krugman, 1995, p. 28).

According to Krugman, 'mainstream economic theory rests on two observations: obvious opportunities for gain are rarely left unexplored and things add up' (1995, p. 74). This formulation is similar to, but subtly different from, the two key principles put forward by Buckley and Casson (1993) – optimisation and equilibrium. There is a difference between optimisation and being self-interested. Buckley and Casson's formulation allows for objectives which are beyond self-interest or 'opportunities for gain'. These may include following ethical injunctions and pursuing altruistic sentiments. Similarly, the truism 'things add up' is valid only ex post, where it is true by definition. Things add up ex ante only in situations of equilibrium – and equilibrium may not always hold. Krugman's justification for this method is that 'what we do when we construct an economic model is to try to use these two principles to cut through the complexities of a situation. And the remarkable thing is how often that succeeds ... the basic principles of economics tell us that there is an unexpected order in the outcome, which is quite independent of the details' (1995, p. 75).

A significant strength of Porter's framework is that it postulates continuous incremental change. Its weakness is that it does not analyse the strategic response to change in a rigorous way. The new agenda in economic modelling, being more dynamic than the old, addresses the point about continuous change head-on. Because of its economic logic, rigour is guaranteed. It is therefore not only a natural successor to the traditional agenda but also a necessary refinement of Porter's work as well.

It could be argued, of course, that the insights of the new agenda should be simply grafted onto the old agenda, rather than developed in a distinct, but complementary, way. But forcing dynamic considerations into an essentially static context results in loss of simplicity (Buckley, 1983). Complex typologies must be developed to distinguish all of the special cases that arise – a process that can clearly be traced in the evolution of Dunning's eclectic theory in response to the growth of IJVs and 'resource-seeking' investment (Dunning, 1977, 1993). Once the complexity of the model approaches the complexity of the phenomena that it attempts to analyse, it ceases to function as a model and becomes simply a description of the situation instead.

7.4   The end of the 'golden age'

During the 'golden age' of Western economic growth, trade was liberalised through GATT and through customs unions, such as the EEC and EFTA.

US mass production technology was transferred through the internal markets of MNEs. Key European industries were transformed. Cheaper motor vehicles created a more mobile society. Female labour force participation increased. Cheaper consumer durables combined with higher incomes raised aspirations to historically unprecedented levels. Mass consumer demand fuelled demand for branded products, such as convenience foods. The glamour of US affluence made US marketing and advertising skills easy to transfer abroad.

The 'golden age' terminated suddenly with the oil price shock of 1973. Imports of manufactured goods from Japan and the newly industrialising countries (NICs) of South-East Asia quickly began to replace domestic production in Western markets – including motor vehicles, which had been one of the 'engines' of Western growth up to that point. The West woke up to the fact that for some time Asian firms had been systematically absorbing Western technologies and adapting them to local conditions. The full consequences of international technology transfer and trade liberalisation were finally being felt.

Traditional international business theory can easily explain how technology transfer to Asia was effected. However, the mechanisms were somewhat more varied than those emphasised by Caves. Technology transfer was effected on government initiative, as well as on the initiative of Western multinationals (Fransman, 1995). Licensing agreements and joint ventures were widely used. The domestic partner was often a 'national champion'. Once it had mastered the technology, the champion diffused it to other firms. Diffusion to other large firms was effected through social networking, factory visits and collaborative research. Diffusion to smaller firms was effected through subcontracting arrangements in which substantial training could be involved. Small firms could also play a direct role in pirating technologies that were easy to copy. 'Reverse engineering' was important too. Product designs were easier to imitate than technologies because patent protection was weaker, and 'me too' designs proliferated as a result.

The price advantage of Asian products stemmed from a number of factors. The weakness of trades unions (often as a direct consequence of political measures) maintained wages at competitive market-clearing levels (Mirza, 1986). The limited scope of social security gave a strong incentive to work. Government expenditure was concentrated on infrastructure investment, such as roads, ports, airports and telecommunications, which reduced the costs of intermediate inputs, such as transport. Investment in large container terminals cut the cost of shipping to

Western markets, for example. Improved domestic communications facilitated 'just in time' production, which economised on inventory costs. Mass production was initiated from the outset to exploit economies of scale to the full. Temporary protection of the domestic market helped to build up demand quickly, and exporting commenced at the outset. A strong desire to save ensured that domestic demand did not crowd out export demand in the long run.

The contrast with the West is clear. During the 'golden age', Western public expenditure was focussed on fighting the 'Cold War' and on building a 'Great Society' or 'Welfare State'. Military expenditures and transfer payments to the poor crowded out productivity-enhancing investment. Rising taxes, it is alleged, discouraged work and risk-taking. The concept of a 'corporate economy' (Marris, 1979) institutionalised collective bargaining and legitimated union strike-threat power. Wage inflation and 'featherbedding' increased costs – particularly the costs of intermediate inputs like transport, which were supplied by highly unionised industries.

A similar set of factors explains why technology transfer succeeded in Asia but failed in Africa. (The Latin American experience lies somewhere between these two extremes.) The deficiencies of European governments were mirrored in their former colonies in Africa. Industrial strategy was based on state-of-the-art technology applied to mega projects rather than on the diffusion and incremental improvement of established techniques (Ergas, 1987). Competition for status between neighbouring nations encouraged lavish public expenditure, financed by foreign borrowing, which could not be repaid when projects failed. Foreign borrowing was also used to finance wars, as well as conspicuous consumption by the political elite. Corruption raised transaction costs. Inward-looking protectionist policies distorted domestic prices and inhibited agricultural development. Industry, though protected, failed to reap economies of scale because of the low growth of the domestic market. When Western MNEs retrenched in the 1970s, they retreated from Africa in order to concentrate on defending their markets at home.

The lessons for international business theory are fairly clear. It is not sufficient to focus exclusively on the choice of mode when analysing technology transfer. As Dunning (1997) has emphasised, full account must be taken of location factors, such as the structure of the host economy, the policies of the host government and the nature of local business culture in explaining the comparative success and failure of FDI.

7.5   Flexibility

Competition from Asia was a visible symbol of a less apparent, but more fundamental change in the business environment, namely, a persistent increase in the amount of volatility with which firms have to contend. Volatility has become much greater since the end of the 'golden age'. There are several reasons for this.

The international diffusion of modern production technology has increased the number of industrial powers, and hence increased the number of countries in which political and social disturbances can impact significantly on global supplies of manufactured products. The liberalisation of trade and capital markets means that the 'ripple' effects of shocks travel farther and wider than before (Casson, 1995). Ripples are transmitted more quickly too: news travels almost instantaneously, thanks to modern telecommunications. Thus speculative bubbles in stock markets spread quickly around the world. Following the breakdown of the Bretton Woods system, exchange rate fluctuations have created a new dimension of financial volatility too.

As a result, any given national market is now affected by a much wider range of disturbances than ever before. Every national subsidiary of a MNE experiences a multiplicity of shocks from around the world. It is no longer the case that a national subsidiary has to respond to shocks originating in its national market alone. The shocks come from new sources of import competition and new competitive threats in export markets too. While most shocks reveal themselves to firms as competitive threats, new opportunities for cooperation may sometimes be presented as well. The awareness of this sustained increase in volatility has led to a search for more flexible forms of organisation.

Increased volatility is not the only reason for greater interest in flexibility. Contemporary culture is very much opposed to building organisations around a single source of monopoly power. The nation state, for example, is under threat from advocates of regional government. The traditional role of the state, to supply defence, can in principle be effected through multilateral defence treaties in which politically independent regions club together for this specific purpose. The demise of the Soviet bloc, and the subsequent political realignment between its member states, may be seen as an example of this kind of cultural change at work. This distrust of monopoly power may be linked to an increase in other forms of distrust, as suggested below.

The aversion to internal monopoly is apparent among MNEs as well. This movement began in the early 1980s when the powerful central research laboratories of high-technology MNEs were either closed down, shifted to the divisions or forced to operate as suppliers to 'internal customers' in competition with outside bodies, such as universities (Casson, Pearce and Singh, 1991). Headquarters' bureaucracies came under attack shortly afterwards, as 'de-layering' got underway. The favoured form of firm has become a federal structure of operating divisions drawing on a common source of internal expertise, but where each division belonging to the federation is free to outsource expertise if it so desires. As with any trend, there has been a tendency for certain advocates to take it to extremes. Just as the 'golden age' was rife with suggestions that oligopolies of hierarchical MNEs would come to dominate world markets, so the 1990s have spawned visions of the 'network firm' and the 'virtual firm'. A factor common to these visions is a 'fuzzy' boundary of the firm, where the firm fades into the market through joint ventures with declining proportional equity stakes. These arguments for fuzzy boundaries are, unfortunately, often based on equally fuzzy reasoning. Fuzzy boundaries can be configured in many different ways. The new research agenda outlined in this chapter places arguments for fuzzy boundaries on a rigorous basis and predicts the specific form that fuzziness will take in each particular case.

It is evident that the search for flexibility has a number of important implications for:

- the external environment of the firm,
- the boundaries of the firm and
- the internal organisation of the firm.

These issues will now be considered in turn.

7.6   External flexibility: The national competitiveness issue

Initial Western reaction to de-industrialisation and the plight of the 'rust-belt' heavy industries was concern over competitiveness. There continues to be considerable debate, however, over what competitiveness really means (Buckley, Pass and Prescott, 1988). Some economists argue, using the Ricardian concept of comparative advantage, that loss of manufacturing competitiveness is a natural consequence of economic maturity (Krugman, 1996). The strength of Western economies no longer lies in manufacturing but in services. Thanks to jet travel, television broadcasting and other technological developments, an increasing number of services, such as tourism and media entertainment, are readily exportable. Consumer demand for services is income-elastic, moreover, so the long-term prospects for the service sector are good. Furthermore, manufacturing is increasingly capital-intensive, whereas many service industries are inherently labour intensive, because they are more difficult to automate. To regain competitiveness, therefore, labour must be shifted out of manufacturing and into services. To eliminate frictional and structural unemployment, this process must be expedited by measures to promote labour market flexibility.

According to this view, Asian countries, being at an earlier stage of industrial development, have exploited labour market flexibility to switch labour out of agriculture and into industry. First-generation workers who have just left the land are often very hardworking, and so, despite their inexperience, this gives a productivity boost to nascent industry. If flexibility can be sustained, then workers can be switched from one industry to another – from textiles to semiconductors, for example – as competition increases from other countries following up the ladder of development. It is in this way that Japan has stayed ahead of competition from the Republic of Korea and Taiwan (China). Such has been the speed of Asian development that several economies, including Singapore, Hong Kong and Japan, have already completed the manufacturing phase and have become major service economies in their own right.

An alternative view of competitiveness emphasises the firm-specific nature of competitive advantage. There are wide differences in productivity between firms in the same industry, it is claimed. Theories of comparative advantage, framed in terms of a representative firm, ignore this (Thurow, 1992). Some firms have major competitive advantages and others have none at all. The competitive advantages of leading Western firms have been eroded by internal failings, it is alleged. It is not that Western workers have lost comparative advantage in manufacturing but that Western firms have lost the ability to manage instead.

The distinction between firm-specific competitive advantage and nation-specific comparative advantages is essentially a question of the period of analysis. Firm-specific competitive advantage is essentially a short-run concept. Firm-specific advantages cannot be taken as given in the long run because they continually obsolesce and have to be regularly renewed (Buckley and Casson, 1976). A nation with a comparative advantage in entrepreneurship will be able to renew firm-specific advantages through sustained innovation, but a nation without such comparative advantage will not. An explanation of loss of competitiveness that emphasises loss of firm-specific advantages is equivalent, from a long-run perspective, to an argument that local comparative advantage in entrepreneurship has been lost. Countries that systematically generate firms with specific advantages are those that have a nation-specific comparative advantage in entrepreneurship.

From this perspective, it is plausible to argue that the West has lost comparative advantage in both manufacturing and entrepreneurship. The first is an unavoidable consequence of economic maturity, but the second is an avoidable consequence of institutional failure and inappropriate business culture. The conflict between the nation-specific view and the firm-specific view is actually a disagreement about whether nation-specific comparative advantage has declined more in manufacturing than in entrepreneurship, or less. Those who adhere to the firm-specific view, which probably includes the majority of international business scholars, implicitly believe that entrepreneurial decline is the major problem and that cultural and institutional changes are required to put it right. The increased volatility of the world economy, and the consequent increase in demand for flexibility, has put Western entrepreneurial failures under the spotlight.

7.7 Restoring competitiveness

Western governments have attempted to restore labour market flexibility through legislation. In the UK, for example, the legal privileges of trades unions (such as secondary picketing) have been reduced, and minimum wage laws relaxed. Qualifications for the receipt of unemployment benefit have been tightened up. Firms have responded in a predictable way. Greater use is made of temporary labour to accommodate peaks and troughs in demand. Full-time workers are expected to work more flexible hours. Work has been subcontracted out to avoid statutory national insurance premiums. The rise in labour-only subcontracting has brought back the 'putting out' system, which was characteristic of the eighteenth-century 'commercial revolution'.

Privatisation has been used to promote greater flexibility in the supply of intermediate products to industry. The UK has privatised 'strategic' heavy industries (steel), public transport (railways and airlines) and utilities (telecommunications, electricity, gas and water). Privatisation allows peripheral activities to be sold off, and complementary activities to be combined, thereby facilitating significant changes in the scope of the firm. Newly privatised enterprises can acquire other newly privatised enterprises or enter into joint venture agreements with them. For the first time in the post-war period, large-scale involvement by MNEs is now possible in most of the utility industries.

Steps have also been taken to improve entrepreneurship. Business education has been expanded, top rates of income tax have been reduced to encourage risk-taking and successful business people have been encouraged to play a more active role in public life in order to raise the status of entrepreneurs. Politicians have increasingly promoted the values of competitive individualism and downgraded the values of organic solidarity, which characterised the 'Welfare State' (Casson, 1990).

Links between universities and business have been strengthened in order to improve the coordination of product development and basic research. This may not directly benefit the nation as much as might have been expected, however. Products researched in one country can be produced in another country, and even exported back to the country where they were researched to compete with local products there. The decentralisation of R&D within large MNEs (Pearce and Singh, 1992) creates internal markets where this kind of transfer can be easily effected. Thus a US MNE could use a wholly owned research laboratory in the UK to tap into government-funded research in order to develop a product to be made in the US for export to the UK. The profits from the product innovation will also accrue to the US – an effect that has been stressed, in a somewhat different context, by Reich (1990).

Government measures to improve competitiveness seem to have been reasonably successful over the past decade. However, it should not be forgotten that the reason why some MNEs continue to produce in Europe for the European market has more to do with the common external tariff of the European Community, and the threat that it might increase, than with the location advantages of Europe per se. Thus tariff considerations and substantial job-creation subsidies have played a major role in the attraction of Asian motor vehicle manufacturers to the UK. Similarly, one of the advantages to foreign firms of producing in the US is that it is easier to adapt product designs to the market using a local production base.

The fact that Asian firms can successfully produce in the West behind a tariff wall suggests that they possess firm-specific advantages of the type generated by sustained entrepreneurship. One of these advantages appears to lie in internal labour market flexibility. There is a tendency in the West to see labour market flexibility as something external to the firm. It is reflected simply in low wage rates. There is less emphasis on firm-specific training, and workers are less versatile than in Asian firms. This is apparent on the shop floor. On-the-job training is weaker, and attention to quality is lower as a result. Machine downtime is greater because workers cannot fix minor repairs, or help each other out when retooling a production line.

In general, Asian firms appear to have taken flexibility more seriously as a production issue. Not only have they invested more in labour versatility but they have invested more in equipment for flexible manufacturing systems too. This is reflected not only in their Asian plants but also in their operations in the West.

7.8   Flexible boundaries of the firm: Networks and joint ventures

The typical US MNE of the 'golden age' was a vertically, as well as horizontally, integrated firm. In consequence, each division of the firm was locked into linkages with other divisions of the same firm. As Asian competition intensified, there was growing recognition of the costs of integration of this kind.

Commitment to a particular source of supply or demand is relatively low-cost in a high-growth scenario, since it is unlikely that any investment will need to be reversed. It is much more costly in a low-growth scenario, where production may need to be switched to a cheaper source of supply, or sales diverted away from a depressed market. The desire for flexibility therefore discourages vertical integration – whether it is backward integration into production or forward integration into distribution. It is better to subcontract production and to franchise sales instead. The subcontracting of production is similar in principle to the 'putting out' arrangement described earlier, but differs in the sense that the subcontractor is now a firm rather than just a single worker.

Disintegration was also encouraged by a low-trust atmosphere that developed in many firms. Fear of internal monopoly became rife, as explained above. Production managers faced with falling demand wished that they did not have to sell all their output through a single sales manager. Sales managers resented the fact that they had to obtain all their supplies from the same small set of plants. Each manager doubted the competence of the others and ascribed loss of corporate competitiveness to selfishness and inefficiency elsewhere in the firm. Divisions aspired to be spun off so that they could deal with other business units instead. On the other hand, managers were wary of the risks that would be involved if they severed their links with other divisions altogether.

A natural way to restore confidence is to allow each division to deal with external business units, as well as internal ones. In terms of internalisation theory, internal markets become 'open' rather than 'closed' (Casson, 1990, p. 37). This provides divisional managers with an opportunity to bypass weak or incompetent sections of the company. It also provides a competitive discipline on internal transfer prices, preventing their manipulation for internal political ends and bringing them more into line with external prices. There are other advantages too. Opening up internal markets severs the link between the capacities operated at adjacent stages of production. The resulting opportunity to supply other firms facilitates the exploitation of scale economies because it permits the capacity of any individual plant to exceed internal demand. Conversely, it encourages the firm to buy in supplies from other firms that have installed capacity in excess of their own needs.

The alignment of internal prices with external prices increases the objectivity of profit measurement at the divisional level. This allows divisional managers to be rewarded by profit-related pay based on divisional profit rather than firm-wide profit. Management may even buy out part of the company. Alternatively, the firm may restructure by buying in a part of an independent firm. The net effect is the same in both cases. The firm becomes the hub of a network of interlocking joint ventures (Buckley and Casson, 1988, 1996). Each joint venture partner is responsible for the day-to-day management of the venture. The headquarters of the firm coordinates the links between the ventures. Internal trade is diverted away from the weaker ventures towards the stronger ones, thereby providing price and profit signals to which the weaker partners need to respond. Unlike a pure external market situation, the partners are able to draw upon expertise at headquarters, which can in turn tap into expertise in other parts of the group.

A network does not have to be built around a single firm, of course. A network may consist of a group of independent firms instead. Sometimes these firms are neighbours, as in the regional industrial clusters described by Best (1990), Porter (1990) and Rugman, D'Cruz and Verbeke (1995). Industrial districts, such as 'Toyota city' have been hailed as an Asian innovation in flexible management, although the practice has been common in Europe for centuries (Marshall, 1919). As tariffs and transport costs have fallen, networks have become more international. This is demonstrated by the dramatic growth in intermediate product trade under long-term contracts. For example, an international trading company may operate a network of independent suppliers in different countries, substituting different sources of supply in response to both short-term exchange rate movements and long-term shifts in comparative advantage.

Flexibility is also needed in R&D. A firm cannot afford to become over-committed to the refinement of any one technology in case innovation elsewhere should render the entire technology obsolete. As technology has diffused in the post-war period, the range of countries with the competence to innovate has significantly increased. The pace of innovation has consequently risen, and the threat of rapid obsolescence is therefore higher as a result. The natural response for firms is to diversify their research portfolios. But the costs of maintaining a range of R&D projects are prohibitive, given the enormous fixed costs involved. The costs of basic R&D have escalated because of the increased range of specialist skills involved, while the costs of applied R&D have risen because of the need to develop global products which meet increasingly stringent consumer protection laws. Joint ventures are an appropriate solution once again. By establishing a network of joint ventures covering alternative technological trajectories, the firm can spread its costs while retaining a measure of proprietary control over new technologies.

The advantage of joint ventures is further reinforced by technological convergence, for example, the integration of computers, telecommunications and photography. This favours the creation of networks of joint ventures based on complementary technologies, rather than on the substitute technologies described above (Cantwell, 1995).

Joint ventures are important because they afford a number of real options (Trigeorgis, 1996) which can be taken up or dropped depending upon how the project turns out. The early phase of a joint venture provides important information which could not be obtained through investigation before the venture began. It affords an opportunity later on to buy more fully into a successful venture – an opportunity which is not available to those who have not taken any stake. It therefore provides greater flexibility than does either outright ownership or an alternative involving no equity stake.

7.9   Flexibility and internal organisation

In a very volatile environment the level of uncertainty is likely to be high. Uncertainty can be reduced, however, by collecting information. Flexibility was defined above in terms of the ability to respond to change. The costs of response tend to be smaller when the period of adjustment is long. One way of 'buying time' to adjust is to forecast change. While no one can foresee the future perfectly, information on the present and the recent past may well improve forecasts by diagnosing underlying long-term trends. Collecting, storing and analysing information therefore enhances flexibility because, by improving forecasts, it reduces the costs of change.

Another way of buying time is to recognise change as early as possible. In this respect, continuous monitoring of the business environment is better than intermittent monitoring because the potential lag before a change is recognised is eliminated. Continuous monitoring is more expensive than intermittent monitoring, though, because more management time is tied up.

Investments in better forecasts and speedier recognition highlight the trade-off between information cost and adjustment cost. This trade-off is particularly crucial when volatility is high. High volatility implies that more information should be collected to improve flexibility, which in turn implies that more managers need to be employed. This is the reverse of the usual recommendation to downsize management in order to reduce overhead costs.

To improve flexibility while downsizing management, the trade-off between information cost and adjustment cost must be improved. There are two main ways of doing this. The first is to reduce the cost of information processing through new information technology (IT). The second is to reduce adjustment costs by building flexibility into plant and equipment, both through its design and its location. A combination of IT investment and flexible plant can reconcile greater flexibility with lower management overheads in the manner to which many MNEs aspire.

The information required for strategic decision making is likely to be distributed throughout the organisation. It is no longer reasonable to assume that all the key information can be handled by a single chief executive, or even by the entire headquarters management team. It is difficult to know in advance where the really crucial information is likely to be found. Every manager therefore needs to have the competence to process information effectively. Managers need to be able to recognise the significance of strategic information that they acquire by chance, and to have the power of access to senior executives in order to pass it on. In other words, ordinary managers need to become internal entrepreneurs.

Few entrepreneurs have sufficient information to make a good decision without consulting other people, however. In a traditional hierarchical firm, the right to consult is the prerogative of top management. If ordinary managers are to have the power to initiate consultation, and act upon the results, then channels of communication within the firm need to be increased. Horizontal communication, as well as vertical communication, must be easy, so that lower level managers can readily consult with their peers.

A natural response is to 'flatten' the organisation and encourage managers to 'network' with each other. This improves the trade-off between local responsiveness and strategic cohesion (Bartlett and Ghoshal, 1987; Hedlund, 1993). Unfortunately, though, there has been some confusion over whether flatter organisations remain hierarchies at all. However, as Casson (1994) shows, the efficient managerial processing of information normally requires a hierarchical structure of some kind. The key point is that the more diverse are the sources of volatility, the greater are the advantages of widespread consultation. The less predictable is the principal source of volatility on any given occasion, the greater is the incentive to allow consultation to be initiated anywhere in the organisation. In practice this means that an increased demand for flexibility is best accommodated by flattening the organisation while maintaining basic elements of hierarchy.

7.10   The costs of flexibility: Engineering trust

If flexibility were costless, then all organisations could build in unlimited flexibility at the outset. In practice, the greater is flexibility, the higher transactions costs become. For example, the flexibility to switch between different sources of supply and demand (described earlier) means that relations with customers and suppliers become more transitory than before. Cheating becomes more likely because the prospect of further transactions between the same two parties is more remote. Direct appeals to the other party's loyalty lose their credibility too.

The same effect occurs when internal entrepreneurship is promoted. Internal entrepreneurs are given more discretion to act upon information that they have collected for themselves, and this increases their opportunity to cheat.

Giving managers a direct stake in the business activities they help to build is one solution. The firm incubates new business units in which particular managers, or groups of managers, have equity stakes. An alternative approach is to appeal to the integrity of managers instead. They are treated well, and in return are expected to be open and honest about what they know.

It is one of the ironies of the 1970s that at a time when personal integrity needed to be high in order to support more flexible organisation, it was allowed to fall very low. The decline of traditional religion, the intellectual cynicism created by two world wars and the rise of mass consumerism have all been blamed for this state of affairs. Communitarians argue correctly that moral values like integrity are most efficiently engineered at the societal level, through family, church and school. But when these institutions fail, they must be engineered to support specific economic relations instead (Fukuyama, 1996). Firms must engineer these values among their employees at their own expense instead (Kotter, 1996). Greater flexibility therefore implies greater costs in promoting a corporate culture that reinforces moral values.

7.11 Interaction of firm flexibility and location flexibility

The desire for flexibility may encourage the firm to produce the same product in several locations so that it can switch production between them as circumstances change. Multiple internal sourcing may therefore be pursued even where some sacrifice of economies of scale is involved. DeMeza and Van der Ploeg (1987), Capel (1992) and Kogut and Kulatilaka (1994) have all emphasised that firms can switch production between alternative locations in response to real exchange rate shocks. The basic idea is that MNEs can combine their superior information on foreign cost conditions with their ability, as owners of plants, to plan rather than negotiate output levels, to switch production more quickly than can independent firms.

This strategy requires, however, that the firm should commit in advance to the locations where it believes it will wish to produce. If it is difficult to foresee where the best locations may lie, then flexibility may be enhanced by subcontracting arrangements instead. Speed of response may be slower, but the range of potential locations is greater. Where short-run volatility predominates, multinational integration may well enhance the value of the firm (Allen and Pantzalis, 1996), but long-run volatility may favour the disintegration of the firm instead.

If a firm is seeking flexibility at one stage of production, then it will experience a derived demand for flexibility at adjacent stages of production. This flexibility is conferred by ease of transport to and from all the locations employed at the adjacent stage. Some locations are inherently more flexible in this respect than others, because they are at nodal points on transport networks. They therefore have low transport costs to a wide range of different destinations. For example, if production is dispersed, then warehousing of finished product should be at an appropriate hub. Greater demand for flexibility concentrates demand for warehousing at such hubs – for example, Singapore (for South-East Asia) and Lille (for North-West Europe).

An MNE that is seeking flexibility in its sources of supply will wish to choose a location where government policy is laissez faire, so that there are no import restrictions. It may be seeking flexibility in the range of products it produces too. This encourages it to seek out locations with a versatile labour force. Flexibility is also conferred by supplier networks that operate with a high degree of trust. Local production needs to be embedded in an impartial legal system and in strong social networks to ensure that trust is high. An 'invisible infrastructure' of mediating institutions, or equivalently, a large endowment of 'social capital', is therefore a feature of the locations that MNEs committed to flexibility are likely to seek out. Flexibility is not just an element of corporate strategy but a component of location advantage too. Such location advantage depends crucially on the nature of local institutions and local culture.

7.12 Flexibility and firm-specific competitive advantage

Flexibility also has implications for firm-specific competitive advantage. Skill in recruiting imaginative employees becomes a competitive advantage when internal entrepreneurship is required. Charismatic leadership by the chief executive may promote loyalty and integrity among key staff. A tradition of informal and consultative management will facilitate the sharing of information among employees. One way of expressing this is in terms of the 'capabilities' or 'competencies' of managers, or the human resources controlled by the firm (Richardson, 1960; Loasby, 1991). In a volatile environment where flexibility is crucial, the key resources of the firm are those that promote internal entrepreneurship. The firm consists not of a single autocratic entrepreneur but a team of entrepreneurs (Wu, 1988) coordinated by a leader who promotes high-trust communication between them.

It is worth noting that the need for flexibility does not necessarily support the idea of a 'learning organization'. To be more exact, flexibility has important implications for what people in a learning organisation actually need to learn. According to Nelson and Winter (1982), learning supports the refinement of existing routines. This is misleading. It suggests that the firm operates in a basically stable environment and merely learns how to do even better what it already does very well. In a volatile environment, however, much of what has been 'learned' from past experience quickly obsolesces. The truly durable knowledge that needs to be learnt in a volatile environment consists of techniques for handling volatility. These techniques include forgetting transitory information about past conditions which are unlikely to recur. But while 'unlearning' or 'forgetting' is important, it is often difficult to do. The difficulty of 'unlearning' helps to explain why so many 'downsizing' and 'de-layering' exercises have identified middle-aged middle managers as targets for redundancy or early retirement. Such people are believed to find it too hard to forget. The 'knowledge' they acquired as junior managers was very relevant during the 'golden age', but has since become obsolete. Some managers have proved sufficiently flexible to be 'retrained', but others have not. Those who were too inflexible to benefit from retraining have been required to leave because their 'knowledge' had become a liability instead of an asset in the more volatile situation of today.

7.13 New techniques of analysis

The key to modelling volatility is to postulate a steady stream of shocks impinging at random on the international business environment. There are exogenous shocks, which are autonomous, and endogenous shocks, which are induced as a consequence of the exogenous ones. The need for simplicity means that many shocks have to be treated as exogenous, even though they are in fact endogenous. The formation of customs unions, the reduction of international shipping costs through containerisation and the breakdown of the Soviet system may all be treated as exogenous random shocks impinging on the global economy. These shocks influence the relative rise and decline of individual nations. This emphasis on the modelling of shocks means that probability theory has a significant role to play in the new research agenda (Dixit and Pindyck, 1994). In particular, the probabilistic foundations of stochastic processes assume particular significance. There is a close link between the collection of information and the refinement of probability measurement, and another link between optimal forecasting and the concept of a 'martingale' (Dempster and Pliska, 1997). These ideas are most extensively developed in the field of financial options, but they can be applied to 'real options' too (Mello, Parsons and Triandis, 1995).

Managers of MNEs perceive the growth and decline of individual national economies as the result of random shocks. Increased volatility in the international economy means that there is greater uncertainty than before about the future growth of any particular economy. For example, there is currently considerable uncertainty about the growth prospects of Thailand and other South-East Asian economies. Theories of rational choice under uncertainty (Hirshleifer and Riley, 1992) are therefore central in analysing corporate behaviour in volatile environments.

Uncertainty can be reduced by gathering information, as noted earlier. Information improves the quality of decision making, but the returns to information diminish at the margin as with any other resource. Efficient search is normally conducted sequentially, and stops when the expected value of the next item of information is just equal to its expected cost of collection. The cheapest information is usually obtained second hand through communication with other people. It can also be obtained as a by-product of other activity. The organisation of a firm may be understood as a rational response to the challenge of collecting the right sort of information in the most appropriate way. This is the major insight of the economic theory of teams (Marschak and Radner, 1972). The organisation effects a division of labour in information processing, and assigns particular managers to particular roles according to where their personal comparative advantage lies. Some are good observers, others are good communicators, while the most entrepreneurial types make the best decision makers. They are all slotted into appropriate niches in the organisation.

The timing of decisions is absolutely crucial in a volatile environment. The right decision may be of little use if it is taken at the wrong time (Rivoli and Salorio, 1996). Committing resources too early to a growing market, for example, means that costs are incurred before adequate revenues can be generated, while deferring until too late means that the market may be permanently lost to competitors (Buckley and Casson, 1981). An important reason for deferring investment is that new information may become available later which would lead to a better decision. This is the central point in the theory of options (Trigeorgis, 1996). Investment is often irreversible, in the sense that the resources committed are illiquid and cannot be fully recovered later through divestment. Deferring a decision on an irreversible investment reduces the risk that the investment may go ahead on a mistaken assessment of the situation (Campa, 1994). The more volatile the environment, the more likely it is to change, and hence the greater the advantage of waiting until all imminent changes have occurred.

It would be wrong to infer, however, that investment is always discouraged by volatility. Investment often leads to the discovery of new information. Suppose, for example, that there are two foreign markets, one of which is known to be similar to the other. Investing in the smaller market involves a smaller commitment than investing in the larger one. A by-product of investment in the smaller market is information about the larger market. This information reduces the risk of investing in the larger one. It therefore pays to invest first in the smaller market, even though the prospects are worse than in the larger one, because the experience gained can be used to improve the later, more important, decision. This idea is central to the Scandinavian model of the internationalisation of the firm (Johanson and Vahlne, 1977).

In general, the growth of MNEs may be understood as a sequence of investments undertaken in a volatile environment, where each investment feeds back information which can be used to improve the quality of subsequent decisions. In this sense, the expansion of the firm is a path-dependent process (Kogut and Zander, 1993). Most expositions of path-dependency assume, however, that the choice of path is essentially myopic, in the sense that decision makers make no attempt to anticipate the kind of information that will get fed back at each stage. This need not be the case, though. An entrepreneurial firm may be able to anticipate how the information that it will obtain in the future depends on the decision that it currently has to make. In this case its managers can exploit the logical structure of this learning process to expand in an optimal manner. The sequence of industries into which the firm diversifies, and the sequence of the countries in which it invests, represents a rational dynamic strategy of growth.

Similarly, strategic divestment in response to competition may also be seen as a consequence of a rational dynamic strategy. In a volatile environment a rational firm will anticipate the possibility of competition by investing in a manner that takes subsequent divestment options into account. It will make only those investments that it is either unlikely to want to divest or which will be easy to divest because the sunk costs involved are relatively low. The typical investment will involve assets that have several alternative uses, and are easy to sell off to other firms. Since assets of this kind are easy to obtain in the first place, through acquisition, the theory suggests that acquisitions and divestment of highly 'liquid' or 'non-specific' assets are likely to play a major role in flexible investment strategies. This is one reason why acquisitions and divestments became more common at the same time that IJVs became more common too. Both are implications of the strategic pursuit of flexibility in a volatile environment.

The pursuit of sophisticated strategies of this kind requires a great deal of information to be shared within the organisation. It is crucial that this information is communicated in an honest manner. Integrity is often assured by repeated interaction, as explained by the theory of non-cooperative games (Kreps, 1990). Alternatively, integrity can be assured by cultural engineering (Casson, 1991) Cultural engineering within a firm can be effected in two main ways. One is by selecting people who have already been subjected to appropriate cultural influences. This explains why many firms recruit selectively from certain communities, educational institutions and ethnic groups. Cultural homogeneity not only improves internal communication but standardises employees on a uniform set of moral values. The alternative is for the firm to recruit people purely on the basis of competence, and standardise the morals through active dissemination of a corporate culture. The first strategy allows the firm to 'free ride' on cultural engineering by other institutions and reduces the demands on the chief executive's leadership role. The second strategy allows the firm to recruit more widely and to tailor the moral system to its specific requirements. MNEs will tend to favour the latter strategy because they need to recruit a range of different nationalities and to combine the expertise of members of very different professional groups.

7.14   An example

What does a scholar pursuing the new research agenda actually *do*? How does the formal specification of a dynamic model differ from that of a static one and how exactly does a dynamic model differ from a 'framework' of the Porter type? A full answer can only be obtained from the literature cited above, but a simple example may clarify the position.

Consider the problem of modelling market entry from a dynamic, rather than a static, point of view (Chi and McGuire, 1996). The most important new point to take into account is that the foreign market can decline as well as grow. Divestment or withdrawal must be considered as serious strategies. Clearly, these strategies do not apply until the market has been entered, but once it has been entered they may need to be used. Static models assume that the market will be constant, while very simple dynamic models, such as Buckley and Casson (1981), only suppose that the market will grow. In a volatile environment a market may grow to begin with, attracting investment, but then go into decline, requiring divestment instead. Such explicit recognition of adverse scenarios is a characteristic of the new research agenda.

Switching between strategies is costly, and the costs depend on both the strategy the firm is switching from and the strategy the firm is switching to. In some cases, switching costs decompose neatly into a cost of exit from the old strategy and a cost of setting up the new strategy. Detailed modelling of such costs is a key element of the new research agenda.

To preserve flexibility it is important for the firm to choose at the outset strategies whose exit costs are low. This tends to favour exporting over host-country production and licensing over internalisation. In other words, it reveals FDI as a high-risk strategy.

Switching decisions can be mistaken, however, because the information upon which they are based is poor. Expected switching costs are reduced by avoiding unnecessary switches. Different strategies afford different opportunities for capturing information from the host environment and feeding it back to inform subsequent switching decisions. The new agenda involves explicit modelling of how the strategy chosen at one stage affects the information available at following stages.

FDI offers better opportunities for information capture than either licensing or exporting, since ownership of assets confers ownership of information too. This means, for example, that if volatility caused the market to unexpectedly grow, then the foreign investor would recognise this quickly. Since it is often cheaper to expand existing capacity than to build from scratch, the foreign investor also faces lower costs of capacity expansion than does an exporter who decides to switch to foreign production at this stage. While exporting continues to confer more flexibility in response to market decline, FDI investment confers more flexibility in respect of market growth.

Is it possible to find a strategy with a better combination of characteristics than either exporting, licensing or FDI? An IJV may provide the answer (Kogut, 1991). Investing in a 50:50 partnership with a host-country producer lays off some of the risks associated with wholly owned FDI. At the same time, information capture remains reasonably good. There is an option to expand capacity if there is unexpected market growth, and a further option to increase commitment by buying the partner out. There is also an easy option to withdraw by selling out to the partner. The partner provides a ready market for divested assets that an ordinary direct investor lacks. There is a downside, of course – an obvious problem is that the partners may themselves become a source of volatility. This is why trust is such an important element in an IJV. In this way the emphasis on risk management within the new research agenda leads to the emergence of new 'compromise strategies', which would be dominated by more conventional strategies were it not for the 'option value' they possess within a volatile environment.

IJV options can only be exercised once, of course, unless the investor switches back to an IJV arrangement at a later date, when they can be exercised all over again. This explains IJV instability as a rational response to the role that IJVs fulfil. An IJV in which the options are never exercised is probably inferior to a wholly owned investment, while an IJV in which the options are exercised at the first available opportunity does not last for very long. When IJVs are chosen because of their option value, it is normally inefficient both to switch out right away or to never switch at all. The optimal timing of a switch is one at which uncertainty about future market growth is dispelled for a reasonable period of time. This implies that the duration of IJVs is, on average, fairly short and relatively variable. The new research agenda provides a simple means of deriving such hypotheses about the period of time for which a given strategy will be pursued.

The globalisation of markets has been a major factor in the growth of volatility, as explained earlier. A feature of many global markets is the use of regional production and distribution hubs, where several neighbouring countries are serviced from the same location. The regional hub, like the IJV, can be understood as a strategy that offers superior flexibility. Just as an IJV offers a compromise ownership strategy, a regional hub offers a compromise location strategy. Because the hub is nearer to each market than is the home location, it reduces transport costs and offers better information capture too. Yet, because it is close to several markets, it avoids exclusive commitment to any one. If one market declines, production can be switched to other markets instead. Provided the shocks affecting the national markets are independent (or less than perfectly correlated, at any rate), the hub provides gains from diversification. These are real gains that only the firm can achieve, as opposed to the financial gains from unrelated product diversification, which have proved disappointing in the past because they are best exploited through the diversification of individual share portfolios instead.

The two strategies of IJV and hub can be combined. Since one is an ownership strategy and the other a location strategy, they can, if desired, be combined directly in an IJV production hub. Closer examination of the issues suggests that this is not normally the best approach, however. The model suggests that a combination of a wholly owned production hub supplying IJV distribution facilities in each national market is a better solution. A hub facility is too critical to global strategy to allow a partner to become involved, because the damage they could do is far too great. Even with a wholly owned hub facility, the combination still affords considerable flexibility to divest or withdraw from any single market. The advantage of the combination is that when divesting the distribution facility can be sold to the partner, while the production capacity can be diverted to markets elsewhere. These options for divestment are combined with useful options for expansion too.

This example illustrates the crucial role that the concepts of flexibility and volatility play in analysing foreign market entry in the modern global economy. Without these concepts it is impossible to fully understand the rationale for IJVs and production hubs. It is also impossible to understand why these strategies have emerged at this particular historical juncture and not before.

While some of the insights of this model can certainly be expressed in terms of a framework, a framework is too crude to analyse the interplay of the different factors in a completely rigorous way. The concepts of adjustment costs and exit costs can already be found in the strategy literature, for example, but even this simple example above is sufficient to show that the interplay of present entry and future exit cannot be properly understood without the aid of a fully specified model. This does not mean that the strategy literature is flawed. The new dynamic agenda is perfectly compatible with much of the existing strategy literature, but it goes beyond it by developing and refining the insights in a way that the strategy framework is unable to do.

7.15   Conclusion

There are many other subjects in international business to which the new agenda can be applied, and many other new techniques which can be used. Enough has been said to indicate the promise that the new agenda holds for future research. The key to success in international business theory is to avoid becoming overwhelmed by the complexity of the issues. New issues, centred on flexibility, call for theory to refocus on the new insights described earlier. The use of economic methodology means that these new issues can be addressed in a simple and elegant way. The traditional agenda has plenty of life left in it yet. But it is not the only agenda. As Arpan (1997) has noted, international business research must change if it is to retain its relevance and its basic simplicity. The new agenda sets out the way in which this can be done.

Notes

The authors are grateful to Jose Paulo Esperanca, Mohammed Azzim Gulamhussen and Filipe Ravara for suggestions regarding the application of real options theory to joint ventures. Useful comments were received from Sarianna Lundan, and anonymous referee.

References

Allen, L. and Pantzalis, C. 1996. Valuation of the Operating Flexibility of Multinational Corporations. *Journal of International Business Studies*, 27(4): 633–53.

Arpan, J. S. 1997. Palabras del Presidente. *AIB Newsletter*, 3(3): 2.

Bartlett, C. A. and Ghoshal, S. 1987. Managing across Borders; New Strategic Requirements. *Sloan Management Review*, Summer, 6–17.

Best, M. H. 1990. *The New Competition: Institutions of Industrial Restructuring.* Oxford: Polity Press.

Buckley, P. J. 1988. The Limits of Explanation: Testing the Internalization Theory of the Multinational Enterprise. *Journal of International Business Studies*, 19(2): 1–16.

——. 1981. The Optimal Timing of a Foreign Direct Investment. *Economic Journal*, 91: 75–87.

——. 1983. New Theories of International Business: Some Unresolved Issues, in M. C. Casson (ed.) *The Growth of International Business.* London: Allen & Unwin, 34–50.

——. 1988. A Theory of Co-Operation in International Business, in Farok J. Contractor & Peter Lorange (eds), *Co-Operative Strategies in International Business.* Lexington, MA: Lexington Books, 31–53.

——. 1993. Economics as an Imperialist Social Science. *Human Relations*, 46(9): 1035–52.

——. 1996. An Economic Model of International Joint Venture Strategy. *Journal of International Business Studies*, 27(5): 849–76.

——. and Casson, M. C. 1976. *The Future of the Multinational Enterprise.* London: Macmillan.

——. and Carter, M. J. 1996. The Economics of Business Process Design: Motivation, Information and Coordination within the Firm. *International Journal of the Economics of Business*, 3(1): 5–25.

——. and Chapman, M. 1996. Economics and Social Anthropology – Reconciling Differences. *Human Relations*, 49(9): 1123–50.

——., Christopher, P. L. and Prescott, K. 1988. Measures of International Competitiveness: A Critical Survey. *Journal of Marketing Management*, 4(2): 175–200.

Campa, J. M. 1994. Multinational Investment under Uncertainty in the Chemical Processing Industries. *Journal of International Business Studies*, 25(3): 557–78.

Cantwell, J. 1995. Multinational Enterprises and Innovatory Activities: Towards a New Evolutionary Approach, in J. Molero (ed.), *Technological Innovation, Multinational Corporations and the New International Competitiveness.* Chur: Harwood Academic Publishers, 21–57.

Capel, J. 1992. How to Service a Foreign Market under Uncertainty: A Real Option Approach. *European Journal of Political Economy*, 8: 455–75.

Casson, M. C. 1990. *Enterprise and Competitiveness.* Oxford: Clarendon Press.

——. 1991. *Economics of Business Culture.* Oxford: Clarendon Press.

——. 1994. Why are Firms Hierarchical? *International Journal of the Economics of Business*, 1(1): 3–40.

——. 1995. *Organization of International Business.* Aldershot: Edward Elgar.

——. Pearce, R. D. and Singh, S. 1991 A Review of Recent Trends, in Mark C. Casson (ed.), *Global Research Strategy and International Competitiveness.* Oxford: Blackwell, 250–71.

Caves, R. E. 1996. *Multinational Enterprise and Economic Analysis.* Cambridge: Cambridge University Press. Second Edition.

Chi, T. and McGuire, D. J. 1996. Collaborative Ventures and Value of Learning: Integrating the Transaction Cost and Strategic Option Perspectives on the Choice of Market Entry Modes. *Journal of International Business Studies*, 27(2): 285–307.

DeMeza, D. and van der Ploeg, F. 1987. Production Flexibility as a Motive for Multinationality. *Journal of Industrial Economics*, 35(3): 343–51.

Dempster, M. A. H. and Pliska, S. R. (eds). 1997. *Mathematics of Derivative Securities*. Cambridge: Cambridge University Press.

Dixit, A. and Pindyck, R. S. 1994. *Investments under Uncertainty*. Princeton, NJ: Princeton University Press.

Dunning, J. H. 1977. Trade, Location of Economic Activity and the Multinational Enterprise: The Search for an Eclectic Approach, in B. Ohlin, P. O. Hessleborn and P. M. Wijkman (eds), *The International Location of Economic Activity*. London: Macmillan.

——. 1993. *Multinational Enterprises in the Global Economy*. Wokingham, Berkshire: Addison-Wesley.

——. 1997. *Alliance Capitalism and Global Business*. London: Routledge.

Ergas, H. 1987. Does Technology Policy Matter? in B. R. Guile and H. Brooks (eds), *Technology and Global Industry*. Washington, DC: National Academy Press, 191–245.

Fransman, M. 1995. *Japan's Computer and Communications Industry*, Oxford: Oxford University Press.

Fukuyama, F. 1996. *Trust*. Harmondsworth: Penguin.

Geringer, J. M. and Hebert, L. 1989. Control and Performance of International Joint Ventures. *Journal of International Business Studies*, 20(2): 235–54.

Hedlund, G. 1993. Assumptions of Hierarchy and Heterarchy: An Application to the Multinational Corporation, in S. Ghoshal and E. Westney (eds), *Organization Theory and the Multinational Corporation*. London: Macmillan, 211–36.

Hirshleifer, J. and Riley, J. G. 1992. *The Analytics of Uncertainty and Information*. Cambridge: Cambridge University Press.

Hood, N. and Young, S. 1994. The Internationalization of Business and the Challenge of East European Business, in P. J. Buckley and P. N. Ghauri (eds), *The Economics of Change in East and Central Europe*. London: Academic Press, 320–42.

Johanson, J. and Vahlne, J -E. 1977. The Internationalization Process of the Firm – A Model of Knowledge Development and Increasing Foreign Market Commitments. *Journal of International Business Studies*, 8(1): 23–32.

Kogut, B. 1991. Joint Ventures and the Option to Expand and Acquire. *Management Science*, 37(1): 19–33.

——. and Kulatilaka, N. 1994. Operating Flexibility, Global Manufacturing, and the Option Value of a Multinational Network. *Management Science*, 40(1): 123–39.

Kogut, B. and Zander, U. 1993. Knowledge of the Firm and the Evolutionary Theory of the Multinational Corporation. *Journal of International Business Studies*, 24(4): 625–45.

Kotter, J. 1996. *Leading Change*. Cambridge, MA: Harvard Business School Press.

Kreps, D. M. 1990. *Game Theory and Economic Modelling*. Oxford: Oxford University Press.

Krugman, P. 1995. *Development, Geography and Economic Theory*. Cambridge, MA: MIT Press.

——. 1996. The Myth of Asia's Miracle, in Paul Krugman, *Pop Internationalism*. Cambridge, MA: MIT Press.

Lall, S. and Streeten, P. 1977. *Foreign Investment, Transnationals and Developing Countries*. London: Macmillan

Loasby, B. J. 1991. *Equilibrium and Evolution*. Manchester: Manchester University Press.

Marglin, S. A. and Schor, J. B. 1990. *The Golden Age of Capitalism: Reinterpreting the Post-War Experience*. Oxford: Clarendon Press.

Marris, R. L. 1979. *The Theory and Future of the Corporate Economy and Society*. Amsterdam: North-Holland.

Marschak, J. and Radner, R. 1972. *Economic Theory of Teams*. New Haven, CT: Yale University Press.

Marshall, A. 1919. *Industry and Trade*. London: Macmillan.

Mello, A. S., Parsons, J. E. and Triantis, A. J. 1995. An Integrated Model of Multinational Flexibility and Hedging Policies. *Journal of International Economics*, 39 (August): 27–51.

Mirza, H. 1986. *Multinationals and the Growth of the Singapore Economy*. London: Croom Helm.

Nelson, R. and Winter, S. G. 1982. *An Evolutionary Theory of Economic Change*. Cambridge, MA: Harvard University Press.

Pearce, R. D. and Singh, S. 1992. *Globalising Research and Development*. London: Macmillan.

Porter, M. E. 1990. *The Competitive Advantage of Nations*. London: Macmillan.

——. 1991. Towards a Dynamic Theory of Strategy. *Strategic Management Journal*, 12 (Special Issue): 95–117

Reich, R. B. 1990. Who is us? *Harvard Business Review*. 68(1): 53–65.

Richardson, G. B. 1960. *Information and Investment*. Oxford: Oxford University Press.

Rivoli, P. and Salorio, E. 1996. Foreign Direct Investment under Uncertainty, *Journal of International Business Studies*, 27(2): 335–54.

Rugman, A. M., D'Cruz, J. R. and Verbeke, A. 1995. Internalisation and De-Internalisation: Will Business Networks Replace Multinationals? in G. Boyd (ed.), *Competitive and Cooperative Macromanagement: The Challenge of Structural Interdependence*. Aldershot: Edward Elgar, 107–28.

Thurow, L. C. 1992. *Head to Head: The Coming Economic Battle among Japan, Europe and America*. New York: Morrow.

Trigeorgis, L. 1996. *Real Options*. Cambridge, MA: MIT Press.

Wu, S -Y. 1988. *Production, Entrepreneurship and Profits*. Oxford: Blackwell.

8
Analysing Foreign Market Entry Strategies: Extending the Internalisation Approach

Empirical studies of FDI have become much more ambitious in scope over the last 30 years. In the 1960s, the main focus of the Hymer-Kindleberger theory (Hymer, 1976; Kindleberger, 1969) and the product cycle theory (Vernon 1966) was exporting versus FDI. In the 1970s the internalisation approach identified licensing, franchising and sub-contracting as other strategic options. The resurgence of mergers and acquisitions in the 1980s – often as a 'quick fix' route to globalisation – highlighted the choice between greenfield ventures and acquisitions. At the same time, the growing participation of US firms in IJVs drew attention to the role of cooperative arrangements.

In the 1990s, the role of FDI in 'transitional' or 'emerging' economies (East and Central Europe, China, Vietnam, etc.) has brought back into focus some of the classic issues of the 1960s: the 'costs of doing business abroad' and the importance of 'psychic distance'. It has renewed interest in the general questions as to why some modes of entry offer lower costs than others and why certain circumstances seem to favour certain modes over others.

Linking all these issues together generates a high degree of complexity. Although the eclectic theory has been regularly revised and updated to accommodate the changing foci of applied research, it is too much of a 'paradigm' or 'framework' and too little of a 'model' to provide detailed advice on research design and hypothesis testing (Dunning, 1980). Complexity appears to have created a degree of confusion among scholars, which only a formal modelling exercise can dispel.

The model presented below has three distinctive features. First, it is based on a detailed schematic analysis that encompasses all the major market entry strategies. In existing literature most strategies are appraised as alternatives to exporting, or as alternatives to greenfield

FDI. It is unusual to see a direct comparison between, say, licensing and joint ventures, or between franchising and subcontracting. The present model permits any strategy to be compared with any other strategy. It is therefore particularly useful when the leading strategies in contention do not include either exporting or conventional FDI.

The second feature of the model is that it distinguishes clearly between production and distribution. Historically, a large proportion of initial FDI relates to foreign warehousing and distribution facilities. Production facilities only come later, if at all. The distinction is obvious in empirical work, but it has not been properly reflected in theory up until now. The result has been some confusion as to how theory should be applied to situations in which investment in distribution has a prominent role.

Finally, the model takes account of the strategic interaction between the foreign entrant and its leading host-country rival after entry has taken place. Following recent developments in industrial organisation theory (as summarised, for example, in Tirole, 1988), it is assumed that the entrant can foresee the reaction of its rival and take this into account at the time of entry. It is argued that this theoretical refinement is of the utmost practical importance in explaining the choice between greenfield investment and acquisition as entry modes.

The model concentrates on FDI for market access reasons and excludes resource-orientated FDI and offshore production.

8.1   Historical development of the theory

Much of the early literature on foreign market entry concerned the choice between exporting and FDI (for previous overviews, see Root, 1987; Young et al., 1989; Buckley and Ghauri, 1993). The cost-based view of this decision suggested that the firm must possess a 'compensating advantage' in order to overcome the 'costs of foreignness' (Hymer, 1976; Kindleberger, 1969). This led to the identification of technological and marketing skills as the key elements in successful foreign entry (Hirsh, 1976; Horst, 1972). This tradition of firm-specific advantages (Caves, 1971; Rugman, 1981) connects with the literature on core competences arising from the Penrosian tradition (Penrose, 1959; Prahalad and Hamel, 1990). Sequential modes of internationalisation were introduced by Vernon's 'Product Cycle Hypothesis' (1966), in which firms go through an exporting phase before switching first to market-seeking FDI and then to cost-orientated FDI. Technology and marketing factors combine to explain standardisation, which drives location decisions.

8.1.1 Internalisation

Buckley and Casson (1976) envisaged the firm as an internalised bundle of resources which can be allocated between product groups and between national markets. Their focus on market-based versus firm-based solutions highlighted the strategic significance of licensing in market entry. Entry involves two interdependent decisions – on location and mode of control. Exporting is domestically located and administratively controlled, foreign licensing is foreign located and contractually controlled and FDI is foreign located and administratively controlled. This model was formalised by Buckley and Casson (1981) and empirically tested by Buckley and Pearce (1979), Contractor (1984) and others.

8.1.2 Stages models of entry

The Scandinavian 'stages' models of entry suggest a sequential pattern of entry into successive foreign markets, coupled with a progressive deepening of commitment to each market. Increasing commitment is particularly important in the thinking of the Uppsala School (Johanson and Wiedersheim-Paul, 1975; Johanson and Vahlne, 1977). Closely associated with stages models is the notion of 'psychic distance' which attempts to conceptualise and, to some degree, measure the cultural distance between countries and markets (Hallen and Wiedersheim-Paul, 1979). For a more recent view see Casson, 1994.

8.1.3 Non-production activities

In explaining foreign market servicing policies, the role of non-production activities must be made explicit. The location of research activities is widely debated, especially in relation to spatial agglomeration (Kogut and Zander, 1993). There is also an extensive literature on the entry aspects of marketing and distribution (Davidson and McFetridge, 1980), much of it in a transactions cost framework (Anderson and Coughlan, 1987; Anderson and Gatignon, 1986; Hill, Hwang and Kim, 1990; Kim and Hwang, 1992; and Agarwal and Ramaswani, 1992).

8.1.4 Mergers and acquisitions versus greenfield ventures

Stopford and Wells (1972) examined takeovers versus acquisitions as part of the their analysis of the organisation of the multinational firm. The predominance of entry via takeovers in most advanced economies has stimulated a number of empirical studies (Dubin, 1975; Wilson, 1980; Zejan, 1990; Hennart and Park, 1993), which have drawn on both the internalisation perspective and the strategy literature (Yip, 1982). Particular attention has been paid to the costs of adaptation and cultural integration that are encountered in the case of mergers. The theoretical issues have recently been surveyed by Svensson (1996) and Meyer (1997).

8.1.5 Joint ventures versus wholly owned subsidiaries

The recent literature on IJVs is immense and has spawned some innovative developments in international business theory and much insightful empirical work based on extensive data sets (Contractor and Lorange, 1988; Beamish and Killing, 1997). Buckley and Casson (1988, 1996) summarise the conditions conducive to IJVs as: (i) the possession of complementary assets; (ii) opportunities for collusion, and (iii) barriers to full integration – economic, financial, legal or political (see also Beamish, 1985; Beamish and Banks, 1987; Kogut, 1988; Hennart, 1988; and Contractor, 1990).

The IJV literature has focused particularly on partner selection, management strategy and the measurement of performance. Partner selection is examined by Beamish (1987), who relates selection to performance, Harrigan (1988b), who examines partner asymmetries, and Geringer (1991). Kogut and Singh (1987, 1988) relate partner selection to entry method. Management strategy in IJVs is analysed by Killing (1983) and Harrigan (1988), while Gomes-Casseres (1991) relates strategy to ownership preferences.

The performance of IJVs is the subject of much debate. It cannot be assumed that joint venture termination indicates failure – an IJV may end precisely because it has achieved its objectives. Similarly, the restructuring of joint ventures and alliances may indicate the exploitation of the flexibility of the organisational form, rather than a response to underperformance – see Franko (1971), Gomes-Casseres (1987), Kogut (1988, 1989), and Blodgett (1992). Other analyses of IJV performance include Geringer and Hebert (1991), Inkpen and Birkenshaw (1994) and Woodcock, Beamish and Makino (1994). Nitsch, Beamish and Makino (1996) relate entry mode to performance, and Gulati (1995) examines the role of repeated ties between partners as contributing to success – an interesting attempt to encompass 'cultural' variables.

8.1.6 Cultural factors

The relationship between (national) culture and entry strategy is explicitly examined (using a reductionist version of Hofstede's (1980) cultural classification) by Kogut and Singh (1988) (see also Shane, 1994). Cultural barriers are utilised in an examination of foreign market entry by Bakema, Bell and Pennings (1996), and a 'cultural learning process' is invoked by Benito and Gripsrud (1994) to help explain the expansion of FDI.

8.1.7 Market structure and entry strategy

It is one of the contributions of this chapter to introduce market structure issues into the modelling of entry decisions. The relationship between entry behaviour and market structure was emphasised in Knickerbocker's (1973) study of oligopolistic reaction, which set up a game-theoretic structure for competitive entry into key national markets. Flowers (1976) and Graham (1978) emphasised 'exchange of threats' in their respective studies of European and Canadian investment in the US and two-way investment between the US and Europe. Yu and Ito (1988) more recently examined oligopolistic reaction and FDI in the US tyre and textiles industry. Graham (1992) laments the lack of attention to competitive structure in the international business literature, where the entrant is effectively a monopolist (Buckley and Casson, 1981). Indeed, Casson's (1985) study of cartelisation versus multinationalisation is one of the few economic models of multinational industrial organisation available.

8.1.8 Summary

Location costs, internalisation factors, financial variables, cultural factors, such as trust and psychic distance, market structure and competitive strategy, adaptation costs (to the local environment) and the cost of doing business abroad are all identified in the literature as playing a role in determining firms' foreign market entry decisions. The model which follows includes all these variables, and analyses their interactions in a systematic way.

8.2 The model

The model applies the economic theory of FDI presented in Buckley and Casson (1976, 1981), Buckley (1983), Casson (1991) and Buckley and Casson (1996) to the set of issues identified in the literature review above. Although the model involves a number of apparently restrictive assumptions, these assumptions can, if necessary, be relaxed, at the cost of introducing additional complications into the analysis. The assumptions are not so much restrictions upon the relevance of the model as indicators of key contextual issues on which every researcher into foreign market entry must pass judgement before their analysis begins. If some of the assumptions seem unfamiliar then it is because few researchers have actually made their assumptions sufficiently explicit in the past.

8.2.1 The entrant

1. A firm based in a home country is seeking to sell for the first time in a foreign market. The emphasis on first-time entry makes it important to distinguish between the one-off set-up costs of an entry mode and the recurrent costs of subsequent operation in that mode. It is assumed, unless otherwise stated, that recurrent operations take place in a stable environment.

2. Foreign market demand for the product is infinitely elastic at a price p_1 up to a certain volume at which it becomes totally inelastic. For example, each customer may desire just one unit of the product, which they value at p_1 and when everyone has bought that unit no more can be sold however far the price is dropped. The volume at which demand becomes inelastic is determined by the size of the foreign market, x.

3. The focus of the model on market entry makes it appropriate to distinguish between production activity *(P)* and distribution activity *(D)*. Distribution links production to final demand. It comprises warehousing, transport, and possibly retailing too. Distribution must be carried out entirely in the foreign market, but production may be located at either home or abroad.

4. The entrant's production draws upon proprietary technology generated by research and development activity *(R)*. Effective distribution depends upon marketing activity *(M)*. Marketing involves investigating customers' needs and maintaining the reputation of the product by giving customers the service they require.

5. The entrant has no foreign activity *M* at the time of entry, and consequently lacks market knowledge. This knowledge can be acquired through experience (learning from mistakes) at the time of entry, incurring a once-and-for-all cost of entry, m. The knowledge can be obtained in other ways as well, as described below. One of the keys to successful entry strategy is to acquire *M* in the most appropriate way.

6. The flow of technology from *R* to *P* defines the first of three 'intermediate products' in the model. The second is the flow of marketing expertise from *M* to *D*. The third is the physical flow of wholesale product from the factory or production unit *P* to the distribution facility *D*. (The internal flow of information between *R* and *M* is not discussed as it is a fixed cost, which is the same for every form of market entry considered in the model.)

7. Production at home means that the product must be exported. Exporting incurs transport costs and tariffs that foreign production avoids. On the other hand, foreign production incurs additional costs of communicating the technology, e.g., training foreign workers. Foreign production may also result in the loss of economies of scale. Exporting increases the utilisation of the domestic plant and allows it to be extended at low marginal cost. All of these factors are summarised in the net additional cost of home production, z, which is equal to transport costs and tariffs *less* savings on account of training costs and economies of scale.

8. The firm may enter the foreign market either by owning and controlling
  * P and D;
  * P only;
  * D only; or
  * Neither P nor D.
In the second case, it uses an independent distribution facility, which is franchised to handle the product. In the third case, it either exports from its home production facility, or subcontracts to an independent local facility. In the final case, the firm licences an independent local firm to both produce and distribute the product. Because there is only one host-country rival (see 14 below), the possibility that the firm could subcontract to one firm and franchise another is ignored.

9. The transaction cost of operating an external market is normally greater than that of an internal one. The availability of alternative incentive structures in an internal market reduces the costs of haggling and default (Hennart, 1982). Indeed, it is assumed in the present model that the transaction cost of obtaining marketing expertise from an external consultant, rather than from the firm's own M activity, is prohibitive. The entrant can tap into an established M activity only by franchising the local rival, forming a joint venture with the rival or acquiring its distribution facility.

10. The cost of external transfer of technology is also high, but acceptably so. One of the main problems in transferring technology is to monitor the output of the production process to make sure that the contract is being complied with. This is easier to do under a subcontracting agreement, where the product is 'bought back' than under a licensing agreement, where it is not. The transactions costs of a subcontracting agreement exceed the internal costs of technology transfer by t_1 while the costs of licensing exceed internal costs by $t_2 \geq t_1$.

11. When the ownership of P differs from that of D then the flow of intermediate products between them is effected through an external

market. When compared to the alternative of vertical integration of P and D, this incurs additional transaction costs, t_3.

12. Entry of any type can be effected by either greenfield investment or acquisition. Under greenfield investment the firm uses its funds to pay for the construction of a new facility. Under acquisition it uses its funds to purchase the facility second-hand as a going concern instead. This is done by acquiring the equity in the firm which previously owned the facility.

13. An effective internal market requires a high degree of trust within the organisation. This trust is not available immediately after an acquisition. It costs q_1 to build trust in technology transfer when a P facility is newly acquired. It costs q_2 to build trust in the transfer of marketing expertise when a D facility is newly acquired and q_3 to build trust in the transfer of intermediate product when either P or D (but not both) is newly acquired.

8.2.2 The host country rival

14. The firm faces a single local rival who previously monopolised the foreign market. At the time of entry, this rival operates as a fully integrated firm. It has the expertise, conferred by an activity M, which the entrant lacks. However, the local rival has higher costs because of inferior technology, on account of having no activity R.

15. It is assumed that in all bargaining (for example, over an acquisition) the local rival plays an essentially passive role. The rival does not bargain for a share of the entrant's profits, but simply ensures that it receives full opportunity earnings for the resources it surrenders to the entrant firm. The rival realises that the entrant has a superior technology, and believes that when confronted with such a competitor its best strategy is to exit the industry by selling to the entrant those resources it wishes to buy and redeploying the others to their best alternative use.

16. If the entrant uses the rival's production facility, then a cost of adaptation is incurred. This is because the entrant uses a different technology from the rival, and equipment must be modified accordingly. This applies regardless of whether the entrant acquires the facility outright, or merely licences, or subcontracts to the rival firm. However, the rival may have local production expertise, which the entrant lacks, providing savings to offset against the adaptation cost. The net cost of adaptation may therefore be negative. A negative adaptation cost, in this context, signifies that the cost of adapting the entrant's technology to local conditions using a greenfield plant is higher than the cost of adapting an existing local plant to the entrant's technology.

17. By contrast, use of a rival's *D* facility incurs no adaptation cost. This is because warehouses are normally more versatile than production plants. Use of the rival's *D* facility always brings with it the marketing expertise associated with *M*.

18. The rival's *P* and *D* facilities are the only existing facilities that can meet the needs of the market. Other local firms cannot enter the market, and the rival firm itself cannot invest in additional facilities. Under these conditions, acquisition of either a *P* or *D* facility gives the entrant monopoly power: Acquisition of a *D* facility gives the entrant a monopoly of final sales, while acquisition of a *P* facility gives the entrant a monopoly of supplies to *D*. Greenfield investment, however, confers no monopoly power because it eliminates no rival facility: greenfield investment in *D* creates duopoly in the sourcing of final demand, while greenfield investment in *P* creates duopoly in the sourcing of *D*.

19. When the rival retains ownership of both its *P* and *D* facilities, then it remains a potential competitor. Although it may have switched some of its facilities out of the industry, it can, in principle, re-enter by switching them back again. If it has contracted out its *P* facility under a subcontracting arrangement, or contracted out its *D* facility under a franchising arrangement, then it can, in principle, re-enter competition when the agreements expire. Under a subcontracting arrangement, the entrant and the rival remain potential competitors in the final product market, since each has its own distribution facility. Any attempt by the entrant to charge the full monopoly price would encourage the rival to switch to producing its own output instead. The entrant must persuade the rival not to compete by reducing its price to a 'limit price' $p_2 < p_1$, at which it just pays the rival to keep its distribution facility out of the industry. Under a franchising arrangement, the local rival retains the option of switching back to supplying its distribution facility from its own production plant. To discourage this, the entrant must set an intermediate output price, which is equivalent (after deduction of distribution costs) to the same limit price p_2. The final customers pay the monopoly price, since the franchisee is the sole distributor, but the difference between the monopoly price and the limit price accrues to the franchisee. In either case, therefore, the persistence of rivalry costs the entrant $s = (p_1 - p_2)x$ in lost sales revenue.

20. Matters are slightly different in the case of a licensing agreement. It is assumed that licensing is a long-term agreement, as opposed to short-term agreements like subcontracting and franchising. A licence, it is supposed, involves either an outright purchase of the right to use the technology or a long-term agreement for the whole of the period

over which patent protection is likely to extend. The licence agreement therefore confers effective monopoly power on the local licensee, but at the same time allows the entrant to appropriate all the monopoly rents by negotiating suitable terms for the licence agreement.

21. Apart from licensing, the only way to avoid the competitive threat is acquisition. Acquisition of either the rival's *P* or *D* facility will do. It is assumed that the costs at which these facilities can be acquired are equivalent to the cost of new construction under a greenfield strategy (although acquisition incurs additional conversion costs, as explained above).

8.2.3   Joint ventures

22. Joint ventures are owned 50:50 by the two firms. Either the *P* or *D* plant, or both, can be jointly owned. It is assumed that when an IJV is undertaken, the partner is always the local rival. If both *P* and *D* are jointly owned, then they are both part of the same IJV, and so the market in intermediate output is internalised within the IJV. The IJV does not involve new facilities; it is assumed to be a 'buy in' by the entrant to the local firm. This means that IJV production incurs the costs of adaptation described above. Greenfield IJVs can easily be included in the model, although its complexity increases considerably as a result. Because the local rival contributes its facilities to the IJV, the IJV enjoys monopoly power in the same way that an acquisition does.

23. When an IJV is linked to one of the entrant's wholly owned activities, the relevant intermediate product market is only partially internalised. It is assumed, however, that once the appropriate degree of trust has been built up, the market can operate as though it was fully internal. The relevant costs of building trust are j_1 for technology transfer, j_2 for marketing expertise and j_3 for intermediate output flow.

24. Where both entrant and rival possess *P* facilities with which to source an IJV *D* facility, they employ the IJV to maintain a monopoly price, but compete to supply it. The competition from the rival's *P* facility forces the entrant to supply the IJV at a limit price, and so allows the rival to obtain half the monopoly rent through its share in the IJV, even though it does not actually supply the IJV itself. If both entrant and rival possess *D* facilities able to draw upon an IJV *P* facility, then they can maintain a monopoly price by competing for a franchise to handle all the output. This forces the entrant to bid up the price for IJV output such that the profits are again shared with the rival through its stake in the IJV.

25. Learning costs m, adaptation costs a and trust-building costs $j_i, q_i (i = 1,2,3)$ are once-and-for-all set-up costs that are financed by borrowing at the given interest rate r. By contrast, the home location cost premium z and the transaction costs $t_i (i = 1,2,3)$ are recurrent costs incurred each period.

8.2.4 Defining the strategy set

The basic approach is to determine the set of all possible market entry strategies, to measure the profitability of each and to identify the most profitable strategy. The dimensions of the strategy set are defined by the following issues:

(1) where production is located;
(2) whether production is owned by the entrant;
(3) whether distribution is owned by the entrant;
(4) whether ownership is outright, or shared through an IJV; and
(5) whether ownership is obtained through greenfield investment or acquisition.

The first four issues determine 12 main strategies of market entry. These 12 strategies are listed on the left hand side of Table 8.1, and summarised schematically in Figure 8.1. Six of these strategies have different variants generated by the fifth issue. These variants are indicated on the right hand side of the table. The figure distinguishes linkages involving the flow of information from R to P and M to D, and linkages involving the flow of physical product from P to D, and from D to final demand. Location is distinguished by the columns, and ownership by the rows. Ownership by the entrant is also identified by shading; facilities owned by the local rival are shown as clear. The strategies associated with each particular linkage are indicated by the numbers 1–12 in the figure.

8.2.5 Deriving the profit equations

A profit equation for each variant of each entry strategy can be derived by applying the assumptions given above to the schematic illustrations in Figure 8.1. Certain elements of cost and revenue are common to all the profit equations, and it simplifies matters to net these out. This generates a set of summary profit equations in which profitability is expressed in terms of deviations from a profit norm. An appropriate norm is the profit generated by pursuing strategy 1 under ideal conditions, in which the firm is already acquainted with the local market and there is no indigenous rival. The profit norm is

Table 8.1 Twelve entry strategies and their variants

Ref.	Type	Description	Variants
1.	Normal FDI	Entrant owns foreign production and distribution facilities.	1.1 Both facilities are greenfield. 1.2 Both facilities are acquired. 1.3 Production is greenfield and distribution is acquired. 1.4 Distribution is greenfield and production is acquired.
2.	FDI in production	Entrant owns foreign production, but uses independent distribution facilities.	2.1 Production is greenfield. 2.2 Production is acquired.
3.	Subcontracting	Entrant owns foreign distribution, but uses independent production facilities.	3.1 Distribution is greenfield. 3.2 Distribution is acquired.
4.	FDI in distribution	Entrant exports to own distribution facility.	4.1 Distribution is greenfield. 4.2 Distribution is acquired.
5.	Exporting/franchising	Entrant exports to independent distribution facility.	
6.	Licensing	Entrant transfers technology to independent integrated firm.	

7.	Integrated JV	Entrant jointly owns on integrated set of production and distribution facilities.	
8.	JV in production	Entrant jointly owns foreign production, but uses an independent distribution facility.	
9.	JV in production	Entrant jointly owns foreign distribution, but subcontracts production to an independent facility.	
10.	JV exporting	Entrant exports to a jointly owned distribution facility.	
11.	FDI/JV combination	Entrant owns foreign production and jointly owns foreign distribution.	11.1 Production is greenfield. 11.2 Production is acquired.
12.	JV/FDI combination	Entrant owns foreign distribution and jointly owns foreign production.	12.1 Distribution is greenfield. 12.2 Distribution is acquired.

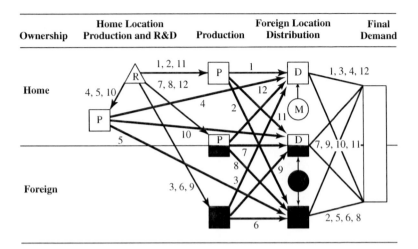

Figure 8.1   Twelve entry strategies and their variants.

the revenue generated by sales at the monopoly price p_1, less the cost of greenfield foreign production, *less* the cost of greenfield foreign distribution, *less* the cost of internal technology transfer to a greenfield foreign plant, *less* the cost of internal transfer of goods from production to distribution.

If the actual profits of each strategy are compared with this norm, then every strategy incurs some additional cost. The relevant cost expressions are given in Table 8.2. The subscripts applied to the cost symbol c refer to the strategies and their variants listed in Table 8.1. The variables on the right hand side have already been explained when introducing the assumptions of the model. Set-up costs are multiplied by the rate of interest to convert a once-and-for-all cost into a continuous equivalent.

To see how the profit equations are derived, consider strategy 2. This involves FDI in production, with sales being handled by the rival firm. There are two variants of this strategy, depending upon whether the production plant is acquired or not. The only international transfer of resources under this strategy involves technology, which moves across the column boundary from R to P. The transfer is internalised because no change of ownership is involved. Change of ownership only occurs where the flow of intermediate output from P to D crosses the row boundary. From D the product is distributed to the entire foreign market, as indicated by the flow fanning out from D.

Table 8.2 Costs of alternative strategies compared with the profit norm

$c_{1.1}$						$+s$	$+rm$
$c_{1.2}$		rq_1	$+rq_2$		$+ra$		
$c_{1.3}$			$+rq_2$	$+rq_3$			
$c_{1.4}$		rq_1		$+rq_3$	$+ra$		$+rm$
$c_{2.1}$				t_3		$+s$	
$c_{2.2}$		rq_1		$+t_3$	$+ra$		
$c_{3.1}$		t_1		$+t_3$	$+ra$	$+s$	$+rm$
$c_{3.2}$		t_1	$+rq_2$	$+t_3$	$+ra$		
$c_{4.1}$	z					$+s$	$+rm$
$c_{4.2}$	z		$+rq_2$	$+rq_3$			
c_5	z			$+t_3$		$+s$	
c_6		t_2			$+ra$		
c_7		rj_1	$+rj_2$		$+ra$		
c_8		rj_1		$+rj_3$	$+ra$		
c_9		t_1	$+rj_2$	$+rj_3$	$+ra$		
c_{10}	z		$+rj_2$	$+rj_3$		$+s/2$	
$c_{11.1}$			$+rj_2$	$+rj_3$		$+s/2$	
$c_{11.2}$		rq_1	$+rj_2$	$+rj_3$	$+ra$		
$c_{12.1}$		rj_1		$+rj_3$	$+ra$	$+s/2$	$+rm$
$c_{12.2}$		rj_1	$+rj_2$	$+rj_3$	$+ra$		

The advantages of this particular strategy are two-fold. It internalises the transfer of technology within the entrant firm, and it internalises the transfer of marketing expertise within the local firm. This can only be achieved, however, by externalising the flow of intermediate output, which generates the transaction cost premium term t_3, which appears in the expressions for both $c_{2.1}$ and $c_{2.2}$. This is, in fact, the only term that is common to both expressions. The remaining terms are all accounted for by the difference between greenfield and acquisition methods of FDI. The greenfield strategy avoids the cost a of adapting an existing plant to the needs of a new technology. Thus the term ra, which appears in the expression for $c_{2.2}$ does not appear in the expression for $c_{2.1}$. The greenfield strategy also means that the internal transfer of technology is not bedevilled by a lack of trust, which arises when the production facility is acquired instead. The cost of building trust in internal technology transfer, rq_1, therefore appears in $c_{2.2}$, but not in $c_{2.1}$.

The compensating advantage of the acquisition strategy is that it does not add to overall capacity in the foreign country. Indeed, because the entrant faces a single local rival, acquisition of the rival's production facility effectively prevents the rival from entering into competition with the entrant firm. Given that under strategy 2 the local firm retains control of distribution, it can threaten to source distribution from its own production plant instead of from the entrant's plant. Although the entrant may be able to constrain this threat in the short term by signing an exclusive franchise contract with its local rival, in the long run this contract will expire, and the threat will reappear. Only acquisition of one of the rival's facilities can eliminate this threat altogether. This means that the greenfield strategy incurs a loss of revenue as compared to the acquisition strategy equal to s.

8.2.6　Dominance relations

Theory predicts that the strategy with the lowest cost will be chosen. Which strategy is chosen depends on the relative magnitude of the different variables on the right hand side of Table 8.2. The easiest way to understand the general properties of the solution is first to eliminate any strategies that are clearly dominated by others, and then to compare the remaining ones in terms of the major trade-offs involved.

Whether strategies are dominated or not depends upon what restrictions are imposed upon the right-hand-side variables. So far, the only restrictions implied by the assumptions are $m, r, s, j_i, q_i, t_i > 0 \, (i = 1, 2, 3)$ and $t_2 \geq t_1$. In particular, the variables a and z are unrestricted in sign. Under these conditions, only two of the strategies are dominated, namely the bottom two in the table:

$$c_{12.1} > c_8; \, c_{12.2} > c_8.$$

These strategies involve a production IJV and a wholly owned sales subsidiary. They are inferior to a production IJV combined with the franchising of sales. This shows that if the entrant is to partner the IJV in production, then there is no point in buying back the product to distribute it afterwards.

Once additional restrictions are imposed, further dominance relations emerge. For example, if the net cost of home production is positive, $z > 0$, then all the export strategies are dominated by equivalent strategies involving greenfield foreign production:

$$c_{4.1} > c_{1.1} \, ; c_{4.2} > c_{1.3} \, ; c_5 > c_{2.1} \, ; c_{10} > c_{11.1}.$$

This illustrates the important point that location effects are independent of internalisation effects in models of this kind.

If the net cost of technological adaptation of existing production facilities is positive, $a > 0$, then it follows that

$$c_{3.1} > c_{1.1}.$$

This means that the strategy of investing only in a greenfield distribution facility is inefficient compared to the strategy of investing in a greenfield production facility as well. Put simply, subcontracting production is not a good idea when the net cost of adapting existing plant to the new technology is positive.

So far, no use has been made of restrictions on transactions costs. Suppose now that external market costs exceed the costs of building trust in internal markets after acquisition. In the context of production, this means that $t_1 > rq_1$ from whence it follows that

$$c_{3.2} > c_{2.2}$$

$$c_9 > c_{11.2}$$

The first inequality shows that subcontracting production in conjunction with the acquisition of a distribution facility is more costly than franchising distribution in conjunction with the acquisition of a production facility. The second inequality shows that subcontracting production in conjunction with a jointly owned distribution facility is more costly than acquiring a production facility in conjunction with a jointly owned distribution facility. These results underline the fact that high transaction costs in technology markets, combined with easy trust-building post-acquisition, discourage subcontracting and favour acquisition instead.

The process of elimination through dominance can be continued by postulating that the cost of building trust is lower after an acquisition than it is within a joint venture: $q_i < j_i \, (i = 1, 2, 3)$. Not surprisingly, this eliminates several IJV strategies – though not all:

$$c_7 > c_{1.2} \; ; \; c_{11.1} > c_{1.3} \; ; \; c_{11.2} > c_{1.3}$$

It is inefficient to combine an IJV distribution facility with a production facility that is either wholly or jointly owned. Obviously, if the cost of building trust were thought to be lower in an IJV then the inequalities would be the other way round, and the three acquisitions-based strategies would be eliminated instead.

It is not only inequality restrictions that can be used to generate dominance relations: equality restrictions can be used as well. For example, if the costs of building trust after acquisition are the same in each internal market, $q_i = q(i = 1,2,3)$, then:

$$c_{1.4} > c_{1.2} > c_{1.3}$$

This means that it is inefficient to acquire production when distribution is wholly owned; it is better to use greenfield production and acquire distribution instead.

If in addition the costs of building trust within IJVs are also the same in all markets, $j_i = j(i = 1,2,3)$ then:

$$c_8 > c_{1.3}$$

It is better to combine greenfield production with the acquisition of a distribution facility than to undertake an IJV in production, and franchise distribution to the partner firm.

Finally, consider two further restrictions. The first asserts that the cost of learning about a foreign market through a greenfield distribution facility exceeds the transaction cost of an external intermediate product market; $rm > t_3$. It follows that

$$c_{1.1} > c_{2.1}$$

so that it is cheaper to combine greenfield production with greenfield distribution rather than with an independent distribution facility.

The second restriction asserts that the transaction cost of the external intermediate product market exceeds the cost of building trust in that market following an acquisition, $t_3 > rq_3$. It follows that (given that $q_1 = q_2$ from an earlier restriction)

$$c_{2.2} > c_{1.3}$$

so that it is cheaper to combine greenfield production with acquired distribution than to acquire production and franchise distribution instead.

8.2.7   Properties of the solution

By carrying the process of elimination so far, only three of the original strategies are left in contention:

1.3. greenfield production combined with acquired distribution;
2.1. greenfield production combined with franchised distribution; and
6. licensing.

The choice between these strategies is governed by six of the original variables: a, q, r, s, t_2, t_3. The solution is to choose:

$$1.3. \text{ if } q \le (t_3 + s)/2r, (t_2/r) + a$$

$$2.1. \text{ if } t_3 + s \le 2qr, t_2 + ra$$

$$6. \text{ if } t_2 + ra \le 2qr, t_3 + s$$

It can be seen that strategy 1.3 is preferred wherever the cost of acquisition q is low. This is reasonable because 1.3 is the only one of the three strategies that involves acquisition. Strategy 2.1 is preferred when the transaction costs of the external market in intermediate output, t_3, are low, and when the loss of monopoly profits from competitive distribution, s, is small. This is reasonable because strategy 2.1 is the only one to involve an arm's length sale of intermediate output, and the only one to leave the local rival in a position to compete. Strategy 6 is preferred when the transactions costs of licensing a technology, t_2, and adapting local production facilities, a, are low. This is reasonable because the licensing strategy is the only one of the three to utilise existing production facilities; the other two use only existing distribution facilities instead.

8.2.8 Deriving the propensity to adopt a given strategy

The logical structure of the model means that a change in any variable that increases the cost of certain strategies tends to inhibit the adoption of these strategies and encourage the adoption of alternative strategies instead. These alternative strategies are the ones whose costs are independent of the variable concerned. Indeed, apart from the rate of interest, r, and the cost of competition, s, every variable that enters into several cost functions enters into each of them in the same way. It is therefore impossible for a change in any variable of this kind to induce any switch between the strategies whose costs depend upon it.

In the case of r, however, the impact varies according to the particular set-up costs involved, and so the impact of r upon the choice of any strategy cannot be determined unless the relative size of different set-up costs is known. An increase in r reduces the propensity to adopt any strategy that involves a set-up cost compared to any strategy that does not. If a strategy with a positive set-up cost has a lower set-up cost than the best alternative strategy, then an increase in r will increase the propensity to adopt this strategy. Because its set-up cost is smaller than that of the best alternative, the strategy is more likely to be chosen when r is high.

In the case of s, the impact of an increase favours distribution joint ventures at the expense of wholly owned greenfield distribution facilities, but favours distribution acquisitions and licensing at the expense of both. The net effect on joint venture distribution strategies therefore depends upon whether the best alternative to joint ventures is greenfield distribution, or acquisitions or licensing instead.

The implications of these general principles for the strategies of acquisition, franchising and licensing discussed above are summarised in Table 8.3. The table indicates whether an increase in a given variable is likely to increase or decrease the propensity to adopt that strategy in preference to the other two. A question mark indicates that the direction of the effect cannot be known unless relative set-up costs are specified – in this context, the relative cost of building trust after an acquisition, q, and the relative cost of adapting a licensee's production plant, a. If $2q < a$ then an increase in r will favour acquisition and discourage licensing, so that r will have a negative effect on licensing. The effect on acquisition will remain indeterminate, however, because although it becomes more favoured relative to licensing, it becomes less favoured relative to franchising. The direction of the effect therefore depends upon whether licensing or franchising is the best alternative to acquisition. If $2q > a$ then an increase in r will favour licensing and discourage acquisition, so that an increase in r will have a negative effect on acquisition. The effect on licensing will remain indeterminate, however, because although it becomes more favoured relative to acquisition, it becomes less favoured relative to franchising.

The wider implications of these principles are summarised in Table 8.4. The results reported in the table apply to the market entry

Table 8.3 Comparative static analysis of the effects of changes in the values of the explanatory variables on the choice between the three dominant strategies

	a	q	s	t_2	t_3	r
1.3 Acquisition	+	−	+	+	+	?
2.1 Franchising	+	+	−	+	−	+

Notes:
a Adaptation cost of production plant
q Cost of building trust to access marketing expertise through a newly acquired distribution facility
s Value of profit-sharing collusion
t_2 Additional transaction cost incurred by licensing technology
t_3 Additional transaction cost incurred in using an external market for the wholesale product
r Rate of interest

Table 8.4 Comparative static analysis of the effects of changes in the values of the explanatory variables on the propensity to adopt each possible entry mode

	a	j_1	j_2	j_3	m	q_1	q_2	q_3	r	s	t_1	t_2	t_3	z
1.1	+	+	+	+	−	+	+	+	+	−	+	+	+	+
1.2	−	+	+	+	+	−	−	+	?	+	+	+	+	+
1.3	+	+	+	+	+	+	−	−	?	+	+	+	+	+
1.4	−	+	+	+	−	−	+	−	?	+	+	+	+	+
2.1	+	+	+	+	+	+	+	+	+	−	+	+	−	+
2.2	−	+	+	+	+	−	+	+	?	+	+	+	−	+
3.1	−	+	+	+	−	+	+	+	?	−	−	+	−	+
3.2	−	+	+	+	+	+	−	+	?	+	−	+	−	+
4.1	+	+	+	+	−	+	+	+	+	−	+	+	+	−
4.2	+	+	+	+	+	+	−	−	?	+	+	+	+	−
5	+	+	+	+	+	+	+	+	+	−	+	+	−	−
6	−	+	+	+	+	+	+	+	?	+	+	−	+	+
7	−	−	−	+	+	+	+	+	?	+	+	+	+	+
8	−	−	+	−	+	+	+	+	?	+	+	+	+	+
9	−	+	−	−	+	+	+	+	?	+	−	+	+	+
10	+	+	−	−	+	+	+	+	?	?	+	+	+	−
11.1	+	+	−	−	+	+	+	+	?	?	+	+	+	+
11.2	−	+	−	−	+	−	+	+	?	+	+	+	+	+

Notes:

a Adaptation cost of production plant

j_1 Cost of building trust to support technology transfer in a production joint venture

j_2 Cost of building trust to access marketing expertise through a distribution joint venture

j_3 Cost of building trust to support a flow of the wholesale product to, or from, a joint venture

m Cost of acquiring knowledge of the market through wholly owned distribution

q_1 Cost of building trust to transfer technology to a newly acquired production facility

q_2 Cost of building trust to transfer marketing expertise to a newly acquired distribution facility

q_3 Cost of building trust to support a flow of wholesale product to, or from, a newly acquired facility

r Rate of interest; s Value of profit-sharing collusion

t_1 Additional transaction cost incurred by subcontracting production

t_2 Additional transaction cost incurred by licensing technology

t_3 Additional transaction cost incurred in using an external market for the wholesale product

z Net additional cost of serving the foreign market by export rather than production in the host market

problem in its most general form. The additional assumptions used to derive the dominance relations above are now set to one side. A wide range of hypotheses are generated by this table. A comprehensive discussion of all of them is beyond the scope of a single chapter. Some of the results are fairly obvious, and appear in an intuitive form in the extant literature. Other results are more surprising. In some cases, the element of surprise is a consequence of the specific assumptions that have been made in order to simplify the model. In other cases, the element of surprise indicates a hypothesis which is plausible when considered in depth, but not immediately obvious to the intuition.

8.3   Discussion of results

Some of the more obvious results are as follows:

(1) An increase in z, caused by higher tariffs, transport costs, or a loss of economies of scale in domestic production, encourages production abroad. It encourages both licensing and wholly owned production. This underlines the importance of keeping the distinction between *location* effects and *internalisation* effects very clear in any discussion of foreign market entry strategy.

(2) An increase in a, reflecting a highly specific type of entrant's technology, discourages acquisition and licensing, and favours greenfield production.

(3) An increase in the cost of building trust, q, discourages acquisition and favours either greenfield investment or arm's length contractual arrangements.

(4) A high cost of learning about the foreign market through experience, m, encourages acquisition, licensing and franchising and discourages subcontracting or greenfield investment in distribution.

(5) A high transaction cost for intermediate output, t_3, encourages the vertical integration of production and distribution. This can be achieved either by the foreign entrant investing in both production and distribution, by the entrant exporting to a wholly owned distribution facility, or the entrant licensing the technology to a vertically integrated domestic firm. It can also be achieved by forming a vertically integrated IJV.

(6) A high transaction cost for arm's length technology transfer, t_1, favours FDI over arm's length arrangements, like subcontracting.

In general, subcontracting is not a very attractive mode of foreign market entry. This is because it does not give access to the domestic rival's marketing expertise. It also leaves the domestic rival in a strong competitive position, since the contractual commitment to the entrant is of a short-term nature and the rival's distribution facility is not committed at all. The reason why subcontracting is so often used is because of another motive for entering a foreign country, and that is for access to local resources – notably cheap labour for off shore processing. This motive, though important, is excluded from the present chapter. This shows how important it is to distinguish different strategic motivations when discussing institutional arrangements in international business.

Three interesting and less obvious results are as follows:

(1) The existence of large monopoly rents, associated with a high cost of competition, s, favours strategies which give the entrant long-term control over either the domestic rival's production facilities, or the domestic rival's distribution facilities. It favours acquisition over greenfield investment in either production or distribution. It also favours long-term arrangements, like licensing, over short-term arrangements, like subcontracting and franchising.
(2) Joint ventures in distribution are a useful mode of market entry when high costs of learning by experience, m, discourage greenfield distribution, high costs of building trust, q_1, discourage the acquisition of distribution facilities, high costs in the arm's length intermediate output market, t_3, discourage franchising, and high costs of arm's length technology transfer, t_2, discourage licensing. However, joint ventures in production do not make much sense as a means of market entry unless the production joint venture is part of an integrated joint venture that handles distribution as well.
(3) In general, the analysis confirms that market structure is a crucial factor in the choice between greenfield investment and acquisition. Entry through greenfield investment increases local capacity and intensifies competition, whereas entry through acquisition does not. This explains why governments so often compete to attract inward greenfield investment, while taking a restrictive attitude to acquisitions at the same time.

8.4 Implications for future research

The model is very flexible, in the sense that it is easy to modify the assumptions to address other issues. It can be extended to include two host country rivals, or two entrants vying with each other to enter the same market. This requires extending the analysis from duopoly to three-firm oligopoly. Introducing a third player not only increases the scope for competition, but also introduces new opportunities for cooperation. The model can be rendered more dynamic by allowing entrants to determine the timing of entry – a particularly important consideration where growing markets, such as China or Eastern Europe, are concerned.

The host government plays a very passive role in the present model. Strategic interactions between the host government and the entrant can be introduced. The host government may offer tax incentives in return for commitments on local value added, or 'job creation' which affect the choice of entry mode. Bargaining may take place over subsidies. Political risk may discourage FDI and encourage the use of arm's length contracts instead. The possibilities for the firm to minimise global tax liabilities through transfer pricing can also be taken into account.

The model can be extended to take account of foreign investment in services, as well as manufacturing. It already takes an important step in the direction of analysing service industries by introducing marketing and distribution activities in addition to production. By modifying the assumptions about the physical relationship between production and distribution in various ways, the model can be applied to a wide range of service industries.

There are many smaller ways in which the model can be modified as well. The analysis of duopolistic rivalry can be refined using models of Bertrand and Cournot competition (Gorg, 1998). The formation of IJVs through greenfield investment can be introduced to supplement the 'buy in' strategy assumed above. Finally, the role of host-country production expertise can be modelled in greater detail by making more explicit the function of adapting foreign technology to local production conditions.

Notes

A preliminary version of this chapter was presented to the Annual Conference of the Academy of International Business (UK chapter) at Leeds University in April 1997, the Conference on International Firms, Strategic Behaviour and International Location at the University of Paris I, Pantheon-Sorbonne in May 1997, and the Joint Annual Conference of the ESRC Industrial Economics Network and the International Economics Study Group at Nottingham University, June 1997. The authors are grateful to the discussants for their comments. The chapter has also benefited from the suggestions of three anonymous referees.

References

Agarwal, S. and Ramaswami, S. N. 1992. Choice of Foreign Market Entry Mode: Impact of Ownership, Location and Internalization Factors. *Journal of International Business Studies*, 23: 1–27.

Anderson, E. M. and Coughlan, A. T. 1987. International Market Entry and Expansion via Independent or Integrated Channels of Distribution. *Journal of Marketing*, 51: 71–82.

——. and Gatignon, H. 1986. Modes of Foreign Entry: A Transaction Costs Analysis and Propositions. *Journal of International Business Studies*, 17: 1–26.

Bakema, H. G., Bell, J. H. J. and Pennings, J. M. 1996. Foreign Entry, Cultural Barriers and Learning. *Strategic Management Journal*, 17: 151–66.

Beamish, P. W. 1985. The Characteristics of Joint-Ventures in Developing and Developed Countries. *Columbia Journal of World Business*, 20: 13–20.

——. 1987. Joint Ventures in Less Developed Countries: Partner Selection and Performance. *Management International Review*, 27(1): 23–37.

——. and Banks, J. C. 1987. Equity Joint Ventures and the Theory of the Multinational Enterprise. *Journal of International Business Studies*, 18: 1–15.

——. and Killing, J. P. (eds). 1987. *Cooperative Strategies*, 3 volumes, *North American Perspectives, European Perspectives, Asian Pacific Perspectives*. San Francisco, CA: New Lexington Press.

Benito, G. R. G. and Gripsrud, G. 1992. The Expansion of Foreign Direct Investments: Discrete Rational Locational Choices or a Cultural Learning Process? *Journal of International Business Studies*, 23: 461–76.

Blodgett, L. L. 1992. Factors in the Instability of International Joint Ventures: An Event History Analysis. *Strategic Management Journal*, 13: 475–81.

Buckley, P. J. 1983. New Theories of International Business: Some Unresolved Issues, in Mark Casson (ed.) *The Growth of International Business*. London: Allen and Unwin, 34–50.

——. and Casson, M. 1976. *The Future of the Multinational Enterprise*. London: Macmillan.

——. 1981. The Optimal Timing of a Foreign Direct Investment. *Economic Journal*, 92(361): 75–87.

——. 1988. A Theory of Cooperation in International Business, in Farok J. Contractor and Peter Lorange (eds), *Cooperative Strategies in International Business*. Lexington, MA: Lexington Books.

——. 1996. An Economic Model of International Joint Ventures. *Journal of International Business Studies*, 27(5): 849–76.

Buckley, P. J. and Ghauri, P. N. 1993. *The Internationalization of the Firm*. London: Dryden Press.

Buckley, P. J and Pearce, R. D. 1979. Overseas Production and Exporting by the World's Leading Enterprises. *Journal of International Business Studies*, 10(1): 9–20.

Casson, M. 1985. Multinational Monopolies and International Cartels, in P. J. Buckley and Mark Casson, *The Economic Theory of the Multinational Enterprise*. London: Macmillan.

——. 1991. Internalization Theory and beyond, in Peter J. Buckley (ed.), *New Horizons in International Business: Research Priorities for the 1990s*. Aldershot: Edward Elgar, 4–27.

——. 1994. Internationalization as a Learning Process: A Model of Corporate Growth and Geographical Diversification, in V. N. Balasubramanyam and David Sapsford (eds), *The Economics of International Investment*. Aldershot: Edward Elgar.

Caves, R. E. 1971. International Corporations: The Industrial Economics of Foreign Direct Investment. *Economica*, 38: 1–27.

Contractor, F. J. 1984. Choosing between Direct Investment and Licensing: Theoretical Considerations and Empirical Tests. *Journal of International Business Studies*, 15(3): 167–88.

——. 1990. Ownership Patterns of US Joint Ventures and Liberalisation of Foreign Government Regulation in the 1980s: Evidence from the Benchmark Surveys. *Journal of International Business Studies*, 21: 55–73.

——. and Lorange, P. (eds). 1988. *Cooperative Strategies in International Business*. Lexington, MA: Lexington Books.

Davidson, W. H. 1980. The Location of Foreign Direct Investment Activity: Country Characteristics and Experience Effects. *Journal of International Business Studies*, 11(2): 9–22.

Dubin, M. 1975. Foreign Acquisitions and the Spread of the Multinational Firm. DBA Thesis: Graduate School of Business Administration, Harvard University.

Dunning, J. H. 1980. The Location of Foreign Direct Investment Activity, Country Characteristics and Experience Effects. *Journal of International Business Studies*, 11: 9–22.

Flowers, E. B. 1976. Oligopolistic Reaction in European and Canadian Direct Investment in the United States. *Journal of International Business Studies*, 7: 43–55.

Franko, L. G. 1971. *Joint Venture Survival in Multinational Corporations*. New York: Praeger.

Geringer, J. M. 1991. Strategic Determinants of Partner Selection Criteria in International Joint Ventures. *Journal of International Business Studies*, 22(1): 41–62.

——. and L. Hebert. 1991. Measuring Performance of International Joint Ventures. *Journal of International Business Studies*, 22(2): 249–63.

Gomes-Casseres, B. 1987. Joint Venture Instability: Is it a Problem? *Columbia Journal of World Business*, 22(2): 97–107.

——. 1991. Firm Ownership Preferences and Host Government Restrictions. *Journal of International Business Studies*, 21: 1–22.

Gorg, H. 1998. Analysing Foreign Market Entry: The Choice between Greenfield Investments and Acquisitions. Trinity College, Dublin, Technical Paper 98/1.

Graham, E. M. 1978. Transatlantic Investment by Multinational Firms: A Rivalristic Phenomenon. Journal of Post-Keynesian Economics, 1: 82–99.

——. 1992. The Theory of the Firm, in P. J. Buckley (ed.), *New Directions in International Business*. Cheltenham; Edward Elgar.

Gulati, R. 1995. Does Familiarity Breed Trust? The Implications of Repeated Ties for Contractual Choices in Alliances. *Academy of Management Journal*, 28(1): 85–112.

Hallen, L. and Wiedersheim-Paul, F. 1979. Psychic Distance and Buyer-Seller Interaction. *Organisasjon, Marknad och Samhalle*, 16(5): 308–24. Reprinted in Buckley and Ghauri, 1993.

Harrigan, K. R. 1988a. Joint Ventures and Competitive Strategy. *Strategic Management Journal* 9: 141–58.

——. 1988b. Strategic Alliances and Partner Asymmetries, in F. J. Contractor and Peter Lorange (eds), *Cooperative Strategies in International Business*. Lexington, MA: Lexington Books.

Hennart, J -F. 1982. *A Theory of Multinational Enterprise*. Ann Arbor, MI: University of Michigan Press.

——. 1988. A Transaction Costs Theory of Equity Joint Ventures. *Strategic Management Journal*, 9: 361–74.

——. and Park, Y-R. 1993. Greenfield vs Acquisition: The Strategy of Japanese Investors in the United States. *Management Science*, 39: 1054–70.

——. 1994. Location, Governance and Strategic Determinants of Japanese Manufacturing Investment in the United States. *Strategic Management Journal*, 15(6): 419–36.

Hill, C. W. L., Hwang, P. and Kim, C. W. 1990. An Eclectic Theory of the Choice of International Entry Mode. *Strategic Management Journal*, 11: 117–28.

Hirsh, S. 1976. An International Trade and Investment Theory of the Firm. *Oxford Economic Papers*, 28: 258–70.

Hofstede, G. 1980. Culture's Consequences: International Differences in Work-Related Values. Beverly Hills, CA: Sage.

Horst, T. D. 1972. Firm and Industry Determinants of the Decision to Investment Abroad: An Empirical Study. *Review of Economics and Statistics*, 54: 258–66.

Hymer, S. H. 1976. The International Operations of National Firms: A Study of Direct Foreign Investment. Unpublished 1960 PhD thesis, Cambridge MA: MIT Press.

Inkpen, A. C. and Birkenshaw, J. 1994. International Joint Ventures and Performance: An Interorganizational Perspective. *International Business Review*, 3(3): 201–17.

Johanson, J. and Vahlne, J-E. 1977. The Internationalization Process of the Firm – a Model of Knowledge Development and Increasing Foreign Market Commitments. *Journal of International Business Studies*, 8(1): 23–32.

——. and Wiedersheim-Paul, F. 1975. The Internationalization of the Firm – Four Swedish Cases. *Journal of Management Studies*, 12: 305–22.

Killing, J. P. 1983. *Strategies for Joint Ventures*. New York, NY: Praeger.

Kim, W. C. and Hwang, P. 1992. Global Strategy and Multinational's Entry Mode Choice. *Journal of International Business Studies*, 23: 29–53.

Kindleberger, C. P. 1969. *American Business Abroad*. New Haven, CT: Yale University Press.

Knickerbocker, F. T. 1973. *Oligopolistic Reaction and Multinational Enterprise*. Boston, MA: Harvard University Press.

Kogut, B. 1988. Joint Ventures: Theoretical and Empirical Perspectives. *Strategic Management Journal*, 9: 319–32.

——. 1989. The Stability of Joint Ventures: Reciprocity and Competitive Rivalry. *Journal of Industrial Economics*, 38 (2): 183–98.

——. and Singh, H. 1987. Entering the United States by Joint Venture: Industry Structure and Competitive Rivalry, in F. J. Contractor and Peter Lorange, *Cooperative Strategies in International Business*.

——. 1988. The Effect of National Culture on the Choice of Entry Mode. *Journal of International Business Studies*, 19(3): 411–32.

Kogut, B. and Zander, U. 1992. Knowledge of the Firm, Combinative Capabilities and the Replication of Technology. *Organization Science*, 3: 383–97.

——. 1993. Knowledge of the Firm and the Evolutionary Theory of the Multinational Corporation. *Journal of International Business*, 24: 625–45.

Meyer, K. E. E. 1997. Determinants of Direct Foreign Investment in Transition Economies in Central and Eastern Europe. PhD thesis, University of London.

Nitsch, D., Beamish, P. and Makino, S. 1996. Entry Mode and Performance of Japanese FDI in Western Europe. *Management International Review*, 36: 27–43.

Penrose, E. 1959. *The Theory of the Growth of the Firm*. London: Basil Blackwell.

Prahalad, C. K. and Hamel, G. 1990. The Core Competence and the Corporation. *Harvard Business Review*, May: 71–91.

Root, F. R. 1987. *Entry Strategies for International Markets*. Lexington, MA: Lexington Books.

Rugman, A. M. 1981. *Inside the Multinationals: The Economics of Internal Markets*. London: Groom Helm.

Shane, S. 1994. The Effect of National Culture on the Choice between Licensing and Direct Investment. *Strategic Management Journal*, 15: 627–42.

Stopford, J. M. and Wells, Jr. L. T. 1972. *Managing the Multinational Enterprise: Organization of the Firm and Ownership of Subsidiaries*. London: Longman.

Svensson, R. 1996. *Foreign Activities of Swedish Multinational Corporations*. Uppsala: Department of Economics, Uppsala University, Economic Studies 25.

Tirole, J. 1988. *The Theory of Industrial Organization*. Cambridge, MA: MIT Press.

Vernon, R. 1966. International Investment and International Trade in the Product Cycle. *Quarterly Journal of Economics*, 80: 190–207. Reprinted in Buckley and Ghauri, 1993.

Wilson, B. 1980. The Propensity of Multinational Companies to Expand through Acquisitions. *Journal of International Business Studies*, 12(2): 59–65.

Woodcock, C. P., Beamish, P. and Makino, S. 1994. Ownership-Based Entry Mode Strategies and International performance. *Journal of International Business Studies*, 25: 253–73.

Yip, G. 1982. Diversification Entry: Internal Development Versus Acquisition. *Strategic Management Journal*, 3: 331–45.

Young, S., Hamill, J. Wheeler, C. & Davies, J. R. 1989. *International Market Entry and Development*. Hemel, Hempstead: Harvester Wheatsheaf.

Yu, C-M. & Ito, K. 1988. Oligopolistic Reaction and Foreign Direct Investment: The Case of the US Tyre and Textiles Industries. *Journal of International Business Studies*, 19: 449–60.

Zejan, M. C. 1990. New Ventures or Acquisitions: The Choice of Swedish Multinational Enterprises. *Journal of Industrial Economics*, 38: 349–55.

9
The Moral Basis of Global Capitalism: Beyond the Eclectic Theory

9.1 Introduction

John Dunning's work has taken a distinctive turn in recent years. He has placed greater emphasis on policy, and addressed much wider issues than before (see, for example, Dunning, 1993). This is particularly evident in his latest book *Global Capitalism at Bay?* (2000). The title not only echoes Raymond Vernon's *Sovereignty at Bay* (1971) but conveys Dunning's concern that capitalism's survival depends not only upon international trade and technology transfer but upon the efficiency of the institutions that support them. Institutional efficiency depends in turn on the legitimacy conferred by moral systems.

The Festschrift for John Dunning, which was published on his retirement from Reading (Buckley and Casson, 1992), naturally concentrated on the technical aspects of his eclectic theory, which he had elaborated during the 1980s. The focus was the interplay of ownership, location and internalisation advantages in the foreign investment decision. The range of issues addressed by the eclectic theory has expanded considerably since that time. The eclectic theory is now concerned as much with the general institutional framework of international business and the political economy of government intervention as it is with specific issues relating to the foreign investment decision. Reflecting this shift of emphasis, the present chapter focuses exclusively on wider issues of this type – and in particular on the issues raised in the first two chapters of his most recent book. These chapters address the future of capitalism and the Christian response to it. They contain little reference to the original technical concerns of the eclectic theory; indeed, the multinational enterprise is relegated to the status of just one of several institutions of global capitalism. His work still remains 'eclectic' – but in the sense of embracing not only economics and business studies but also politics, ethics and religion.

In his Raul Prebisch lecture, Dunning (1994) suggested that a 'G7' of the world's spiritual leaders be convened in order to 'establish common ground rules for the values and behaviour of their followers' (Dunning, 1994, 33). Despite his generally optimistic view of the impact of globalisation, Dunning feared that without some consensus of spiritual values among people of goodwill from widely different cultures, any gains in material welfare which global interdependence might bring, could be completely destroyed by a clash of civilisations, the like of which is 'too terrible even to contemplate' (see also Huntingdon, 1996).

Dunning argues that a synthesis of economic liberalism and strong communitarianism is required to optimise the performance of the modern global economy (see also Hood, 1998). He does not consider the dismantling of the present global system as either probable or desirable. He is clear that changes need to be made to the present order, but he remains agnostic on whether change is best effected using a 'top-down' or 'bottom-up' approach.

This chapter argues that Dunning overlooks the way in which modern global capitalism actively undermines the moral order on which it depends for its long-term survival. A sharp distinction is drawn between the early capitalism that evolved around the time of the Commercial and Industrial Revolutions and the global capitalism of today. Early Western capitalism was embedded in a strongly religious culture, whereas modern Western capitalism is embedded in a highly secular one. Early capitalism developed in a world of relatively slow communication, where people, goods and information all travelled at about the same speed, in contrast to contemporary capitalism, where information travels at almost the speed of light. In particular, modern mass media had not been invented at this stage: the closest equivalent to a modern satellite television channel was a local newspaper, which would carry only a limited amount of advertising.

The traditional religion that incubated early capitalism embodied important insights into human nature which have been lost in the modern secular world (Skutch, 1970). Modern elites view human nature through the lens of modern social sciences, which have popularised misleading views of human nature, as explained later. As a result, the contemporary mass media disseminate a large amount of disinformation about human nature, encoded in entertainment and 'lifestyle' advertising (Earl, 1986). Contemporary mass media amplify the distortions effected by modern social sciences by selective emphasis on those ideas that serve their private interests. This disinformation undermines the spirit of community which Dunning recognises as being so important for social stability. Economic liberalism cannot be combined with a spirit of community, as Dunning proposes, so long as contemporary capitalism assumes its current cultural form. Sound social policies cannot be derived from an erroneous view of human nature.

From this perspective the problem facing the modern world is not a clash between different civilisations, based on different religious traditions, which will disturb an otherwise stable secular world built on the foundations of free trade. The confrontation in Seattle shows that it is not divisions between East and West, or between Christians, Moslems and Jews, that are most likely to bring down global capitalism, but discontents among Western consumers – the very people that capitalism has made materially rich but left spiritually poor.

9.2   Plan of the chapter

The remainder of the chapter is structured as follows. Section 9.3 examines the religious context in which early Western capitalism developed. It argues that the potential excesses of profit-seeking behaviour were curbed by self-imposed emotional sanctions – in particular, by a strong sense of guilt that would be incurred by unethical business dealings. While the Protestant ethic did much to legitimate business as a 'calling', it established definite limits on how far businessmen could pursue profit at the expense of broader social objectives. Religious sanctions kept transactions costs low at a time when commercial law was relatively underdeveloped and competition in local markets was normally weak.

Many of the insights into human nature provided by Protestant Christianity can be discerned in other religious traditions too, as Dunning has pointed out. A common theme is that people have both a higher nature and a lower nature. The higher nature is associated with deliberate conscious decision making, based on logic and calculation. Decisions are based on mental models, and involve the pursuit of long-term objectives, the most important of which is peace of mind. The lower nature is largely governed by subconscious decisions, in which an unexpected stimulus generates an immediate response. The objectives that govern these decisions are concerned with fulfilling a small number of powerful drives concerned with aggression, procreation, pursuit of social dominance and so on. This view has much in common with the argument of Alexander Pope's *Essay on Man*: 'Two principles in human nature reign, Self-love, to urge, and Reason, to restrain' (Pope, 1733, p. 62).

There is an underlying rationality to the lower nature, concerned with the biological survival of a race or tribe in a highly volatile environment. The resultant behaviour is, however, badly adapted to a civilised society where volatility is handled through complex social institutions. The power of the drives is such, however, that considerable self-control must be exercised in order to override them (Ainslie, 1992; Charlton, 1988). Moral systems punish lapses of self-control, and thereby sustain a civilised society (Casson, 1998).

Opinions have always differed, however, on the amount of self-control that needs to be applied. Section 9.4 considers modern opinion on this issue, and in particular the Freudian view. It argues that the modern Freudian view of human nature is seriously misleading in certain respects. While Protestantism may have overestimated the importance of certain forms of self-control, modern Freudianism almost certainly underestimates it. Some people are sufficiently self-aware to recognise their need for self-control, but others are not. People who lack such self-awareness are vulnerable to manipulators, who may persuade them that self-control is not required. Manipulators have a good command of the arguments relating to self-control, and can use them to persuade others of their views. They are especially good at advancing reasons for relaxing self-control, and Freudian rhetoric is admirably suited to this purpose. It is argued that modern capitalism is based on the systematic use of mass marketing to undermine consumer self-control. The techniques used were not available in earlier times – for example, television advertising. But equally, the message would have proven unacceptable in earlier times because Protestant convictions would have caused the arguments to be rejected. The decline of Protestantism, and religious belief in general, combined with the growth of mass media means that modern capitalism is based on a culture that is exceptionally lax in its attitude to self-control. As a result, manipulation of consumers, and consequent consumer discontent, is rife.

Section 9.5 examines some of the moral ambiguities of capitalism in greater detail. Ideologically, capitalism represents a systematic attempt to harness private self-interest for the public good. It tries to achieve this by constraining the pursuit of self-interest by competition and the law. It accepts that only a moderate degree of success can be achieved. It therefore tolerates a situation where entrepreneurs make exaggerated claims for their products, and bluff in negotiations by withholding information. It supports the pragmatic maxim of 'buyer beware' to cover situations in which neither competition nor law can fully address the problem.

Socialism does not make moral compromises of this kind, but it depends on a quite Utopian view of human nature to make it work. Its morality, though in one sense secular, is even more severe than that of the strictest Protestant sect. Because of its extreme demands, well-intentioned socialist experiments often degenerate into tyrannies whose excesses are even worse than those of capitalism. Protestantism accepts that the lower nature can never be completely eradicated, and that sin and temptation are therefore ever-present realities. Capitalism accepts this verdict too. Capitalism works best, however, when it uses internal moral constraints to control the excesses of the entrepreneur, as well as the external constraints of competition and the law.

Section 9.6 argues that the present moral weakness of global capitalism first began to emerge over 100 years ago. It argues that the present moral vacuum, in which self-control has atrophied, is not caused solely by the decline of Protestant Christianity but the subsequent decline of alternative secular ideologies too: scientific progressivism, socialism, imperialism and so on.

Sections 9.7–9.9 consider the impact of globalisation. A major effect of globalisation has been to open up new economic linkages between low-wage workers in newly industrialised and newly liberalised economies and wealthy consumers in mature industrial economies. This has benefited Western consumers and non-Western labour, and penalised unskilled Western labour. On balance, it has significantly advanced international economic development, considered in purely materialistic terms.

Globalisation has, however, been marred by many of the excesses of the secular capitalist economy alluded to earlier. Many of these excesses have been perpetrated by multinationals involved in marketing branded consumer products, and by multinational banks promoting credit. The producers have targeted inexperienced consumers, such as affluent young people in Western economies, while the banks have targeted inexperienced borrowers, such as Third World governments.

Globalisation has generally weakened the power of nation states to implement economic policies at the national level. Many of the complaints against globalisation have come from those who favour the use of national industrial policies to facilitate innovation and growth. It can be argued, however, that the major weakness of national policies is the inability of governments to call advertisers and the mass media to account. The power of the multinational media in a global economy has revealed a potential weakness in modern democracy – namely, the unwillingness of party politicians to constrain the media in case the media should take revenge by undermining their electoral prospects using hostile propaganda.

Sections 9.10 and 9.11 summarise the conclusions and discuss possible ways of improving the performance of global capitalism. It is argued that in the long run the necessary improvements in the moral basis of capitalism can only be effected by the revitalisation of traditional religious views of human nature, and a consequential reformulation of certain aspects of social science theory. As a short-term measure, statutory controls should be placed on the programme content of the mass media and on the advertising of branded products. Because of the multinational nature of the entertainment and media industries this may require international agreements. Such agreements may be difficult to negotiate because of the opposition of certain governments who face constitutional constraints and/or a powerful industry lobby. This may well set the scene for further confrontations of the kind witnessed in Seattle.

9.3   The protestant ethic and its decline

The development of capitalism in Western Europe is often ascribed to the influence of Protestantism (Weber, 1930). This is a controversial thesis (Robertson, 1933). It is grossly inadequate as a monocausal explanation because it fails to take account of the growth of capitalism in late-nineteenth-century Catholic Europe – for example, France and Italy. On the other hand, it is consistent with the prominent role of Protestant nonconformist sects in the British Industrial Revolution.

An interesting feature of Protestantism is that it undermined a traditional source of authority – namely the Papacy – and replaced it with the direct accountability of the individual to God. It thereby discouraged conformity of thinking and encouraged individuals to think more independently, and even to express open dissent. Individuals continued to affiliate to groups, but they now decided for themselves, as a matter of conscience, to which groups they should belong. In this way Protestantism encouraged individualism.

Protestantism was promoted by the availability of printing, and by the translation of the Bible into local languages, which meant that people could afford to purchase and read the Bible for themselves. This in turn provided a great stimulus to literacy. The Word of God was now presented in an impersonal codified form (Dark, 2000).

Protestantism also promoted the idea of human rationality. People no longer needed to rely on a priesthood to interpret religious truth for them: they could engage with truth directly for themselves. In other words, they could 'cut out the middleman' in their relations with God. Protestantism also presented a novel view of this relationship with God. Celebration of the Eucharist was played down, and prayer and study were played up. The net effect was to replace passive participation in a communal ritual with proactive private prayer and study.

It also became possible to interpret the Bible in distinctive ways. For example, an analogy could be drawn between a commercial contract and God's 'contract' with his creation. God would always keep his side of any contract, and so people should keep their side of a contract too. Equally, those who did not keep their side of a contract would be punished. They would certainly be punished in the afterlife, and possibly in this life as well. The contractarian interpretation of scripture fitted in well with the Commercial Revolution which was getting underway at the time.

The spread of Protestantism was effected by conversion. Catholics were an obvious target to begin with. Protestant preachers emphasised that nothing short of genuine repentance could deliver people from their sins. Purchasing indulgences from the Pope would do no good at all. The message of repentance requires people to be conscious of their sins. They need to reflect on all the things that they have done wrong. Only when they feel guilty, and are full of remorse, are they ready to make themselves right with God. Even then, those who enjoy sinning may attempt to have the 'best of both worlds' by deferring repentance until their deathbed.

To emphasise the importance of immediate repentance, the Protestant preacher would emphasise the many different forms that sin can take – for example, sins of omission, which are easily overlooked, as well as sins of commission, which are normally easier to recall. He would emphasise that death is an ever-present risk, and dwell on the endless torments of hell that awaited the unprepared. In modern parlance, the Protestant preacher was 'selling' religion. He first created the problem – sin – and then offered the solution – salvation – which was available exclusively through the church. Unlike the Catholic church, however, the solution had to be administered by the individual themselves and not by a priest (or saints) interceding on their behalf. Because the cure was more onerous, the problem had to be presented as more urgent and acute. Repentance could not be taken lightly in the Protestant church, and so the 'salesmanship' needed to be of a high order.

The techniques of persuasion employed by the Protestant preacher were really quite modern. To market a truly innovative product it is always necessary to explain to potential customers why the product is needed. Unless the product resolves some problem, it is pointless for the customer to spend their money on it. While the problem may not be one of guilt, it is often one of shame. People may be ashamed of the spots on their face, or dandruff in their hair, or that they are not as tall as they would like to be. The answer may be a new brand of soap, a new shampoo, or a new style of shoe; in each case purchasing the product helps to make the consumer feel less ashamed than before.

It might be said that the analogy with guilt is rather weak because guilt is a feeling that is purely subjective while shame reflects an external social reality. But this ignores the fact that modern advertisers may create illusory problems: for example, people can be led to believe that they suffer from 'body odour' on the flimsiest of evidence, and thereby induced to purchase unnecessary deodorant spray. In fact, the reverse is the case: some advertisers would defend their strategies explicitly on the subjectivist grounds that their products exist merely to make people feel better, and for no other reason at all. It has been said, for instance, that the housewife is the only real expert on washing powders because she alone knows what shape and colour of box she likes her powder to be delivered in. According to this view, the role of the producer is not to educate the housewife that the colour of the box makes no difference to the contents but to discover what colour she desires and to match it as closely as possible.

More fundamentally, the Protestant preacher's emphasis on guilt may not have been so misplaced as modern opinion would suggest. It depends a lot on what the Protestant preacher wanted to make people feel guilty about. Insofar as he condemned dishonesty and breach of contract, for example, his efforts will have served to reduce transactions costs in the economy (Casson, 1991). If he preached on the Fall of Man, then he may have argued that work is not merely an unavoidable chore, but is actually good for the soul. Once mankind has been expelled from the Garden of Eden, there is no alternative for the great majority to making the best of a life of toil. Making people feel guilty about idleness helps to overcome the shirking problem and raise productivity.

But if the role of the Protestant preacher was to promote economic performance, why did he also emphasise the forgiveness of sins? Surely an enduring sense of guilt for an unforgivable sin is a more powerful deterrent than a temporary feeling of guilt that can be quickly redeemed? The Protestant preacher was, however, too good an intuitive psychologist to overlook the need for forgiveness. Many sins are committed in the heat of the moment, through a temporary lapse of self-control. Self-control requires scarce resources, such as willpower – which are in limited supply (Vance, 1985). Thus no amount of preaching can eliminate sin altogether, as the story of the Fall of Man confirms. If one sin were enough to condemn a person forever, then having sinned once they might as well go on to sin as many times as they liked, for the final result – eternal damnation – would be the same. By 'cleaning the slate', forgiveness creates an incentive not to sin again. Although it reduces the expected cost of sin, it does not eliminate it altogether, because the emotional cost of temporary guilt remains. In general, if sins are associated with antisocial activity, then a Protestant sense of guilt fulfils a useful purpose by curbing anti-social behaviour. In a Protestant community, fear of guilt can not only improve economic performance but improve quality of life as well.

One reason why traditional Protestant values have fallen out of favour is that guilt was associated not just with antisocial behaviour in general but with sex in particular. The Bible lays great emphasis on sex, since it is the first reported sin. Before the advent of modern contraceptives, associating guilt with sex outside of marriage was a highly cost-effective method of population control. When marriage was accessible only to males with the means to support a family, strict observance of the Protestant ethic ensured that children were reared by parents with adequate means to support them.

Even before the appearance of modern contraceptives, the association of guilt with extramarital sex had been attacked by psychoanalysts – notably Sigmund Freud – who argued that it could lead to subsequent problems within marriage too. More generally, it led to repression of sexual drives, which was bad for the individual's health (Sulloway, 1979). Fear of sexual guilt could turn potentially well-balanced people into neurotics, it was suggested. Christianity had an obsession with sex, it was suggested, and had, quite unnecessarily, turned a major source of pleasure into a major cause of guilt.

There is a problem with this view, however, which continues to cause difficulties in the global economy of today. Because the sexual impulse is so strong, control of sexual drives is a paradigm for the exercise of self-control as a whole. It is not only sexual drives that need to be controlled but various forms of aggression too. A person who cannot control their sexual impulses may be unable to cope with anger, envy or other emotions. The basic problem is that any sort of self-restraint can cause neurosis if carried to extremes, and so tackling neurosis simply by relaxing self-control removes an important check on aggression and undermines social behaviour as a whole (Ellenberger, 1970). Freud himself was aware of this issue, but most of his professional followers chose to ignore it (Freud, 1930).

The weakening of self-control, and the liberalisation of attitudes to sex, give modern capitalism some distinctive features compared to its earlier form. For example, an important form of self-control has traditionally related to saving. To resist the temptation to purchase consumer novelties on impulse, people often commit to long-term savings schemes – from save-as-you-earn schemes through to 'Christmas clubs' and the like (Thaler and Sheffrin, 1981). At the same time, business interests counter with credit cards and hire purchase schemes that allow people to consume temporarily beyond their current means. They employ slogans such as 'Take the waiting out of wanting' and 'Go on, treat yourself, you deserve it'. Such advertising directly undermines the individual consumer's self-control.

Another example is the way in which modern advertising promotes products as instruments of sexual seduction – for example, motor cars, alcoholic drinks, chocolate boxes, bubble bath and so on. Indeed, it seems that there is hardly any product advertised on television that cannot be given a similar treatment. The difficulty here lies with the fact that only a tiny minority of consumers are offended by this genre of advertising, and that once the genre is accepted, the advertiser who exploits the sexual connotation of the product most effectively is generally the one that gains the largest market share. Regulators lack the will to interfere if consumers do not protest, since they do not wish to appear out of step with public opinion. Conversely, if consumers were widely offended then regulation would be unnecessary, since advertisers would find the advertising counterproductive – people would either not watch the advertisements, or would watch the advertisements but then boycott the product.

The reason why people are not offended is that they believe that taking offence is a kind of psychological weakness (indeed, it is quite common for warnings about the contents of magazines or television programmes to be addressed to 'people who are easily offended'). The fact that taking offence can be a valuable aid to self-control is overlooked.

A standard defence of such advertising is that it is aimed at rational individuals, who are perfectly capable of managing their own affairs, and do not require any protection from an interfering 'nanny state'. The concept of rationality employed in this argument is far removed, however, from the concept of rationality employed in Protestant thought. The rational Protestant invests in control devices to stop his lower animal nature getting the better of his higher spiritual one. Rationality is a higher-order function, given to man by God to enable him to control his lower nature, and to be exercised by act of will. This act of will allows the power of reason to prevail over the power of aggression and sexual drives. The exercise of the will stems from the individual's commitment to their religious faith. While this commitment is emotional, it is a higher-order emotion that differs fundamentally from the emotions that dominate the lower nature.

The unwillingness of regulators to play a 'nanny' role in the modern era of global capitalism shows just how far traditional moral leadership has fallen into decay. The classic role of the moral leader was to promote personal commitment to exercise self-control. Today the people who occupy traditional leadership roles – including priests and intellectuals, as well as politicians and regulators – have lost confidence in the message about self-control. Guilt has become an unfashionable word, and forgiveness has become just an excuse for doing nothing about antisocial behaviour. The idea that perpetrators of antisocial acts should be asked to repent would seem extraordinary to many citizens of the modern global economy.

9.4   Modern views of human nature: An evaluation

Few people today, therefore, agree with the Protestant view set out above. The views of Freudians, libertarians and neoclassical economists are far more influential. Table 9.1 summarises the main differences between these modern views and the strict Protestant view described above. It also compares these views with the view of human nature advanced in this chapter.

In contrast to the strict Protestant view, a typical Freudian psychoanalyst would argue that it is the higher nature, rather than the lower nature, that is the major source of problems. Excessive self-control means that civilisation produces mass neurosis. It encourages people to be dishonest by denying the existence of their lower nature altogether. This repression forces the lower nature to surface through disturbing dreams and psychosomatic illnesses. The cure is to condemn the higher nature as fundamentally hypocritical, to 'get in touch with your feelings', and to indulge your lower nature whenever possible. The only moral constraint is that one person's self-indulgence should not be at the expense of others.

Table 9.1   The rhetoric of moral manipulation: Five views of human nature compared

		Distinguish higher and lower nature?
Protestant	Yes	Higher nature must completely subdue lower nature. A strong sense of guilt will deter sin and so improve social and economic coordination.
Freudian	Yes	Higher nature may go too far by repressing feelings associated with the lower nature. This leads to ill-health. Higher nature must respect the truth regarding biological imperatives. Lower nature must be indulged, except when other people are likely to get hurt in the process.
Libertarian	No	There is a single nature. To say that it is either high or low is an unscientific value judgement. The single nature may be identified, in emotional terms, with a lower nature in search of continuous excitement through novelty and experimentation. Its powers of reason are substantial, however, and in this sense it corresponds to the higher nature. It fears the law. It recognises the imperatives of competition. This is all that is necessary to maintain social order.
Neoclassical economist	No	For reasons of analytical parsimony it is convenient to assume that there is a single nature, to equate it with the selfish motives of the lower nature, and to assume that people are fully rational in pursuing their selfish motives. Issues that cannot be dealt with within this framework will be studied by other social sciences instead.
This paper	Yes	The Protestant position is correct in principle, but too unforgiving. Freudianism suppresses the higher nature, and so makes people unable to cope with a legitimate sense of guilt. Libertarianism is unworkable because it ignores unavoidable imperfections in legal and market institutions. Neoclassical economics is too partial to provide a holistic approach to the issue. Freudian and Libertarian positions (and to some extent the neoclassical one) are exploited for profit by modern marketing techniques. Globalisation allows these techniques to be refined to an unprecedented level.

A Libertarian would take a rather similar view. If one person's self indulgence occurs at the expense of someone else then the other person should be compensated through a market process. With a full set of markets people can be completely free to experiment with any form of self-indulgence that appeals to them. For those who like excitement, the 'weirder' and 'freakier' the indulgence, the better. In fact, a typical Libertarian would assert that the higher nature can be dispensed with completely as an analytical device, because it is simply a vestige of a primitive religious age that preceded the modern enlightenment. The only controls required on self-indulgence are legal ones, protecting the individual property rights on which the market economy is based. The only civil role for the state is to uphold the law, and not to act as 'nanny' by giving spurious moral guidance to its citizens.

Many neoclassical economists hold rather similar, though less extreme, views. They would argue for assuming a single rather than a dual human nature simply on grounds of analytical parsimony. They would identify this single nature with the lower nature because it is easier to model the selfish and material preferences associated with the gratification of basic drives than it is to model the altruistic motives associated with the higher nature. Furthermore, since neoclassical economics is very much concerned with competition for scarce resources, it is natural to emphasise the aggressive side of human nature that is evident in competition. Indeed, some neoclassical economists would like to synthesise their subject with sociobiology, and explain people's preferences as an outcome of a biological struggle for survival. This approach will naturally tend to emphasise the kind of motivations associated with the lower nature.

An important feature of the Freudian, Libertarian and neoclassical views is that they provide an excellent form of propaganda for those who would like to weaken the degree of self-control that is exercised within society. There are a number of vested interests that would like to do this. Prominent among these are firms producing products that are most easily sold to people who lack self-control. For example, cosmetics can be sold as devices for attracting casual sexual partners, while motor cars can be sold as aggressive weapons, encouraging prospective owners to drive them in a dangerous manner. Cheap products can be sold as 'impulse' buys, while more expensive products can be sold to impatient consumers by offering hire purchase credit. Advertising can attack the notion of self-control by showing the happy consumer as an uninhibited one – this is particularly noticeable in the promotion of alcoholic drinks. Consumers can be flattered into thinking of themselves as being rational in the higher sense, when they are only being rational in the lower sense; they can then be duped, for example, into making enormous 'savings' on items in a bogus 'sale'.

The principal types of product whose sales can be expanded through undermining self-control are summarised in Table 9.2. The left-hand

Table 9.2   Who benefits most from self-control? A comparative analysis by type of control

Drive	Examples of products whose promotion tends to undermine self-control	Main beneficiary of self-control
Aggression	Sporting motor cars Spectator sports involving physical contact	Others
Sex	Cosmetics Pornography	Equal
Greed & envy	Status products: conspicuously expensive branded luxuries	Self
Impatience	Consumer credit 'Impulse' buys, e.g. snack foods	Self
Fear & anxiety	Insurance purchased on impulse	Self
Rest & relaxation	Passive activities: watching TV, social drinking	Self

column identifies six main drives associated with the lower nature, each of which calls for a particular type of self-control. Examples of relevant products are given in the middle column. The final column indicates whether the costs that arise from undermining self-control are borne mainly by the individual or society. For example, undermining control of aggression is likely to increase outbursts of anger and violence, which will tend to damage other people even more than it damages the angry or violent person themselves, but conversely, stimulating greed and envy is likely to damage the person who becomes greedy or envious more than it damages the people whom they envy.

The fact that people are damaged directly by loss of self-control raises the question of why they willingly allow their self-control to be undermined. If it were only other people that suffered then it could be said that they allowed themselves to be manipulated for purely selfish motives. The type of people who are most likely to be manipulated against their own self-interest are those who lack self-awareness. They do not understand themselves, and so are willing to believe things about themselves that are not true. Another factor is low self-esteem. They may believe that there is something wrong with themselves, and feel that they do not know what it is. They look to others to provide an answer. They look, in particular, to people who appear confident and cheerful, because they suppose that these people know how happiness is achieved. It follows that people who appear confident and happy, and who have a good command of the rhetoric of self-control, can influence other people. These confident-looking people are potential manipulators.

9.5 The moral ambiguity of capitalism

It would be a great mistake to suppose that before the advent of modern mass communication the morality of capitalism was impeccable. Capitalism has always suffered from serious moral ambiguities (Knight, 1935). To put the present situation in its proper historical context, it is important to appreciate where these moral ambiguities lie. While the morality of capitalism has declined during the age of globalisation, it has declined from what has always been, at best, a mediocre level.

Markets are the focus of activity in the capitalist system. Market equilibrium harmonises individual decisions. Markets have ideological significance because of the claim that they harness self-interest for the public good. In Bernard Mandeville's (1729) *Fable of the Bees*, Private Vices promote the Public Virtue because the market rewards people for supplying other people's wants, while according to Adam Smith's (1776) principle of the Invisible Hand, the discipline of competition constrains the exercise of market power. Markets emerge naturally because opportunities for 'buying cheap and selling dear' encourage entrepreneurs to set-up shop, permitting goods to be traded more conveniently than before (Kiev, 1994). In pursuing their private profit, entrepreneurs unintentionally benefit everyone else as well.

But entrepreneurship is a morally ambiguous role. To maximise their profit, entrepreneurs may drive hard bargains with their customers and suppliers. They do not tell their customers the prices for which they purchased the goods they are reselling, and they do not tell their suppliers the price at which they can resell. They are allowed to bluff about these issues if they wish (Casson, 1982). Bluffing is not considered lying, although the effect is much the same: with successful bluffing, the buyer pays more than he needs to, and the seller receives less than he could get (Bok, 1978). The constraint on bluffing is not an ethical one but a practical one. It is competition from other entrepreneurs, who enter the market when the profit margin is too great. The competitive system works because rival entrepreneurs cannot be trusted to keep out of the market when profits are higher than elsewhere. Thus the buyers and sellers can trust the entrepreneur only because the entrepreneur cannot trust his fellow entrepreneurs to collude with him. No one can trust anyone else, and the system works only because everyone plays off everyone else against each other!

For many consumers, quality is just as important as price. Once again, the entrepreneur has an opportunity to bluff. For example, many consumer products are addictive – either for biological reasons – such as tobacco and drugs – or because there is a lifestyle that reinforces habitual consumption of the good – for example, gambling (Becker and Murphy, 1981; Warburton, 1990). A consumer's higher nature would warn them off such products, if information about the dangers of the product were to hand. But the entrepreneur can withhold information on addictive properties; indeed, he may even promote the product with special introductory offers designed to 'hook' the inexperienced consumer.

Consumers can also be manipulated through flattery. The neoclassical economist's notion of the fully rational consumer is very useful to entrepreneurs from this point of view. Consumers are told that they are sophisticated and cosmopolitan, and are complimented on their choice of the firm's product. This puts them off their guard, and increases their willingness to commit to a purchase. The fact that economic agents are only fully rational when they are fully informed, and that advertising often does little to inform the customer, is quietly forgotten in the process.

Another kind of quality problem arises when individual items of a product are defective. This is connected, not with promotion of the product, or negotiation of price, but the enforcement of contracts. Reputation can sometimes be used to solve such problems. It relies on the entrepreneur's enlightened self-interest, but only works well when he has regular contact with his customers. Competition alone cannot solve this type of problem. In the absence of reputation effects, enforcement requires a system of law. When the law itself is weak, the maxim is 'buyer beware'. Under these conditions, the market becomes a place that is safe only for the 'streetwise' customer.

To protect the naive consumer, a variety of institutional checks and balances have been set up at different times and places, including consumers' associations and statutory regulatory bodies. Growing suspicions of employers were a major factor in the growth of trade unions in the late nineteenth-century. It is recognised more generally that naive people may be manipulated into entering all sorts of contracts on terms that they may later regret (Moore, 1962). In extreme cases, people are prevented from entering into contracts at all, on the grounds that if they enter these contracts they are probably being manipulated. This explains the widespread prohibitions of slavery and prostitution.

The idea that the market economy is a place for streetwise people is most apparent where stock markets are concerned. The valuation of stocks and shares provides an opportunity for people to pit their wits against others by speculating on the future. Opportunities for bluffing are enormous where stock market trading is concerned. Professional traders can manipulate market opinion by disseminating disinformation to naive investors, while keeping genuine information to themselves. This disinformation causes people to underestimate risks, and exposes them to serious capital losses. Many critics of capitalism have focused on the instabilities created by stock market 'bubbles', and the crises that occur when they collapse, in which many innocent people suffer, such as the employees of bankrupt firms who lose their jobs.

It is evident that manipulation is very much at the core of market capitalism. It is involved in bargaining and negotiation, especially where competition is weak. It is involved in advertising lifestyle products and withholding information about addictive properties. It is involved in engineering stock market bubbles, where naive investors are enticed into buying shares in firms they know little about.

Manipulation can involve either withholding information, supplying disinformation or deliberately undermining self-control. All three aspects can often be combined in a single message. The marketing of lottery tickets, for example, may involve playing down the risk of addiction, exaggerating the chances of winning, and promising instant euphoria to the winner as well.

Manipulation is not, of course, a monopoly of market capitalism. All social systems involve manipulation of one sort or another. The distinguishing feature of market capitalism is that manipulation is decentralised, and that selfish manipulation is condoned. Table 9.3 identifies two dimensions of a social system, according to whether manipulation is centralised or decentralised, and whether it is supposed to be selfish or altruistic. Intuitively, the decentralisation

Table 9.3 Two dimensions of a socio-economic system: Degree of decentralisation and degree of altruism

Degree of responsibility for others (level of trust)	Centralised manipulation (collectivism)	Decentralised manipulation (individualism)
Selfishness (Low trust)	1. Tyranny	3. Market capitalism
Altruism (High trust)	2. Utopian socialism	4. Protestantism

dimension, which appears as the horizontal axis, measures the extent of individualism in the system, while the altruism dimension, which runs vertically, measures the degree of trust between ordinary people. Market capitalism emerges as an individualistic low-trust system. Socialism, in its purest form, represents a collectivist high-trust system, although in practice, as its leaders become corrupt, it tends to degenerate into tyranny – the collectivist low-trust form. Protestantism supports an individualistic high-trust society, which explains why, historically, it has provided a useful antidote to the moral excesses of pure market capitalism.

The moral excesses of market capitalism stem from the way in which everyone is encouraged to manipulate everyone else for their own gain, and that way that smarter people are allowed to keep the profits they win from the naive. These profits are treated as legitimate because all the participants in the market game are assumed to be sufficiently rational to look after themselves. The problem is that many people are neither so well informed, nor so self-aware, as they believe, and as a result they are 'easy prey' for selfish manipulators.

9.6   Antecedents of moral decline

The moral basis of capitalism, as it stands today, reflects the profound secularisation of Western society during the twentieth century. The intellectual origins of this secularisation can be traced back to the impact of Darwin and Lyell, whose scientific researches served to undermine the literal interpretation of the Bible on which popular support for Christianity in general, and Protestantism in particular, was based. This decline increased the problems caused by the moral ambiguities of capitalism, as described above.

Darwin's evolutionary theory highlighted the biological and behavioural similarities between animals and humans, thereby emphasising man's lower nature. It provided an intellectual justification, of sorts, for the growing hedonism of the 'naughty nineties', and of bohemian intellectual society in the Edwardian period just before World War I. By identifying the 'self' with animal appetites, avant-garde artists could flout convention and breach sexual taboos on the grounds that they were merely being 'true to themselves'. The manner in which 'science' appeared to have defeated 'religion' also reinforced the rationalist view of human nature, which was already well developed in France. The higher nature became identified with reason, and the lower nature with emotion. The role of the higher nature was to indulge the lower nature in such a way as to maximise pleasure and minimise pain. Morality became purely prudential. Enlightened self-interest became the criterion by which actions were judged. Within these prudential limits individuals pursued a hedonistic lifestyle through utilitarian calculation.

This culture was very similar to modern Western culture, and it is tempting to argue that modern culture has simply taken up where Edwardian culture left off at the outbreak of World War I. Matters are not quite so simple as this, however. At the turn of the century, secular replacements for religion were at hand to offer hope for the future.

- Science provided a basis for Utopian schemes in which poverty could be abolished forever. Technological developments in the field of electricity and chemistry seemed to offer unlimited potential for the future. Science became a noble calling, offering exciting careers to young people who in an earlier generation would have been destined for the church.

- Socialism offered a scientific basis for social and economic reform. Although anticlerical and pro-scientific, there were moral similarities to Protestant Christianity. Socialist intellectuals dedicated their lives to building a 'New Jerusalem' to replace the old one (Pick and Anderton, 1999). The excesses of capitalism, when freed from the constraints of Protestant self-control, were already evident in the monopolistic practices of the great cartels and trusts. 'Muck-raking' journalism had exposed the venality of 'fat-cat directors'. The parasitic bourgeois capitalist was doomed – he would be swept away by efficient state-owned enterprises run in the interests of society as a whole. By participating in this revolution, idealistic young supporters would win themselves a place in history – the nearest thing to immortality available in the secular world.

- For those who did not subscribe to the scientific or socialist agendas, Imperialism was at hand. Exporting parliamentary institutions and honest government to 'primitive' societies was a noble calling too – even if some of the 'beneficiaries' lost their land rights in the process. The excitement of foreign travel, coupled with the security of a career in government service, made diplomacy and administration a rewarding challenge.

- Finally, for those who were not of an intellectual turn of mind, there was war. As imperial rivalry among European nations led to military conflict, there was plenty to excite the patriotic imagination. Prior to the 'industrialisation' of warfare, it was still possible to contemplate a glorious death on the battlefield with some degree of equanimity.

These different ideologies were not as incompatible at the time as they might seem today. Although many socialists disapproved of international warfare, they were still prepared to contemplate class-based civil war in the interests of the Revolution. Although many scientists also disapproved of war, others found it a major stimulus to invention. Imperial expansion provided scientists with new data on plants, races and societies, and provided reformers with an outlet for philanthropy and missionary work.

One by one these secular ideologies became discredited.

- The unprecedented loss of life in the trenches of World War I, followed by the aerial bombardment of civilian targets in World War II, undermined the perceived legitimacy of war. In the nuclear stand-off of the Cold War, many Europeans came to believe that it was 'better to be Red than Dead'. Vietnam provided a similar turning point in the USA. Enlightened self-interest, rather than patriotic fervour, came to dominate attitudes to war.
- Imperialism succumbed to socialism. Indigenous leaders from the colonies who went to study in Western universities were quick to see the relevance of socialist doctrine to their country's situation. The exploitative class was clearly the colonial capitalist, and the exploited were the indigenous people. The fact that indigenous people were often excluded from the higher echelons of management and administration in their own countries only made the socialist scenario appear an even better fit. The historical links between colonisation, slavery and military conquest persuaded the imperial elites that their position was morally untenable, and 20 years after the end of World War II decolonisation was virtually complete.
- Socialism could not save itself either. It was based on an intellectual critique of capitalism, and was largely untried in terms of practical policy. The socialist leader commanded enormous power, and therefore needed enormous self-control. The ideology of altruistic collectivism quickly succumbed to tyranny. Postcolonial socialist states suffered from government corruption and civil wars. In the developed world, the post-war Western experiment with socialism focused on the creation of the welfare state. But when services were provided free, it became difficult to limit demand. Because of the heavy fiscal burden of social security payments, taxes were seen as unfair by those who worked hard. The final 'nail in the coffin' of the post-war socialist experiment was the demise of the Soviet system, as symbolised by the fall of the Berlin Wall.

- Finally, science – the great hope of the late nineteenth-century – also became discredited. The causes are complex, and the process may yet be reversed. Some of the expectations were clearly excessive – for example, that nuclear fusion would make energy free – and so disillusionment was inevitable. Other concerns arose because science exceeded expectations, rather than falling short – for example, advances in genetics provided opportunities for social engineering that threatened the traditional fabric of society (Bruce, 1997). As pollution rose, and 'wilderness areas' disappeared as a consequence of global of industrialisation, environmentalism became the new creed. Environmentalists began to challenge professional scientific opinion rather than deferring to it. There was a growing suspicion that the pursuit of scientific knowledge for its own sake was being perverted by powerful vested interests in government and industry.

All of these ideologies suffered from the problem of trying to deal with highly complex issues in a very simple form. Because they over-simplified key issues, it was only a matter of time before their weaknesses were exposed. The intellectuals of the late nineteenth and early twentieth centuries thought that they had dethroned traditional religion and put something modern and scientific in its place. Although they often disagreed about what replacement was required, they did not for a moment doubt that it would take a modern scientific form.

But with so many intellectual failures occurring in so short a time, a sense of despair about the value of great social scientific ideas took hold. Intellectuals were forced to admit that they did not always know best. The sense of failure was particularly great in France – the leader of socialist thought in the mid-twentieth century. It seemed that the only acceptable theory was that there was no theory – at least of a modern scientific kind. Thus postmodernism was born. There was a crisis of authority: truth became relative, not absolute, because there was no one to turn to who was sure to be correct. The opinions of an ordinary layman became just as valuable as those of the intellectual. The ordinary citizen could regard themselves as an expert on everything.

Without a reputable body of experts to back them up, politicians began to lose confidence. If the public believed that the public was always right, then politicians might as well pander to this belief. Populist politics became fashionable as politicians increasingly 'led from behind'. This crisis of authority provided great opportunities for the press and media. The press became self-professed experts on the state of public opinion, and began to mount their own single issue campaigns, claiming public opinion as their authority. Their ability to manipulate opinion through selective dissemination of information gave the 'press barons' considerable power. Yet many of their campaigns turned out to be misguided; they showed that the press were no better at solving problems than were the politicians themselves. It seemed that nobody could be trusted – neither official authority figures nor the unofficial opinion leaders who mounted campaigns against them.

9.7   Globalisation of commodity trade and factor movements

Market capitalism, as described above, has inherent global tendencies. These stem directly from the central role of trade in a market system. The tendency of trade to promote globalisation can be seen in the empires of classical antiquity, as well as in the globalisation that occurred in the Age of High Imperialism before World War I (Prior, 2000). This age was the culmination of almost a millennium of incremental development, in which local markets became integrated into regional trading systems, and these trading systems were in turn integrated across continents as a consequence of transoceanic voyages of discovery. This integration of markets is a defining characteristic of globalisation.

Market capitalism also encourages the globalisation of finance and promotes the mobility of labour. Large financial markets offer investors greater liquidity, and more competitive pricing of stocks and shares, combined with greater legal security. This leads to the agglomeration of economic power in major metropolitan centres where financial dealings predominate. Peripheral regions of the integrated economy are plundered for their raw materials, or farmed intensively to feed the urban areas, or relegated to unskilled labour-intensive work. This is simply the imperative of efficiency-seeking in a world of constant change.

This discussion provides a suitable framework for examining some of the major complaints levelled at the World Trade Organization at their 1999 Seattle meeting. The substance of the complaints appears to be that

- the progressive reduction of trade and investment barriers leads to loss of jobs;
- an accelerating pace of technological change leads to greater insecurity of jobs, and to the end of the lifetime employment system;
- inadequate environmental standards lead to increases in pollution which are incompatible with sustainable development;

- greater income inequality emerges, both within countries and between them, creating new social and political divisions;
- destruction of local communities is caused by an extension of global linkages;
- cultural diversity is reduced, because culture is homogenised by standardisation on modern Western values;
- national sovereignty is threatened, and the power of the state is undermined; and
- deregulation of industry and services leads to increased uncertainty, and to greater opportunities for stock-market speculation.

Little can be done to address some of these objections because they hit directly at the logic of the capitalist process (Rugman, 2000). For example, the dynamics of the market system mean that old jobs are destroyed at the same time that new jobs are created, and as this process accelerates, jobs become progressively more insecure. Many of these objections can be addressed fully only by changes which would dramatically reduce the long-run efficiency of the capitalist system. It is perfectly possible, for example, to insist that the metropolitan trading centres be deglomerated, thereby redistributing entrepreneurial profits to more peripheral regions. But the costs of transporting and distributing commodities would increase, and consumers as a whole would be worse off. Similar measures could be applied to deglomerate R&D from major clusters like Silicon Valley to a host of minor ones, but again there would be efficiency losses in terms of innovations foregone. Moreover, it is likely that plans for enforced deglomeration would quickly become distorted by local politics, so that any redistribution of income would mainly favour corrupt officials.

Indeed, contrary to the claims of the Seattle protestors, globalisation confers important benefits. As Table 9.4 indicates, the opening up of trade frees domestic workers from the need to produce for subsistence and allows them to specialise, if they wish, on export production. Provided they work in a free society, they will switch to export production only if they perceive a benefit from doing so. There is little direct evidence that local producers are systematically duped into producing for export markets through selfish manipulation, although it is often alleged by critics of free trade that this is what local moneylenders and export merchants do.

While some of the objections are invalid, however, others have substance to them. The moral ambiguities of the capitalist system generate a range of problems connected with negative externalities of one

Table 9.4   Winners and losers from the globalisation of capitalism

	Winners	**Losers**	**Factor**
Labour	Labour in newly industrialising countries	Labour in mature industrial countries	Reductions in transport costs and tariffs for manufactured goods
Profit earners	Owners of successful globalised firms, or of the firms that supply them	Owners of firms that fail to globalise, or of firms dependent on them	Reduced communications costs facilitate international transfer of proprietary knowledge
Government	Non-interventionist governments with strong respect for property rights	Interventionist governments with weak respect for property rights	Reduced transport and communication costs give increased scope for international specialisation and exploitation of agglomeration economies, providing firms with a wider choice of political regimes from which to operate

sort or another. No set of market contracts can cover all of the issues involved in coordinating a complex global economic system – except at prohibitive transaction cost. It is wrong to suggest that nothing can or should be done about these problems. Consider, for example, the issue of financing mineral industries in developing countries. In a world where entrepreneurial greed was constrained by Protestant guilt, profits in resource-based industries would be voluntarily sacrificed to render development more sustainable. Bankers would think twice before lending large sums of money to inexperienced borrowers, such as the governments of less developed countries. In a more secular society, issues of sustainability and manipulative lending practices can be addressed through statutory regulation, but this requires a high level of intergovernmental cooperation. The institutions of intergovernmental cooperation are often slow and bureaucratic, creating considerable impatience among activists awaiting a policy response. It is inherently wasteful to operate a capitalist system which encourages selfish profit-seeking behaviour, and to then establish a cumbersome intergovernmental bureaucracy to restrict it. Regulating profit seeking through self-restraint is, in principle, a much cheaper option, provided that the moral infrastructure is in place.

9.8   Globalisation and the nation state

It is undoubtedly true that the globalisation undermines the power of the nation state. Historically, the nation state has played almost no role at all in developing international trade. Long-distance trade in Europe first flourished in an age of minor principalities, where merchants obtained safe conducts to attend major fairs. The main role of the state has been to inhibit trade in the interests of national self-sufficiency – often linked to programmes of forced industrialisation and military conquest (Gellner, 1983). Free trade, by contrast, tends to promote peace, by increasing the economic interdependence of economies and improving communication between them. Those who support the capitalist system therefore see little to regret in the weakening of the nation state, since this makes protectionism harder to sustain, and thereby advances the gains from trade.

There is, of course, much more to government policy than the regulation of trade. Nevertheless whatever the field of policymaking, it can be argued that globalisation will on balance tend to improve the quality of government rather than reduce it. Bad governments tend to suffer most from globalisation, while good governments may not only suffer less but may actually benefit from it. One of the advantages of globalisation is that migrants can move from bad states to good ones, thereby improving their economic prospects and quality of life. The consequential loss of tax revenue suffered by bad states, and the increase in tax revenue achieved by good states, provides an incentive for bad states to improve their policies, and this encourages the diffusion of good government throughout the world. Similarly private capital will flow out of countries where property rights are insecure, and into countries where they are secure. Insofar as a prime responsibility of the state is to guarantee property rights, this also penalises bad government and rewards the good.

Many writers who are critical of globalisation believe that the state has an important role in building up national economic power. Like the Mercantilists of the seventeenth century, they seek economic growth through government-led industrial development. Globalisation creates problems for such interventionist industrial policies. For example, the benefits of subsidising the education of scientists and engineers are rendered null and void if the graduates emigrate to higher-paid jobs overseas. Again, the global diffusion of technology means that subsidies to R&D offered in one country may be used to develop new products which are produced in other countries. The efficiency of internal markets for know-how within multinational firms allows knowledge to diffuse more quickly than ever before.

From a global perspective, however, the promotion of national economic growth makes no more sense than does the promotion of regional growth from a national perspective. Taking a moral view of the problem, it could be argued that a more appropriate global objective is international development. From this broader perspective, most of the problems identified above disappear. The enlightened nation state educates people in skills that will serve the global economy rather than the national one. It regards the state-educated workers who emigrate as part of its contribution to world development. The diffusion of R&D is regarded in a similar light. What each government can afford to contribute to international development is dictated by the number of skilled workers that it can retain as its citizens, since these constitute a major group of tax-payers. If the government taxes land – either directly, or indirectly, through an inheritance tax – then it can finance development from this source as well. Countries which are well endowed with natural resources, or occupy a natural entrepôt situation, will perform well in this respect.

Not every nation can realistically expect to attract large numbers of skilled workers or to become an international centre for R&D. Indeed, if every nation were to try to match every other nation in this respect, then economies of agglomeration would soon be lost. Small nation states must come to terms with the fact that, in a modern global economy, they are no more viable as units for subsidy-based industrial policies than were regions in the past.

9.9   The globalisation of communications

The growth of long-distance communication is an aspect of globalisation that has profound cultural effects, because it permits the rapid diffusion of the low-trust capitalist culture that was described above. Long-distance communication takes two main forms. The first is person-to-person communication – such as by telephone – while the second involves broadcasting to a wider public. Radio and television broadcasting allow one person, or a small group of people, to communicate with a very large geographically dispersed audience.

The cultural consequences of broadcasting are much greater than those of the telephone, because so many people can be influenced at the same time. This is particularly true of television. A visual medium is highly effective for gaining and keeping attention, and so its messages can be conveyed in a very powerful way. Television is an ideal medium of mass manipulation.

Television provides mass entertainment as an alternative to local socialisation (Etzioni, 1988; Putnam, 1993). Television appeals to people in search of passive entertainment. These tend to be the same sort of people who are easily manipulated. The more they stay in watching television, the less they go out, and the more their view of the outside world is dependent on television. It is easy for them to obtain a distorted view of human nature. Television has created its own fantasy world of weekly 'soaps', the friendly faces of news readers and chat show hosts and so on. Television drama provides a continual diet of people losing self-control through violence, sex, greed, envy and the like.

Advertisers too want television to attract and retain the attention of the more manipulable people. Commercial pressures therefore encourage what intellectuals would consider to be the 'dumbing down' of entertainment to maximise the number of viewers from the socio-economic groups targeted by the advertisers.

Television has enormous potential for achieving positive social outcomes. It can disseminate expert opinion and promote high-quality debate of major issues. In practice it rarely does these things. To maximise market share the owners of major channels consider it necessary to turn debate into entertainment by structuring it as a quick-fire contest between people of extreme opposing views. The professional manipulator knows that under these conditions it is not the argument, but the memorable 'sound bite', that wins the day. Competition between ideas does not work in the same way as competition between products when played according to the rules of the television audience game. The correct idea is not necessarily the most profitable one, for an incorrect idea may serve to lower consumer resistance to a product and so command more value. Where viewers are passive and uncritical and seek entertainment rather than truth, then the truth or falsity of an idea cannot be inferred from its popularity with the audience.

Not all viewers are so lacking in self-awareness, however. Those who possess both self-awareness and self-control are likely to behave in a distinctive way, however – they are likely to turn the television set off. At any rate, they will be highly selective in their viewing. So far as television advertisers are concerned, this only reinforces their incentive to 'dumb down' their programmes, since they know that the most active people will not be watching in any case.

The self-aware viewer could be forgiven for contemplating the contemporary world of global capitalism with a certain amount of despair. The combination of violent dramas, superficial reporting, documentary exposures and trivial advertising suggest a world that has been totally corrupted by selfish manipulation. The cynical viewer may feel that the public is no longer a group of citizens served by honest politicians but a collection of faceless people manipulated by the media. Behind the media stand vested interests who give an 'angle', 'slant' or 'spin' to every issue in order to present their own interests in the best possible light. They hide their true identity, so that even when people suspect that they are being manipulated they cannot discover by whom.

Under these conditions, the truth is concealed behind the deliberate distortions of those who provide the information. Even if by accident a person heard someone speaking the truth, they probably would not recognise it because they would be bombarded with so much erroneous information at the same time that they could not filter it out.

Fortunately, television is not the only medium in which ideas can be debated. There are other media which seem to be more suitable for this purpose. E-mail is a good example. E-mail combines the options of both private (one-to-one) and public (one-to-many) communication. This flexibility explains its popularity in large dispersed organisations. In particular, e-mail facilitates the development of 'cyber-communities' based on shared interests. Strategic use of e-mail capabilities is a major factor in the success of many pressure groups. Enterprising individuals with strong moral commitments can organise people in different countries around political, social and religious issues. When formalised as multinational non-government organisations fighting single-issue campaigns, they have proved formidable adversaries for slower-footed governments. Effective governmental response on global issues requires intergovernmental cooperation and, as noted earlier, this is often slow because it is channelled through cumbersome bureaucracies.

E-mailing is an ideal activity for people who have specialised interests, and have better things to do in the evening than watch television. E-mailing is not necessarily incompatible with local community involvement, because it provides a suitable means for local groups with common interests to keep in touch with similar groups elsewhere. The cyber-community is an ideal institution for active people who are not prepared to become the passive recipients of television advertising. It is hardly surprising, therefore, if the political agendas of many cyber-communities are strongly opposed to global capitalism.

9.10   Protests against global capitalism reconsidered

The secular ideologies reviewed in section 9.6 provided an outlet for creative talents throughout much of the twentieth century, and their demise leaves a serious vacuum. The protesters at Seattle were struggling to find a relevant language in which to express their discontent. Their demonstrations showed that they did not trust existing international institutions to make the changes that they believe are required. They sensed intuitively that there is a lack of restraint by those who hold economic power – namely by those who influence key decisions about future policy regimes in the global economy. In this sense their attitudes simply reflect the low-trust culture that modern capitalism has created.

Admittedly, many of their criticisms are not new – they echo the criticisms of international capitalism advanced by socialists in the past. Some of their claims may also be misguided. It was shown above, for example, that low-wage workers in developing countries could benefit substantially from global capitalism. But there is always a tendency for people who are making a point to support their position with as many arguments as they can find – good as well as bad. Groups that wish to engage in collective action often have to promote an eclectic position in order to mobilise support as widely as possible.

The analysis in this chapter suggests that the protesters' accusations of bad faith against modern capitalist enterprises may have substance. Some marketing techniques systematically probe for ignorance and lack of self-awareness among the consuming public. Popular brands are targeted at poor consumers, offering them subjective rewards, such as higher status, at a price they cannot afford to pay. Children and young people make easy targets, especially when advertisements can be skilfully designed to undermine parental veto power. When people find the time to relax, and reflect on their experience as consumers, their higher nature intuitively alerts them to the problem. But they cannot easily articulate their feelings because they have been brought up to believe that they are rational all of the time. Even if the products they buy seem useless in retrospect, it has to be admitted that shopping for them seemed like fun at the time (see Frank, 1999). Shopping becomes an end in itself – exercising the impulse to buy being the immediate source of pleasure – and the product is just the excuse. Products have to be thrown away because otherwise storage space would limit indulgence in the shopping experience. On this view, it is when shopping palls, and the meaninglessness of the impulse to buy becomes obvious, that protests become attractive instead. People become angry when they finally have to face the fact that they have been systematically manipulated by the producers of the branded trivia of the modern capitalist system.

9.11   Conclusions

This chapter has highlighted some of the moral ambiguities that lie at the heart of the capitalist system. Capitalism is a system based on private property in which the enlightened pursuit of self-interest plays an important role. It is a system in which people are expected to bluff in negotiations, unless constrained by competitive forces, and are liable to default on transactions, unless constrained by the law. Capitalism accepts the biblical view that mankind has a 'fallen' nature, and attempts to 'make the best of a bad job'.

Historically, capitalism has played an important role in the economic development of civilised society. In itself, however, it has not been the driving force of civilisation. Civilisation is ultimately a moral concept, and the major civilisations of history have derived their moralities from an organised religion or some sense of collective destiny. The modern concept of a society based on the individualistic gratification of material desires is linked, historically, not to the growth of civilisations but to their decline.

The social cost of excessive individualism is increased by the unprecedented opportunities for marketing products through global television advertising. Contemporary individualism is characterised by apathy towards traditional morals. Contemporary values provide a convenient justification for a vegetative existence in front of a television screen. Aggressive individualism dismisses all arguments for self-control. From this perspective, globalisation merely accentuates problems that are already present in the capitalism system. Globalisation itself is morally neutral. In principle, it is ethically sound from an international development perspective, for it allows workers in poorer countries to develop new markets for their products. In practice, globalisation means that the excesses of market capitalism become even greater than they would otherwise have been.

There is a major discrepancy between the private rewards to moral manipulation faced by television advertisers and programme makers on the one hand, and the social benefits on the other. Private rewards are maximised by undermining consumer self-control, while social rewards are maximised by increasing it. The social rewards reflect both the benefits to individual consumers – less disappointment with their lifestyle, lower debt and so on – and the benefits to society as a whole – lower crime, greater vitality of community life and so on.

It is often suggested that nothing can be done to influence the multinational mass media. It is certainly true that the position of a national regulator is often weak – for example, in respect of satellite TV broadcasting. But regulation is not really the main issue. Even in a self-contained economy, a regulator may be unwilling to intervene unless he feels that public opinion is behind him. If the media are sufficiently powerful to mobilise public opinion against any form of 'censorship', then regulation may not be applied even when it could be effective.

From a long-run perspective, the real issue concerns the way in which public opinion is formed. Members of the public cannot make up their own minds on every issue that concerns them, and so they naturally listen to the opinions of leaders on the issue. Because television enjoys such status, it has the power to make its own leaders, who will then promote the views that favour television. But even when other leaders get an opportunity to state their views, they rarely call explicitly for those concerned to exercise greater self-control. The subject of self-control seems to be almost 'taboo' in intellectual circles today.

This brings us to the heart of the problem: modern social science presents a misleading view of human nature, which overlooks the crucial significance of self-control. Many of the misleading views of human nature, as reflected not only in advertising but also in art and drama, derive from intellectual currents in twentieth-century social science (Bailey, 1983; Baxter, 1988). There are, of course, many different versions of social science theory, associated with different disciplines, but this simply means that there is almost always some convenient theory available to those who wish to argue against the use of self-control. Freudian theory is the best example of this, and libertarian economics provides another example.

When suitably popularised, these theories have great appeal. People like to believe that they are fully rational, and can indulge themselves on impulse without fear. People like to be told that they are fully autonomous individuals who do not have to rely on other people for their opinions. As a result, many people fail to appreciate the extent to which their values and beliefs are influenced by other people. By being blind to the risk of manipulation, they become extremely vulnerable to it.

In the long run, the only antidote to this regrettable situation is better social science. The analysis in this chapter suggests that the key to better social science is to concentrate on developing and refining the ideas about human nature that are found in traditional religions, rather than attempting to replace them with some radically different secular alternative.

This is an important theme in Dunning's recent work, and is completely endorsed by the analysis above. The social scientific notions that have failed the capitalist system in the twentieth century were mistakenly developed in opposition to conventional religious ideas, and so they ignored them or even contradicted them. The fact that religious tradition encapsulates insights drawn from observations of human behaviour in all sorts of countries and under all sorts of conditions over thousands of years was ignored. Modern social science was seen as a radical movement that overthrew all tradition, rather than an additional method for gaining insight and wisdom that could be added to the existing stock of knowledge. The metaphysical notions used by traditional religions to express their insights were sufficient grounds for rejecting these insights altogether. The social costs of doing so are now all too evident. Society cannot afford to throw away such valuable 'knowledge capital'. Dunning's recent work hopefully marks a turning in social scientific thought which may ultimately lead to the recovery of much of what has been lost (see also Hahnel and Albert, 1990).

For the past 20 years or so, the spread of Western commercial culture as a result of globalisation may be likened, in some respects, to the diffusion of a 'public bad'. This public bad – a low-trust culture, based on selfish manipulation – gained credibility from the enormous strength of Western technology, to which it appeared to be linked. The rightful reputation that Western technology enjoyed 'softened up' consumers around the world for the low-trust culture that was used to sell the products in which the technology was embodied. But it was a stern moral commitment to basic research, and not cynical individualism, that motivated the scientists who created the powerful ideas on which the new technologies were based. Modern capitalism works in spite of contemporary cynicism, and not because of it.

The same stern commitment is required to motivate future social science research. John Dunning's own career provides a useful model in this respect. His wide-ranging curiosity and careful attention to detail have provided a worthy legacy on which his successors can build. Unlike many other social scientists, he has never divorced his theorising from practical insights into human nature, and has never forgotten the religious ideals with which he was brought up. The need to reconstruct social science on a more reliable basis, as a guide to better global policymaking, is a worthy calling. It is one which will, hopefully, appeal to future generations of scholars. In the study of global capitalism, they cannot do better than follow in John Dunning's footsteps.

References

Ainslie, G. 1992. *Picoeconomics: The Strategic Interaction of Successive Motivational States within the Person.* Cambridge: Cambridge University Press.

Bailey, F. E. G. 1983. *The Tactical Uses of Passion: An Essay on Power, Reason and Reality.* Ithaca, NY: Cornell University Press.

Baxter, J. L. 1988. *Social and Psychological Foundations of Economic Analysis.* Hemel Hempstead: Harvester Wheatsheaf.

Becker, Gary S. and Murphy, K. M. 1988. A Theory of Rational Addiction. *Journal of Political Economy,* 96, pp. 675–700.

Bok, S. 1978. *Lying: Moral Choice in Public and Private Life.* Hassocks, Sussex: Harvester Press.

Bruce, D. M. 1997. Patenting Human Genes – A Christian View. *Bulletin of Medical Ethics,* 124, pp. 18–20.

Buckley, P. J. and Casson, M. (eds). 1992. *Multinational Enterprises in the World Economy: Essays in Honour of John Dunning.* Cheltenham: Edward Elgar.

Casson, M. 1982. *The Entrepreneur: An Economic Theory.* Oxford: Martin Robertson.

Casson, M. 1991. *Economics of Business Culture: Game Theory, Transaction Costs and Economic Performance.* Oxford: Clarendon Press.

Casson, M. (ed.). 1998. *Culture, Social Norms and Economic Behaviour.* Cheltenham: Edward Elgar.

Charlton, W. 1998. *Weakness of Will: A Philosophical Introduction.* Oxford: Blackwell.

Dark, K. R. 2000. Large Scale Religious Change and World Polities, in K. R. Dark (ed.) *Religion and International Relations.* London: Macmillan, 2000, pp. 50–82.

Dunning, J. H. 1994. *Globalisation, Economic Restructuring and Development: The Sixth Raul Prebisch Lecture.* Geneva: UNCTAD.

Dunning, J. H. 2000. *Global Capitalism at Bay?* London: Routledge.

Earl, P. 1986. *Lifestyle Economics: Consumer Behaviour in a Turbulent World.* Brighton: Wheatsheaf.

Ellenberger, H. R. 1970. *The Discovery of the Unconscious: The History and Evolution of Dynamic Psychiatry.* New York: Basic Books.

Etzioni, A. 1988. *The Moral Dimension: Towards a New Economics.* New York: Free Press.

Frank, R. H. 1999. *Luxury Fever: Why Money Fails to Satisfy in an Bra of Excess.* New York: Free Press.

Freud, S. 1930. *Civilisation and its Discontents.* London: Kegan Paul.

Gellner, E. 1983. *Nations and Nationalism.* Oxford: Blackwell.

Hahnel, R. and Albert, M. 1990. *Quiet Revolution in Welfare Economics.* Princeton, NJ: Princeton University Press.

Hood, N. 1998. Business Ethics and Transnational Companies, in Ian Jones and Michael Pollitt (eds), *The Role of Business Ethics in Economic Performance*. London: Macmillan, pp. 193–210.

Huntingdon, S. P. 1996. *The Clash of Civilisations and the Remaking of World Order*. New York: Simon & Schuster.

Kley, Roland. 1994. *Hayek's Social and Political Thought*. Oxford: Clarendon Press.

Knight, Frank H. 1935. *The Ethics of Competition*. London: George Allen & Unwin.

Mandeville, B. 1729/1924. *The Fable of the Bees* (edited by F. B. Kaye). Oxford: Clarendon Press.

Moore, W. E. 1962. *The Conduct of the Corporation*. New York: Random House.

Pick, J. and Anderton, M. 1999. *Building Jerusalem: Art, Industry and the British Millennium*. Amsterdam: Harwood Academic Publishers.

Pope, A. 1733. *An Essay on Man* (edited by Maynard Mack). London: Methuen.

Prior, F. L. 2000. Internationalisation and Globalisation of the American Economy, in Thomas L. Brewer and Gavin Boyd (eds), *Globalising America: The USA in World Integration*. Cheltenham: Edward Elgar.

Putnam, R. D. 1993. *Making Democracy Work: Civic Traditions in Modern Italy*. Princeton, NJ: Princeton University Press.

Reisman, D. 1990. *Theories of Collective Action: Downs, Olson and Hirsck*. London: Macmillan.

Robertson, H. M. 1933. *The Rise of Economic Individualism*. Cambridge: Cambridge University Press.

Rugman, A. M. 2000. *The End of Globalisation*. NewYork: Random House.

Skutch, A. 1970. *The Golden Core of Religion*. London: George Allen & Unwin.

Smith, A. 1776. *An Inquiry into the Nature and Causes of the Wealth of Nations* (Glasgow edition). Oxford: Clarendon Press.

Sulloway, F. 1979. *Freud: Biologist of the Mind*. London: Burnett.

Thaler, R. H. and Sheffrin, H. M. 1981. An Economic Theory of Self-Control. *Journal of Political Economy*, 89(2), 392–406.

Vance, N. 1985. *The Sinews of the Spirit: The Ideal of Christian Manliness in Victorian Literature and Religious Thought*. Cambridge: Cambridge University Press.

Vernon, R. 1971. *Sovereignty at Bay: The Multinational Spread of US Enterprises*. New York: Basic Books.

Warburton, D. M. (ed.). 1990. *Addiction Controversies*. Chur: Harwood Academic Publishers.

Weber, M. 1930. *The Protestant Ethic and the Spirit of Capitalism*. London: George Allen & Unwin.

10
Strategic Complexity
in International Business

10.1 The current challenges facing international business theory

This chapter outlines a progressive research agenda for the field of international business studies. In retrospect there have been significant theoretical achievements in international business (IB) over the past 40 years, but there has also been a loss of focus.

1. A comparison of the periods 1972–82 and 1990–2000 suggests a declining dynamic of theoretical innovation; developments in IB were once ahead of those in related areas, whereas now they seem to follow behind.
2. Every answer raises new questions, but many of the new questions raised in the 1970s literature remain unresolved.
3. The 'strategic alliances' literature exhibits the weaknesses as well as the strengths of a multidisciplinary perspective; there are so many different propositions about different aspects of alliances, often based on different definitions, that it becomes unclear whether they are coherent or not.
4. The debate between transaction costs and resource-based theories has become increasingly sterile.
5. Excessive dependence on case studies means that the 'strategic management' literature increasingly confuses consultancy with research, and equates the development of executive teaching materials with original contributions to knowledge.

If IB is to regain its influence within the social sciences as a whole, it is necessary to reintegrate it into mainstream intellectual debate. One way in which this can be done is to introduce more refined analytical techniques into IB theory. This chapter recommends that the rational action approach to modelling should be expanded in order to address a wider range of IB issues. It provides practical examples of how this can be done, based mainly on our own recent work.

The rational action approach has achieved its greatest successes in addressing economic issues, but it can also elucidate issues in strategic management and organisational behaviour. By working with formal models whose assumptions are explicit it is possible to eliminate ambiguity, and thereby foster informed criticism that serves to eliminate logical error (Elster 1986; Hargreaves-Heap 1989). Modern IB texts tend to present the subject as a multidisciplinary field of research that addresses issues that are specific to international business operations. This was not the view of IB that prevailed at the time of its greatest intellectual vitality in the 1970s, however. Many scholars of that time perceived IB as a field of applied economics – a useful 'laboratory' in which to test general theories against newly gathered statistical evidence (Buckley and Casson 1976).

Since the 1970s the methods of economics have been extended to other fields of social science, such as politics, law and sociology (Buckley and Casson 1993). This has been made possible by the increasing power of rational action modelling techniques. As a result, it is possible to update the 1970s view: IB is now best regarded as a field of applied social science, rather than just a field of applied economics, as before. But in this context social science must be understood, not a collection of different disciplines, each with its own tradition and methodology, but an integrated social science based upon the rational action approach.

This chapter does not present a forecast of how the subject will evolve but simply makes a proposal, with which others may well disagree. It begins with a critique of recent calls for the use of 'softer' theories in IB. In particular, it considers whether the increasing complexity of the IB environment makes formal modelling impractical. It concludes that it does not. Much of what is called complexity, it suggests, is subjective, and merely reflects the confusion of scholars who rely on softer theories. Such confusions can be dispelled by invoking the intellectual rigour of the rational action approach.

Two main sources of complexity are identified. One is the uncertainty involved in long-term planning. It reflects the 'strategic' nature of many IB decisions, such as those concerned with irreversible investments. There is a distinctive set of rational action modelling techniques that is available for analysing such decisions.

Another source of complexity is connected with networks. Networks in IB take both physical and social forms. A physical network comprises a set of production plants, distribution centres and retail outlets. These various facilities are connected by transport infrastructure. Several facilities may be owned by the same firm, depending upon where the boundaries of the firm are drawn. Boundaries of firms that span international boundaries lead to multinational firms. Formal models of IB networks are now available which determine simultaneously where all the boundaries of the different firms within a system are drawn. These models can also incorporate flows of knowledge generated by R&D and marketing activities, as explained below.

Social networks are concerned with communications between decision makers. Networks can be high-trust or low-trust, and either formal or informal. Communication through social networks allows different decision makers to coordinate their decisions. Coordination within a firm involves internal networks, which often take a hierarchical form, whereas coordination between firms involves external networks which typically take a 'flatter' form. Formal analysis of communication costs makes it possible to analyse what kind of networks will emerge to coordinate different types of activity.

10.2   Complexity or confusion?

It is often asserted that the modern global environment is so complex that it is impossible to capture reality with the aid of any formal model. As a result, a good deal of effort has gone into developing heuristic approaches that use analogy and metaphor, rather than formal theory, to articulate key ideas (Parkhe 1993). For example, writers on joint ventures and strategic alliances have argued that as the boundaries of the firm become increasingly 'fuzzy', so theory must become 'fuzzy' too in order to handle the issue. Fuzzy theories are difficult to refute, however, because it is usually unclear what they mean, so that errors in these theories go undetected for a considerable time. Researchers who attempt to build on 'fuzzy' foundations can waste a good deal of time before the weaknesses of their foundations are properly exposed.

Another example of fuzzy thinking arises when people apply general systems theory to try to understand the complexity of the global economy. General systems theory talks a lot about 'complex systems', and so it seems intuitively reasonable that it should be invoked to explain the nature and causes of complex IB phenomena. The fact that the theory is opaque only adds to its credibility so far as the uninitiated are concerned.

But a lot of what is described as 'complexity' is often just confusion. When people do not understand something, they tend to assume that it must be 'complex', and so turn to 'complexity theory' for a solution. This theory introduces them to new jargon such as 'chaos', 'catastrophe', 'emergent properties' and the like (Arthur 1988; Coriat and Dosi 1998). It is suggested that these concepts derive from advanced mathematics, or 'rocket science'. In fact, many of the terms are little more than labels applied to areas of ignorance. While it is true that the mathematical theory of non-linear systems can explain chaotic behaviour, for example, such behaviour has little or nothing to do with the kind of behaviour that is observed in the IB system. If there is some connection, then it has certainly not been spelt out rigorously so far.

Popular perceptions of complexity may also be a response to a quickening pace of change. The world economy of 2010 appears to be radically different from what it was only 50 years ago. It can be argued that radical changes call for radically new theories to explain them. A new brand of IB theory must be developed to meet the intellectual challenges of the new millennium, it may be said. Complexity provides an impressive range of novel jargon for describing change in the IB system. 'The global economy is a dynamic self-organizing system based on co-evolving institutions' seems to be a profound statement, even though it says little more than that the global economy is undergoing change.

Radical changes in theory are very expensive, however, because a whole new set of concepts needs to be developed and disseminated. Investing in radically new theory is extremely wasteful if existing theory is perfectly adequate. This chapter argues that complexity can be addressed perfectly adequately using existing concepts derived from the rational action approach.

10.3   Two concepts of complexity

Systems theorists distinguish between combinatorial complexity and what may be termed organic complexity. Combinatorial complexity is created when a large number of different cases have to be analysed before a decision can be made, and in each case a large number of different factors have to be taken into account. Organic complexity arises because of numerous interdependencies and feedback loops within a system. Everything depends upon everything else in such a way that cause and effect are difficult to disentangle. Organic complexity, it is suggested, cannot be addressed through rational analysis. In organically complex systems agents cannot understand the system of which they form a part. As a result, they have to commit themselves arbitrarily to certain rules, and the interactions between different agents playing according to different rules then generates the very kind of complexity in the system that defies analysis.

The techniques illustrated in this chapter approach complexity as a combinatorial problem. They address combinatorial complexity using a range of simplifying techniques. This reflects a methodological stance that complexity is best addressed by simplifying the representation of reality, rather than by making theory itself more complex. The problem of organic complexity is not ignored altogether, however. Organic complexity is handled by the traditional method of focusing on an equilibrium. For more than a century economists have tackled system interdependencies by analysing the mathematical properties of equilibrium. Systems theorists often ridicule this approach. The fact remains, however, that the qualitative features of a system's dynamic behaviour are largely determined by its equilibrium properties. All stable systems have a propensity to converge to an equilibrium. Systems that exhibit localised instabilities usually do so because they have more than one equilibrium. The number of equilibria is therefore an important guide to the out-of-equilibrium behaviour of a complex system. Although an equilibrium model cannot track the out-of-equilibrium behaviour of a system over time, it can identify the equilibrium to which the system will tend to converge from any given initial condition. For many purposes, this is all that a satisfactory model is required to do.

Certain types of disequilibrium behaviour can also be modelled in mathematical terms. This is normally achieved by assuming that agents follow certain simple myopic rules: the agent makes little attempt to look far ahead (Nelson and Winter 1982). This contrasts sharply with the situation in rational action modelling, where agents are far-sighted. Similarly, in simple disequilibrium models agents do not adapt their rules to the environment in which they operate, as a rational agent would do. These extreme assumptions are relevant in certain special cases: they are useful, for example, in explaining the sudden build-up of traffic jams, the persistence of stock exchange 'bubbles', and the formation of crowds around sensational events. It is not at all clear that they are useful in explaining IB phenomena, however. A successful multinational enterprise is unlikely to be controlled by a myopic rule-driven manager who is unable to adapt his behaviour to the circumstances he is in. It is more likely to be managed by a successful entrepreneur who can take a long-term view of a situation and can adapt his behaviour to different sets of conditions.

Nevertheless it is often claimed that disequilibrium models with system effects can provide a more realistic account of the global economy than a rational action model can. One reason for this is that some disequilibrium models predict that almost anything can happen out of equilibrium. When behaviour is highly sensitive to certain parameter values, which are difficult to measure, it can always be claimed that the model has explained reality because the parameters took on whatever values they needed to. This kind of explanation is vacuous, because as long as key parameter values cannot be independently measured the explanation is impossible to verify.

'Path-dependence' is a good example of this type of non-explanation. Almost any historical aspect of the IB system can be explained in path-dependent terms. Path dependent explanations usually begin with unspecified initial conditions which have been lost way back in the mists of time. 'Given the way things began, and all the things that have happened since, things are bound to be the way they are', goes this kind of explanation. The problem is that data on how things began, and on many of the things that happened since, are usually incomplete. In many applications of path dependence, even the pattern of causation linking one step to the next is unclear. Path dependence can be used to rationalise almost any sequence of events, and can give any simple narrative of events the appearance of a being a scientific test of systems theory.

This is not to deny that path-dependence occurs. Agents are 'locked in' by their actions whenever there are adjustment costs, because their actions cannot be costlessly reversed. But 'lock in' is only a serious problem under certain conditions, and rational action models explain what these conditions are. It is often suggested that 'lock in' is a direct consequence of myopic decision making, but this is incorrect. Everyone is locked in by adjustment costs, whether they are rational or not. Rational agents may be locked in less than irrational ones, however, because when they realise that they still have much to learn about a situation they will choose a course of action which maximises flexibility. To establish that agents are myopic it is necessary to show that they are worse off than a rational agent would have been, and not simply that they were locked in by a situation. Few systems theorists have addressed this crucial issue.

An important reason why 'lock in' is of limited importance in IB is that multinational firms have access to a wide range of factor and product markets. For example, a firm that has over-extended its capacity at an upstream stage of production can use external intermediate products to sell off surplus output to independent downstream firms. Alternatively, the firm could sell off surplus plant and equipment in markets for second-hand assets, or even divest the entire upstream operation as a going concern. All of these strategies incur adjustment costs, of course, but the costs are nowhere near as large as they would be in the absence of the market system. While it is highly desirable for IB theory to take account of adjustment costs, it is unnecessary to suppose that adjustment costs are a major source of instability in the IB system.

10.4   Rational action and international business strategy

During the 1980s and 1990s the concept of strategy came to occupy an important role in the IB literature, although the term was hardly used at all before then (Porter 1991). None of the key theoretical developments of the 1970s invoked the concept of strategy at all. It is interesting to note that very few of the writers who use the concept of strategy regularly ever bother to define the term. Sometimes they employ it simply as a synonym for 'chosen course of action', while in other cases they use it to signal that some particular decision is of crucial importance.

The rational action approach clearly implies that some decisions are more important than others, and indicates why this is the case. A strategic decision may be defined, in rational action terms, as a decision with the following characteristics:

(1) long-term perspective creates a need for inter-temporal planning;
(2) uncertain environment;
(3) information needs to be collected in the most efficient and reliable manner;
(4) irreversible commitment of resources;
(5) the decision determines the context in which future tactical (short-term) decisions are taken: the implications for tactical decisions need to be considered before strategic decisions are made;
(6) there are interactions with other strategists: either competition, cooperation, or both.

There is now a 'critical mass' of rational action technique that can be used to analyse strategic issues. These techniques address strategic complexity through clarification and simplification of the decision problem (see for example Kreps 1990). The repertoire includes the following:

Information costs

- decision theory: rational choice under uncertainty
- sequential analysis
- search theory.

Dynamic optimisation

- optimal timing of investment
- irreversibility and switching costs.

Real option theory

- deferring decisions to avoid mistakes
- valuing flexibility.

Game theory

- Nash equilibria of a non-cooperative game
- sequential games
- repeated games.

There is insufficient space to review all of the relevant techniques at this stage. This chapter focuses on the first three sets of techniques, as these have achieved the widest acceptance in IB theory (see, for example, Allen and Pantzalis 1996; Buckley and Casson 1981; Casson 1995; DeMeza and van der Ploeg 1987). The final set of techniques – game theory – affords major opportunities for IB which have so far been exploited to only a limited extent (Graham 1990).

10.5   Example: Analysing foreign market entry

The application of these new techniques is best illustrated by means of an example. One of the classic issues in IB is foreign market entry strategy (Buckley and Casson 1981, 1998a). This is a decision by a firm in a home country (country 1) to supply the market in a foreign country (country 2). Foreign market entry involves uncertainty, relating to either demand side factors, such as the size of the foreign market, or supply side factors, such as foreign costs of production.

The simplest way of introducing uncertainty into the rational action approach is to assume that decision makers partition the state of the environment into a number of different categories, or 'states of the world', and then assign a subjective probability to each. A sophisticated decision maker may distinguish a large number of different states, whereas a naïve decision maker may distinguish just a few. The simplest categorisation of states is a binary one (Hirshleifer and Riley 1992).

For the sake of simplicity, it is assumed that uncertainty relates to the supply side only, and that the decision maker distinguishes just two states of the world: state 1, in which foreign cost conditions are bad, and state 2, in which they are good. The key issue is whether the foreign market is served by domestic production or foreign production. Under domestic production the foreign market is supplied through exports (strategy 1) while under foreign production (strategy 2) the firm undertakes FDI.

Suppose that the firm is already committed to serving the market, and that market size is fixed, so that the revenue obtained is the same for either strategy. Thus only the costs of the two strategies are different. Production takes place under constant returns to scale, with a unit cost of production c_0 in country 1. Unit cost is c_1 in country 2 when conditions are bad, and c_2 when conditions are good, where $c_1 > c_0 > c_2$. It follows that the firm should export when foreign cost conditions are bad and invest abroad when they are good. The probability that conditions are good is $p(0 \leq p \leq 1)$.

The firm's objective, it is assumed, is to maximise expected profit. This is a reasonable objective for a firm with a large number of shareholders who hold well-diversified portfolios. With given revenues, this translates into minimising expected unit costs. The expected cost of foreign production is $E(c) = (1 - p)c_1 + pc_2$ while the unit cost of domestic production is already known to be c_0. Comparing the expected unit cost of foreign production with the cost of domestic production shows that the firm should produce abroad when $p > p^* = (c_1 - c_0)/(c_1 - c_2)$. In other words, the firm should produce abroad when the probability of good production conditions exceeds a critical level p^*.

A simple way of understanding this result is to recognise that there are two types of error that the firm can make. The first is to reject the export strategy when it is correct (a Type I error), and the second is to accept the export strategy when foreign production is appropriate instead (a Type II error). The nature of these errors, and the costs associated with them, are set out in Table 10.1. The cost of a Type I error is

Table 10.1   Two possible errors in strategic choice under uncertainty

	State 1: Foreign cost conditions bad	State 2: Foreign cost conditions good
Strategy 1	0	Type *II error*
Produce at home: Exporting		$c_0 - c_2$
Strategy 2	Type *I error*	0
Produce abroad: FDI	$c_1 - c_0$	

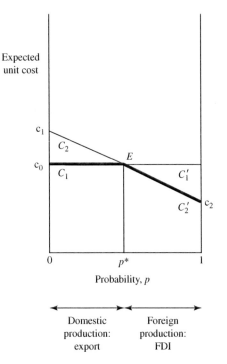

Figure 10.1   Diagrammatic solution of the entry strategy under uncertainty.

$c_1 - c_0$ and the cost of a Type II error is $c_0 - c_2$. It follows that the critical probability value may be expressed as:

p^* = Cost of Type I error/Total cost of both errors.

The solution is illustrated in Figure 10.1. The horizontal axis measures the probability that foreign cost conditions are good and the vertical axis measures corresponding expected unit cost. The horizontal schedule

C_1C_1' indicates that domestic costs are constant, independently of foreign costs, while the downward-sloping schedule C_2C_2' shows that expected foreign costs decrease as the probability of good conditions increases. The minimum attainable expected unit cost is indicated by the thick line C_1EC_2', which is the lower envelope of the two schedules, and has a kink at the switch-point E. The rational decision maker minimises expected costs by choosing to export for low probabilities, to the left of *E*, and to produce abroad for high probabilities, to the right of *E*.

The economic implications of the analysis may be summarised as follows:

(1) Optimists undertake FDI, pessimists export.
(2) The greater the cost of a Type I error relative to the cost of a Type II error, the more optimistic an investor needs to be.
(3) The costs of a Type I error are greater, the higher the cost of foreign production under bad conditions relative to domestic costs; and
(4) The costs of a Type II error are greater the lower the cost of foreign production under good conditions relative to domestic costs.

10.6   Collecting information

It is often suggested that uncertainty is a basic 'fact of life', but this is not quite correct. Uncertainty can be dispelled by collecting information. Even if it cannot be dispelled entirely, its impact can be reduced by narrowing down the margin for error. It is therefore irrational to always passively accept uncertainty.

But how is it possible to know how much information is worth collecting? Rational action modelling provides an answer to this question. All that is required is that the decision maker can estimate the cost of collecting relevant items of information, and attach subjective probabilities to what the results of investigation will turn out to be. This allows the decision maker to estimate both the costs and the benefits of collecting information, and therefore to arrive at a rational information strategy (Casson 2000*a*, chapters 4, 7).

Decision making becomes a two-stage procedure: in the first stage the decision maker decides how much information to collect, and in the second stage he uses the information he has collected to take the decision. These two stages are interdependent, and the rational decision maker arrives at his strategy by considering them in reverse order. He knows that it would be a waste of time collecting information that would not influence his decision. He therefore needs to determine in advance how he would use any item of information if he had it. If he would not use it whatever it turned out to be, then it is a waste of time collecting it. Only when he has decided how he would use it is he in a position to decide whether he wants to collect it or not.

Suppose, for example, that the decision maker could research the costs of foreign production at a cost q. Once he has collected the cost information, he can avoid both the Type I and Type II errors shown in Table 10.1. If he discovers that the conditions are good then he can commit to invest abroad, while if he discovers that conditions are bad then he can export instead. As a result, the expected cost of market entry is $(1 - p) c_0 + p c_2$, which is always lower than the expected cost of either the ordinary export strategy or the ordinary foreign investment strategy, except when the decision maker is certain at the outset what the conditions will be $(p = 0, 1)$.

The expected cost of market entry using information on foreign costs is illustrated by the line $C_1 C_2'$ in Figure 10.2. This figure is similar to Figure 10.1, but with the addition of the research strategy. To evaluate the total cost of the research strategy, the cost q must be added to the cost

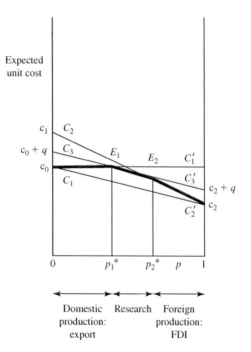

Figure 10.2 Strategy for information gathering.

of market entry. Since this cost is independent of what the information turns out to be, its effect is simply to shift the schedule C_1C_2' in parallel fashion up to C_3C_3'. If the cost of research is suitably low, this will determine two new critical values, p_1^*, p_2^*, at which the decision maker switches into and out of the information-gathering strategy. These critical points are determined by constructing the lower envelope $C_1E_1E_2C_2'$ of the three schedules, and identifying the kinks E_1 and E_2.

The following results may be derived from Figure 10.2:

(1) research is most efficient when uncertainty is high i.e. the probability p is in the mid range

$$p_1^* < p < p_2^*;$$

(2) research is most valuable when the variability of foreign production costs, $c_1 - c_2$, is large; and
(3) the range of probability values for which research is efficient is greater, the lower the research cost, q.

10.7 Using decision trees

The fundamental point about research is that it alters the information set available to the decision maker at the time of the decision. The easiest way to appreciate the significance of this is with the aid of a decision tree. Figure 10.3 uses a decision tree to compare decision making with and without research. Without research, the decision maker acts first and the true situation reveals itself later, whereas with research the situation is revealed before the decision maker acts.

A complete description of a research strategy involves specifying not only what information will be collected but also what the decision maker will do with the information once it has been collected. In the previous example there are only two ways in which it could be used. One of these – to invest if foreign cost conditions are good, and otherwise to export – is obviously sensible, while the alternative – to invest only if foreign cost conditions are bad, is obviously absurd. The use of the information is indicated by the thick vertical lines in the bottom half of the figure.

The gist of this discussion so far may be summarised as follows:

(1) research strategies enlarge the information set available to the decision maker and thereby reduce the risk of error;

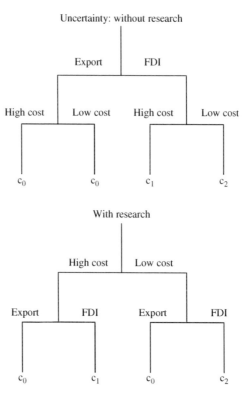

Figure 10.3   Comparison of decision trees with and without research.

(2) research strategies involve rules for using the information that has been collected in the course of the research; and

(3) as new strategies are introduced, new critical points are introduced at which switching between strategies occurs.

10.8   Deferring decisions: Real options

Research is not the only way of augmenting the information set. If a decision maker waits long enough, the information they require may reveal itself anyway. Deferring a decision may save the cost of collecting the information at the outset. The reason why firms do not delay decisions is because there is a cost involved. For example, if market entry will be profitable right away, profits will be lost if entry is deferred.

Furthermore, there is a risk that another firm may enter the market and pre-empt the profit opportunity. Comparing deferment with research, therefore, there is a trade-off between saving information costs on the one hand, and losing revenue on the other.

If market entry decisions were fully reversible then there would be no need to defer a decision at all. A provisional decision would be made on the basis of the information that was freely available at the outset, and when additional information became available this decision would be changed as appropriate. The revenue stream would therefore commence immediately, and the cost of information would be avoided altogether. The only losses would relate to errors made at the outset, and corrected later.

In practice, of course, most decisions are not reversible. If the firm invests in a foreign production plant, for example, it will not be able to sell it off for as much as it cost to build. The 'illiquidity' of the plant means that the firm incurs a capital loss. Similarly, if the firm adapts the plant to some alternative use then adjustment costs will be incurred. Some investments are more readily reversed than others. Strategies that involve reversible investments afford more flexibility than those which do not. High levels of uncertainty favour the selection of flexible strategies, since mistakes are easier to put right (Buckley and Casson 1998b).

10.9 Example: Optimising the dynamics of foreign market entry using research, deferment and switching strategies

The demand for flexibility can be analysed using real option theory (Dixit and Pindyck 1994; Kogut 1991; Kogut and Kulatilaka 1994; Rivoli and Salorio 1996). The specific approach followed here is based on Casson (2000a, Chapter 7). Continuing with the previous example, suppose that there are now two periods, 1 and 2, and that the overall market entry strategy must be set at the beginning of period 1. The first period is short – of unit length, in fact – while the second period is of infinite length. The firm now maximises expected net present value rather than expected profit; it discounts future costs and revenues at a fixed interest rate, r.

Entry into the foreign market is profitable right away, but information about the state of foreign cost conditions is not available until the end of period 1. Both exporting and foreign investment incur a fixed set-up cost, f, which is the same whether it is incurred in period 1 or period 2. An investment in foreign production is much more difficult to liquidate than an equivalent investment in export production: it can be sold off for only h_2 instead of h_1, where $h_2 < h_1 < f$.

At the beginning of period 1 the firm decides whether to carry out research to discover foreign production costs. It also decides whether to invest in foreign production right away, to commit itself to exporting right away, or to defer the decision on the method of market entry until period 2. If it carries out research then it will produce abroad only if it discovers that foreign costs are low; otherwise it will export instead. These commitments will be made right away since with the information at its disposal it has no reason to defer a decision.

In period 2 the firm can reverse any commitments it made in period 1 in the light of new information. Alternatively, if the firm deferred its decision, then it can decide its entry strategy unconstrained by the legacy of previous decisions.

The decision tree is shown in Figure 10.4. There are six dominant entry strategies, which are listed in Table 10.2. If the firm could costlessly obtain all the information it required at the outset then its profit would be

$$v = s\,(1 + r)/r - f - pc_2 - (1 - p)c_0.$$

In practice none of the available strategies can achieve this level of profit, but they can be ranked by their shortfalls compared to this norm. The shortfalls are shown in the right-hand column of the table.

The number of strategies that need to be considered can be reduced using one or more of the following conditions:

1. If the firm exports initially then it will switch to foreign investment when cost conditions turn out to be good (i.e. strategy 5 is preferred to strategy 1) if and only if the sunk costs are lower than the capitalised savings on subsequent production costs:

$$f - h_1 < (c_0 - c_2)\,(1 + r)\,/r.$$

2. If the firm invests abroad initially then it will switch to exporting when cost conditions turn out to be bad (i.e. strategy 6 is preferred to strategy 2) if and only if

$$f - h_2 < (c_1 - c_0)\,(1 + r)\,/r.$$

3. Deferment is preferred to research (i.e. strategy 4 is preferred to strategy 3) if and only if the expected profit lost from the first period trading is less than the costs of research:

$$s < q + c_0 - p(c_0 - c_2) + (fr/(1 + r)).$$

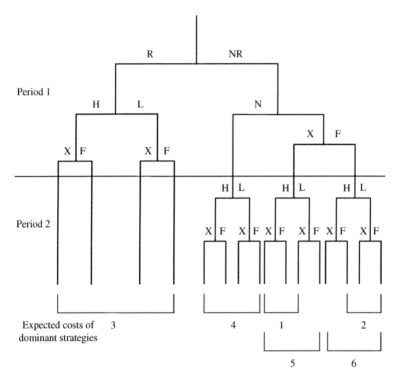

Figure 10.4 Decision tree for integrated research/waiting/switching problem.

Note: F: Foreign direct investment
NR: No research
H: High foreign production costs
R: Research
L: Low foreign production costs
X: Exporting
N: Null strategy

The overall solution can be determined using a four-way comparison: this involves the cheapest from each of the two pairs of strategies (1, 5), (2, 6), together with the research strategy (3) and the deferment strategy (4). The solution is illustrated graphically in Figure 10.5. In contrast to Figure 10.2, which plotted the absolute costs of each strategy, Figure 10.5 plots the costs of each strategy relative to the full-information norm as defined above. The schedule C_1C_1' shows the costs associated with the cheapest of strategies 1 and 5; the schedule C_2C_2' shows the costs associated with the cheapest of the strategies 2 and 6, while C_3C_3' and C_4C_4' show respectively the costs associated with strategies 3 and 4.

Table 10.2 Foreign entry strategy set encompassing research, deferment and switching, assuming that it is always profitable to serve the market

Strategies	Research?	Entry under uncertainty	If cost high	If cost low	Expected cost relative to norm
1. Commit to X	NR	X	X	X	$p(c_0 - c_2)(1 + r)/r$
2. Commit to F	NR	F	F	F	$(1 - p)(c_1 - c_0)(1 + r)/r$
3. Research	R	N	X	F	q
4. Defer	NR	N	X	F	$s - c_0 + p(c_0 - c_2) - fr/(1 + r)$
5. Conditional switch from X to F	NR	X	X	F	$p((c_0 - c_2) + (f - h_1)/(1+r))$
6. Conditional switch from F to X	NR	F	X	F	$(1 - p)((c_1 - c_0) + (f - h_2)/(1+r))$

Note: F: Foreign Direct Investment
N: Null strategy
NR: No research
R: Research
X: Exporting

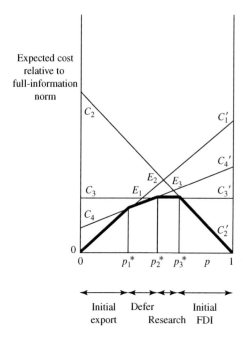

Figure 10.5 Diagrammatic solution of an entry problem encompassing research, deferment and switching.

Because of the way that costs are defined, the horizontal axis represents the base-line performance of the full-information strategy. The figure shows that none of the strategies attains base-line performance except those at the two ends of the axis, where the decision maker is subjectively certain about the level of foreign production costs ($p = 0$, 1). The figure has been drawn to illustrate the case where both research costs and the profits generated by foreign sales are relatively modest. This means that both research and deferment are optimal strategies for certain values of p. There are now three critical probability values at which the firm switches strategies: p_1^*, where the firm switches from initial exporting to deferment; p_2^*, where it switches from deferment to research; and p_3^* where it switches from research to initial FDI.

A selection of the results that can be obtained (in addition to the previous results) is given below:

(1) As the decision maker becomes more optimistic, the chosen strategy switches in turn from exporting to deferment to research to FDI;

some of the steps may be omitted when one of the strategies is completely dominated by the others, but the basic sequence is never reversed;

(2) Deferment is preferred when uncertainty is high, the costs of error are high, set-up costs are high, the interest rate is high, and the cost of research is high;

(3) Switching is more likely to take place, the lower are the losses incurred by liquidating a fixed investment; and

(4) Switching is more likely to take place when foreign costs are highly variable.

10.10   Further extensions of the real options approach to strategy

This approach to modelling strategy is extremely versatile and can be extended in many different ways. The costs of research may depend on the ownership and location of facilities. For example, FDI may generate information about the foreign market as a by-product of the foreign location of production; this may provide a reason for undertaking FDI from the outset – but in a flexible form, so that it can be divested if the market turns out to be poor. Similarly a foreign-owned plant may be more useful in capturing information than a plant operated by a licensee, because ownership gives more effective access to information by-products. Hence not only does information-gathering affect ownership and location strategy but ownership and location strategies affect information-gathering too. Ownership issues are considered in more detail below.

So long as there remains just a single source of uncertainty, most problems of this type can be solved using the graphical technique described above. The following properties of Figure 10.5 are common to all graphical solutions:

(1) The envelope of minimum expected cost, indicated by the thick line, is (weakly) convex;

(2) The convex envelope is constructed from a series of straight-line graphs representing the expected costs of the various dominant strategies;

(3) There are critical probabilities defining the switch-points between strategies;

(4) Changes in the parameters such as costs, sales revenues and interest rates cause the straight-line graphs to shift and/or rotate, and thereby

lead to previously efficient strategies becoming inefficient, and vice versa. This generates a wide range of interrelated hypotheses about the effects of various parameters on the dynamics of foreign market entry under uncertainty.

Additional sources of uncertainty can also be introduced: for example, the reactions of established foreign firms in the foreign market, or the reactions of other potential foreign entrants into that market. In this context it is important to distinguish two types of situation:

(1) The initial entrant wins customer loyalty, and subsequent entrants can only access the 'residual' market that was not captured by the initial entrant; and

(2) There is no customer loyalty, so an initial entrant must subsequently defend their market share through price warfare, or other competitive weapons. The initial entrant can deter followers by making an irreversible commitment to the foreign market, which means that it will always pay him to 'stay and fight' rather than 'quit the market'. The method of entry then becomes important in determining the strength of this threat.

These issues (especially the second) can be analysed using game-theoretic techniques.

10.11   The IB system as a global network

An important source of combinatorial complexity in the IB system lies in its network structure. This network structure was only implicit in the previous analysis, and it now needs to be made explicit.

A simple network structure is represented schematically in Figure 10.6, using a set of conventions established in earlier work (Casson 1995, 1997, 2000a, b). The figure illustrates a two-country world, comprising a home country (country 1) and a foreign country (country 2). It focuses on a single industry, assumed, for convenience, to be a manufacturing industry. Physical processes, such as production and distribution, are represented by square boxes. Each box indicates a facility, such as a factory or warehouse, at a specific location. Flows of tangible products are represented by black lines: thus factory output awaiting distribution flows from production, P, to distribution, D, and onwards from distribution to the final customer, C; the customer may be a group of household consumers, the government,

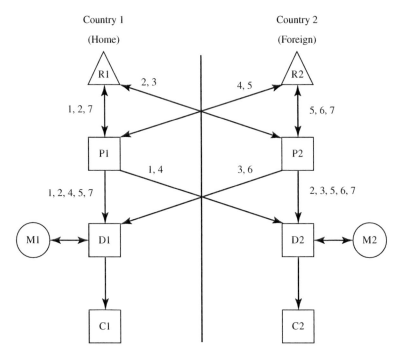

Figure 10.6   Schematic representation of a simple international business system.

Note: The letter indentifying a facility denotes the type of the facility, as described in the text. The number indentifies the country in which the facility is located. The numbers associated with the flows identify the location strategies that involve these flows. The strategies concerned are described in Table 10.5.

or firms in some other industry. The direction of flow is indicated by an arrow.

Intangible flows such as knowledge are represented by grey lines. Two types of knowledge are identified: technological know-how, produced by R&D, and local market knowledge, accumulated through experience in distribution of the product. Technological know-how is generated in scientific laboratories, *R*, indicated by a triangle, while marketing expertise is accumulated by a marketing department, *M*, indicated by a circle. Unlike product flows, which are one-way, knowledge flows are two-way, as indicated by the two arrows on each grey line.

In principle any configuration of production plants, distribution facilities, research laboratories and marketing offices located in any number of different countries can be represented in this way. Mapping out the entire IB system would, of course, prove extremely complex and generate a very complicated diagram (Isard 1956). However, the network structure of the IB system can also be conveniently summarised in tabular form, as indicated in Table 10.3; this tabular form can be more readily expanded to accommodate additional detail as required.

10.12 Levels of aggregation

The IB system can be represented at different levels of aggregation. For example, when discussing international trade and investment flows at a macroeconomic level it may be sufficient to analyse the system in terms of a single representative plant in each country. In this case each of the boxes, triangles, or circles indicates a single representative facility of a given type. The number of facilities of that type in a given country may be indicated by placing a number adjacent to the corresponding box; thus a number 'three' placed adjacent to the box P2 would indicate that there are three production plants in country 2.

By contrast, a microeconomic view of a particular industry in a particular country might require different regional locations to be identified and the transport infrastructure linking these locations to be mapped out, including ports, airports, railway junctions and major road hubs. In general, the existence of specialised nodes where traffic is switched between linkages is fully apparent only with disaggregation.

The extreme of disaggregation occurs when individual workspaces are identified within each plant, and the roles of separate individuals are identified. This level of disaggregation is extremely useful for discussing the organisational structure of the firm, as explained later.

Each element identified at a high level of aggregation appears as a system in its own right when viewed at a lower level of aggregation. There is a hierarchy of sub-systems within the system as a whole. The representation of a system using a high level of aggregation is analogous to the 'desk top' on a computer screen, while a representation using a low level of aggregation opens up the 'windows' to reveal the contents of the drives or files.

Different variants of IB work with different levels of aggregation:

- the individual person
- the firm
- the industry
- the global economy
- the socio-political-ecological system.

Table 10.3 Tabular representation of flows illustrated in Figure 10.6

From/to	R1	R2	M1	P1	P2	D1	D2	C1	C2
R1				Know-how	Know-how				
R2				Know-how	Know-how				
M1						Experience			
M1							Experience		
P1	Feed back	Feed back				Wholesale product	Wholesale product		
P2	Feed back	Feed back				Wholesale product	Wholesale product		
D1		Feed back	Feed back					Retail product	
D2		Feed back	Feed back						Retail product
C1									
C2									

Economic theories of IB such as internalisation theory, and theories of international business strategy, operate at the firm and industry level, and these are the levels on which this chapter focuses.

Scholars working at one level of aggregation often criticise others for making unwarranted assumptions. This sometimes leads to unnecessary controversy. Typically those who work at low levels of aggregation criticise those working at higher levels of aggregation for making sweeping assumptions, while those who work at high levels of aggregation tend to criticise those working at lower levels of aggregation for cluttering their analysis with irrelevant detail and being 'unable to see the wood for the trees'. It is important for those working at one level of aggregation to bear in mind that other scholars work at other levels of aggregation and that considerable care is needed in reconciling work at adjacent levels of aggregation.

It is not only the level of aggregation that is important when describing a system. There is an important distinction between short-run and long-run analysis too. In the short run the IB system comprises a fixed number of facilities which have been inherited from the past. In the long run, by contrast, the number of facilities is variable because new facilities can be created and established facilities may be closed down. In a long-run context it is therefore important to distinguish between actual and potential facilities.

10.13   Implementing the network research agenda

The network view of the IB system is well suited to addressing two of the major issues in IB: the issue of where IB facilities will be *located* and the issue of who will *own* them. These questions can be considered separately or together. It is possible to analyse, for a given pattern of ownership, where facilities will be located. Similarly, for a given pattern of location, it is possible to analyse the structure of ownership. Finally, it is also possible to determine simultaneously what the patterns of location and ownership within the system will be.

Issues of location, considered in isolation from issues of ownership, are addressed by theories of geography and trade. Relevant theories include the Ricardian theory of comparative advantage, the Heckscher-Ohlin-Stopler-Samuelson theory of factor intensities and theories of transport costs and economies of scale (Krugman 1995).

IB theory has tended to concentrate on issues of ownership: in particular, internalisation theory, as developed in the 1970s, focused on the question of why a firm that owned facilities in one country would wish to own facilities in another country, and how it could survive against international competition if it did so. The theory emphasised the gains from internalising knowledge flow, and allowed for gains from internalising intermediate flows of material product too, for example components and raw materials.

A major justification for distinguishing IB as a special field of study is that pattern of ownership used to coordinate international linkages in a network is different from those used to coordinate purely domestic ones. If there was no substantial difference then the international dimension would be of limited significance so far as the interaction of ownership and location are concerned. A key feature of an IB system is that the costs and benefits of internalisation vary according to whether an international or domestic linkage is involved. This cost differential can impact on both ownership and location decisions. Thus a firm may licence internationally a technology that it exploits internally in the domestic market; similarly, it may produce at home instead of abroad because it can only afford to produce abroad by licensing its technology and it is reluctant to do so because of the costs involved.

To illustrate this point it is useful to consider the structure of costs within an IB network. Consider first location strategy. Suppose that in the previous example both the national markets have to be served, and that both are of fixed size. Market sizes are normalised to unity for simplicity. Since the markets cannot be served without distribution facilities, nor without market knowledge, the costs incurred by marketing and distribution activities are sunk costs, and so can be omitted from the analysis. This leaves just the costs that are shown in Table 10.4. The key elements in this table are the production costs in the two countries, c_1, c_2, R&D costs in the two countries, a_1, a_2, costs of transferring technology internationally, m, and the cost of transporting the product internationally, z. All of these costs are assumed to be known for certain; the analysis can be extended to allow for uncertainty by using the techniques described in the earlier part of this chapter.

It is easy to deduce that

1. it is never efficient to carry out research in both countries unless there is production in both countries;
2. when there is research in both countries, it is never efficient to 'cross haul' research by linking R&D in country 1 to production in country 2, and vice versa; and;
3. when there is production in both countries it is never efficient to 'cross-haul' the product by exporting from country 1 to country 2 at the same time as exporting from country 2 to country 1.

Table 10.4 Structure of location costs for the flows illustrated in Figure 10.1 (excluding sunk costs of marketing and distribution)

From/to	R1	R2	P1	P2	D1	D2
R1	Domestic R&D cost; fixed cost: a_2		Domestic transfer cost (zero)	International transfer cost; fixed cost: m		
R2		Foreign R&D cost; fixed cost: a_2	International transfer cost; fixed cost: m	Domestic transfer cost (zero)		
P1			Domestic production cost; unit cost: c_1			
P2				Foreign production cost; unit cost: c_2	International transport cost; unit cost: z	Domestic transport cost (zero)

Table 10.5   Dominant locational strategies

Location Strategy	Description	Active facilities	Cost
	Research in country 1 only		
1	Export from country 1	R1, P1	$a_1 + 2c_1 + z$
2	Produce in both countries	R1, P1, P2	$a_1 + m + c_1 + c_2$
3	Export from country 2	R1, P2	$a_1 + m + 2c_2 + z$
	Research in country 2 only		
4	Export from country 1	R2, P1	$a_2 + m + 2c_1 + z$
5	Produce in both countries	R2, P1, P2	$a_2 + m + c_1 + z$
6	Export from country 2	R2, P2	$a_2 + 2c_2 + z$
	Research in both countries		
7	Produce in both countries	R1, R2, P1, P2	$a_1 + a_2 + c_1 + c_2$

Note: All the strategic utilise both distribution facilities $D1$, $D2$; these are omitted from the third column for reasons of simplicity

It follows that just seven location strategies need to be distinguished. These seven strategies dominate all other conceivable strategies, in the sense that one of these seven strategies will always afford the lowest overall system cost. The dominant strategies are listed in Table 10.5. Note that because of locational specialisation, strategies 1–6 utilise only some, and not all, of the available facilities.

The optimal location strategy is derived by comparing the costs set out in the final column of the table and identifying the strategy associated with the lowest cost. The following principles characterise an efficient location strategy in general terms:

1. Produce in both countries if and only if international transport costs exceed the savings from concentrating all production in the lower cost country:

$$z > max \ [c_1 \ c_2] - min \ [c_1 c_2]$$

2. Research in both countries if and only if producing in both countries, and if the cost of transferring technology exceeds the cost of researching in the higher-cost country:

$$m > max \ [a_1 \ a_2]$$

3. Produce and research in different coun tries if and only if the cost of transferring technology is less than the smaller of the savings in

research costs and production costs achieved by switching one of the locations:

$$m < min\left[\left|a_2 - a_1\right|, \left|c_2 - c_1\right|\right]$$

4. If producing and researching in the same country, choose the country for which the sum of research and production costs is lowest:

   choose country 1 if $(a_2 - a_1)(c_2 - c_1) > 0$, otherwise choose country 2.
5. Similarly, if producing and researching in different countries, choose the combination for which the sum of research and production costs is lowest:

   choose to research in 1 and produce in 2 if $(a_2 - a_1)(c_2 - c_1) > 0$, otherwise choose the opposite combination.

10.14   Transaction costs: Optimising ownership patterns

From a network perspective, ownership patterns are driven by the need to minimise the costs of coordinating the system. Each facility is allocated an owner. Since no two owners can own the same facility outright, the ownership strategies of different firms constrain each other: what is owned by one firm cannot be owned by other firms as well. Although ownership can be shared through joint ventures, the partners must still harmonise their strategies, so that their shares add to 100 per cent. The interdependence of ownership strategies is missing from conventional expositions of internalisation theory, which focus on the strategies of a single firm. This weakness is often mitigated by assuming that the firm invests in new facilities, such as a greenfield production plant, but the problem remains when discussing takeovers, where several firms may be competing to acquire the same facility, and only one of them can succeed. In general, the internalisation strategies of all firms in a system need to be analysed simultaneously, and this can only be done using a network approach.

The pattern of ownership that emerges in an IB system depends crucially on the structure of transactions costs (Coase 1937). For present purposes transaction costs may be equated with the costs of coordinating linkages, although a more refined analysis would distinguish different aspects of transaction costs (Casson 2000a, Chapters 3, 5).

The transaction costs associated with any given linkage in a network depend, in general, upon three main factors:

(1) the nature of the flow along the linkage and, in particular, whether the flow is an intangible flow of knowledge ($i = 1$) or a tangible flow of product ($i = 2$);
(2) whether the flow is internal to a firm ($j = 1$), or external, connecting two independent firms ($j = 2$); and
(3) whether the flow is domestic ($k = 1$) or international ($k = 2$).

The transactions cost incurred by the IB system is the sum of the transaction costs associated with the individual linkages utilised by the system. The linkages that are active at any one time depend on the location strategy that is being used. Thus different location strategies, when applied in conjunction with a given pattern of ownership, are liable to generate different transaction costs, as well as different location costs.

The total cost of the system is the sum of the transaction costs and the location costs. In general, there is a trade-off between location costs and transaction costs, because economising on location costs through the international rationalisation of research and production locations will tend to increase the number of international linkages, and international linkages typically incur higher transaction costs than purely domestic ones. In order to mitigate the increase in transaction cost patterns of ownership may change. In this way, changes in the system driven by location factors may induce a change in patterns of ownership; conversely, changes in ownership patterns may induce changes in location strategies, although in practice this effect appears to be less common.

When all the different location strategies are permuted with all the different ownership patterns, a very large number of possible system structures emerge. All of these structures can, however, be ranked in terms of their overall system costs, and so in principle the least-cost configuration of the system can always be ascertained. Although it is complex, the problem remains finite.

The solution of this problem determines how many different firms will exist within the system, and where their individual boundaries will lie. Firms must be large enough to internalise all the linkages that benefit from internalisation, but small enough to allow other linkages to be external instead. The importance of internalising knowledge flows means that a higher proportion of knowledge flows will be internal to firms than will flows of ordinary products. It follows that the boundaries of firms will be determined mainly by the structure of knowledge flows, and only secondarily by the structure of product flows. This highlights a major difference between the IB literature and some of the other literature on transaction costs (e.g. Williamson 1985) where the emphasis of internalisation is erroneously placed on ordinary product flows.

For many purposes, however, it is unnecessary to consider all of the permutations referred to above. IB scholars are typically interested in more specific issues which can be 'projected out' of the network model. For example, they are primarily concerned with the coordination of international linkages rather than domestic linkages. They also tend to be concerned with the choice between a subset of all the possible location strategies discussed above.

Consider, for example, the issue of foreign market entry strategy, as discussed in the first part of this chapter. Before internalisation theory was developed it was normally assumed that FDI was the natural form of the local production strategy. Internalisation theory pointed out that licensing was also an option. The network model presented above indicates that there are other options too. Foreign market servicing involves establishing a link between the R&D carried out in the home country (country 1) and the marketing and distribution of the product carried out in the foreign country (country 2). This involves two separate linkages: a flow of knowledge between R&D and production and a flow of product between production and R&D. Either of these flows can be internal or external to the firm (see Table 10.6). Under the export strategy the flow of knowledge is domestic but the flow of product is international, whereas under local production the converse applies: the flow of knowledge is international and the flow of product is domestic. As a result, different location strategies generate different pattern of transactions costs, and the resulting differences in transactions costs can influence the choice of location strategy. They also determine the form of ownership structure used to implement the chosen location strategy.

Suppose, for example, that internalisation of knowledge flow is always cheaper than external knowledge flow, but that the internalisation of product flow is only cheaper where domestic rather than international linkages are concerned. Under these conditions it always pays to internalise the linkage between production and R&D. The structure of transaction costs for knowledge flow implies that the cheapest foreign production strategy involves FDI rather than licensing. The structure of transaction costs for product flow implies that foreign production will be integrated with foreign distribution, so that FDI in production implies FDI in distribution too. It also implies, however, that exporting will be carried out at

Table 10.6 Alternative contractual arrangements for linking domestic R&D to foreign distribution

	Domestic production	Foreign production
Internalise knowledge flow		
Internalise product flow	(1)	(2)
	FDI in distribution	FDI in production & distribution
	$t_{111} + t_{212}$	$t_{112} + t_{211}$
Externalise product flow	(3)	(4)
	Export to independent foreign sales agent	FDI in production; sell through an independent foreign sales agent
	$t_{111} + t_{222}$	$t_{112} + t_{221}$
Externalise knowledge flow		
Internalise product flow	(5)	(6)
	Licence a firm that undertakes FDI in distribution	Licence a foreign producer that integrates forward into distribution
	$t_{121} + t_{212}$	$t_{122} + t_{211}$
Externalise product flow	(7)	(8)
	Licence an exporter that sells through an independent foreign sales agent	Licence a foreign producer that sells through an independent local agent
	$t_{121} + t_{222}$	$t_{122} + t_{221}$

Note: It is assumed that the domestic market is always supplied through domestic production. Domestic distribution is either integrated with domestic production, or undertaken by an independent agent, whichever affords the lower transaction costs. This decision can be made independently of all other decisions and, since it does not bear directly on IB strategy, is omitted from the analysis.

arm's length, so that domestic production will be sold to an independent distributor in the foreign market. So far as the domestic situation is concerned, domestic production will be integrated with domestic distribution, so that the firms will be vertically integrated in both countries.

The actual choice between exporting and FDI depends on the structure of both location costs and transaction costs. The costs of domestic

R&D are common to both strategies. The exporting strategy derived above incurs transaction costs

$$t_1 = t_{111} + t_{222}$$

while the FDI strategy incurs transaction costs

$$t_2 = t_{112} + t_{211}$$

where t_{ijk} is the transaction cost associated with a flow of type i through a market of type j along a linkage of geographical type k (as defined above). Combining these expressions with the expressions for location costs in Table 10.5 shows that FDI is preferred to exporting when:

$$z + c_1 - c_2 > m + t_2 - t_1.$$

This condition states that the savings in international transport costs *plus* any savings in production costs effected by FDI must exceed the costs of international technology transfer *plus* any additional transaction costs that stem from internationalising internal technology transfer *less* any savings in distribution costs that arise from using an internal domestic market rather than an external international one. This result demonstrates how embedding an analysis of foreign market entry within a network view can enrich understanding of the issue.

10.15   The distribution of information within a global system

In the first part of this chapter foreign market entry was discussed from the standpoint of an individual firm, whereas in the second part it has been discussed from the standpoint of the overall system. In the first part the existence of the firm was given, whereas in the second part the structure of the firm emerged from an analysis of internalisation. The first part also assumed uncertainty, whereas the second did not. Intuitively, the system perspective is that of an all-knowing planner who controls the whole system, while the firm perspective is that of a decision maker who only understands a part of the system – specifically, that part of the system to which their personal knowledge and experience relates. Another difference is that the planner begins from scratch and moves directly to the optimal configuration, whereas the individual decision maker is constrained by the legacy of their previous decisions.

The link between the system-wide view of the planner and the partial view of the individual firm is that in a private enterprise economy, where individual entrepreneurs compete to establish firms, competition between them will tend to drive the system towards the planner's system-wide optimum (Hayek 1937; Richardson 1960). Different entrepreneurs will select different locations for their facilities and choose to operate with different boundaries for their firms. They will compete to own facilities in highly desirable locations. The entrepreneurs with the most efficient strategies will be able to outbid those with less efficient strategies, and so competition for the ownership and control of scarce resources will reward those entrepreneurs whose partial plans are most closely aligned with the system-wide optimum.

In practice, of course, there is no planner who possesses all the information of the kind required to fully optimise the system. Planning has encountered numerous problems at national level, and these would only be further compounded if planning were attempted at the global level. This does not mean that the network view is irrelevant, however, because for reasons already noted a well-functioning private enterprise economy will tend to converge on the optimum through incremental trial and error. Competition between individual entrepreneurs within the system leads to a pooling of local knowledge – the knowledge being encoded in the prices that the entrepreneurs quote when bidding for the use of facilities and when competing for customers. So long as the competitive system remains stable, therefore, the network approach will successfully identify the long-run tendencies in the system by identifying the equilibrium to which it is converging through localised iterations.

Because an individual entrepreneur perceives only a small part of the global system, he faces considerable uncertainty regarding the consequences of his decisions. He cannot track the full implications of any decision that he makes. Conversely, because decision making has been decentralised to many different entrepreneurs like himself, he is continuously exposed to unexpected changes caused by decisions made by other people – notably his customers and his competitors. The efficiency with which the global system works will therefore depend on the skill of entrepreneurs in handling uncertainties of this kind.

10.16   Social networks and organisations

An important strategy for handling uncertainty is to construct a network of contacts that act as sources of information (Ebers 1997). An entrepreneur can develop two main types of network for this purpose. First, he can build a network involving other entrepreneurs, who own independent firms, and secondly he can turn his own firm into a networking organisation. External networks may encompass not only other firms but governments, banks and opinion-leaders too. Internal networking may involve a hierarchical structure of reporting based on authority relations, or a flatter structure where people of similar status consult with each other.

There is insufficient space to describe in detail how social networks can be analysed using the rational action approach. It is sufficient to note that the rational action approach explains very simply why people are motivated to join social networks in order to gain access to information. Networks generate efficiency gains by exploiting the 'public good' property of knowledge and information. The rational action approach also explains how social and physical networks interact. Social networks are used to coordinate physical networks, for example, by planning the flow of product along the linkages between facilities. At the same time, social networks utilise physical networks as inputs as, for example, when people travel to face-to-face meetings by road, rail or air.

It is worth noting that the rational action approach to social networks has significant implications for the modelling of organisational behaviour within multinational firms (Egelhoff 1991). Where a large amount of information on the global environment needs to be routinely collected, a division of labour may be introduced that allows different members of an internal network to specialise in collecting different sorts of information. Where multiple sources of uncertainty are involved, multiple sources of information are normally required. The information obtained from these various sources needs to be synthesised for decision-making purposes. This requires communication between the specialists involved. Some of the communication may be 'intermediated' by other specialists, and these intermediators may sometimes take overall responsibility for the decisions. Thus the nature of the division of labour applied to information processing determines the organisation of the multinational firm.

The efficiency of internal communication is a major factor in the overall cost of decision making, and hence a major determinant of the performance of the firm. The 'entrepreneurial' qualities of the firm's key decision makers govern its ability to synthesise information successfully. This in turn affects the overall quality of decisions (e.g. the frequency with which potential mistakes are avoided) and so determines overall performance.

The organisation of decision making can be introduced into the previous model of foreign market entry under uncertainty by formally splitting the final period into an infinite number of sub-periods, and allowing new information of a particular type to become available each period. Foreign costs of production fluctuate from one period to the next, and foreign output in each period therefore needs to be adjusted in response. This encourages the firm to invest in information systems for predicting changes in cost. It also encourages the firm to invest in highly versatile capital equipment, thereby establishing a link between the structure of the organisation and the type of physical capital that it employs (Capel, 1992).

10.17   Conclusion

All of these research avenues need to be fully explored before any claim that the challenge of complexity warrants the introduction of more radical or unorthodox techniques into IB theory can be accepted. It is only sensible to follow the simplest and most straightforward path of theoretical development before investing too heavily in untried concepts and techniques. This chapter has suggested that the most productive theoretical developments in IB over the next ten years or so are likely to be those that build upon the rational action approach.

When the rational action approach is developed along the lines described above, many of the notions found in systems theory emerge in their proper light. Rule-driven behaviour, of the kind assumed in systems theory, is shown to be a rational response to information costs (Baumol and Quandt 1964). It is only rational in certain types of environment, however: in other environments, entrepreneurial improvisation is shown to be the order of the day.

Economy of coordination calls for a division of labour in information processing, and this in turn calls for cooperative behaviour of a social nature. It is rational to adapt the rules governing social behaviour to the long-term features of the environment within which decisions have to be made. The environment differs between locations, and it is therefore to be expected that there will be differences between locations in the kinds of rules that are used. In other words, social interactions will follow different rules in different places.

It is not expected that everyone will agree with these recommendations. But the onus is on those who disagree to set out their own agenda with a similar degree of analytical rigour and to demonstrate that their favoured approach can deliver practical results. Talking about 'strategy' or 'complexity' in non-specific ways may be adequate for consultancy assignments, or for teaching certain types of courses, but it is not an adequate response to the research challenges that currently face IB.

References

Allen, L. and Pantzalis, C. 1996. Valuation of the Operating Flexibility of Multinational Corporations. *Journal of International Business Studies*, 27/4: 633–53.

Arthur, B. W. 1988. Competing Technologie s: An Overview, in Giovanni Dosi, C. Freeman, R. Nelson, G. Silverberg and L. Soete (eds), *Technical Change and Economic Theory*. London: Francis Pinter.

Baumol, W. J. and Quandt, R. E. 1964. Rules of Thumb and Optimally Imperfect Decisions. *American Economic Review*, 54/1: 23–46.

Buckley P. J. and Casson, M. C. 1976. *The Future of the Multinational Enterprise*. London: Macmillan.

——. 1981. The Optimal Timing of a Foreign Direct Investment. *Economic Journal*, 91:75–87.

——. 1993. Economics as an Imperialist Social Science. *Human Relations*, 46/9: 1035–52.

——. 1998a. Analysing Foreign Market Entry Strategies: Extending The Internalisation Approach. *Journal of International Business Studies*, 29/3: 539–61.

——. 1998b. Models of the Multinational Enterprise. *Journal of International Business* Studies, 29/1: 21–44.

Capel, J. 1992. How to Service a Foreign Market Under Uncertainty: A Real Option Approach. *European Journal of Political Economy*, 8: 455–75.

Casson, M. C. 1995. *Organization of International Business*. Aldershot: Edward Elgar.

——. (1997). *Information and Organisation: A New Perspective on the Theory of the Firm*. Oxford: Clarendon Press.

——. (2000a). *Economics of International Business: A New Research Agenda*. Cheltenham: Edward Elgar.

——. (2000b). *Enterprise and Leadership: Studies on Firms, Networks and Institutions*. Cheltenham: Edward Elgar.

Coase, R. H. (1937). The Nature of the Firm. *Economica*, NS, 4: 386–405.

Coriat, B. and Dosi, G. (1998). The Institutional Embeddedness of Economic Change: An Appraisal of the 'Evolutionist' and 'Regulationist' Research Programmes, in K. Nielsen and E. J. Johnson (eds), *Institutions and Economic Change*. Cheltenham: Edward Elgar.

DeMeza, D. and Van der Ploeg, F. 1987. Production Flexibility as a Motive for Multinationality. *Journal of Industrial Economics*, 35/3: 343–51.

Dixit, A. and Pindyck, R. S. 1994. *Investments under Uncertainty*. Princeton, NJ: Princeton University Press.

Ebers, M. (ed.). 1997. *The Formation of Inter Organizational Networks*. Oxford: Clarendon Press

Egelhoff, W. G. 1991. Information processing theory and the Multinational Enterprise. *Journal of International Business Studies*, 22/3: 341–68.

Elster, J. (ed.). 1986. *Rational Choice*. Oxford: Blackwell.

Graham, E. M. 1990. Exchange of Threat Between Multinational Firms as an Infinitely Repeated Game. *International Trade Journal*, 4: 259–77.

Hargreaves Heap, S. 1989. *Rationality in Economics*. Oxford: Blackwell.

Hirshleifer, J. and Riley, J. G. 1992. *The Analytics of Uncertainty and Information*. Cambridge: Cambridge University Press.

Isard, W. 1956. *Location and Space Economy*. Cambridge, MA: MIT Press.

Kogut, B. 1991. Joint Ventures and the Option to Expand and Acquire. *Management Science*, 37/1: 19–33.

Kogut, B. and Kulatilaka, N. 1994. Operating Flexibility, Global Manufacturing, and the Option Value of a Multinational Network. *Management Science*, 40/1: 123–39.

Kreps, D. M. 1990. *Game Theory and Economic Modelling*. Oxford: Oxford University Press.

Krugman, P. 1995. *Development, Geography and Economic Theory*. Cambridge, MA: MIT Press.

Nelson, R. and Winter, S. G. 1982 *An Evolutionary Theory of Economic Change*. Cambridge, MA: Harvard University Press.

Parkhe, A. 1993. 'Messy' Research, Methodological Predispositions, and Theory Development in International Joint Ventures. *Academy of Management Review*, 18: 227–68.

Porter, M. E. 1991. Towards a Dynamic Theory of Strategy. *Strategic Management Journal*, 12 (Special Issue): 95–117.

Richardson, G. B. 1960. *Information and Investment*. Oxford: Oxford University Press.

Rivoli, P. and Salorio, E. 1996. Foreign Direct Investment under Uncertainty. *Journal of International Business Studies*, 27/2: 335–54.

Von Hayek, F. A. 1937. Economics and Knowledge. *Economica*, NS, 4: 33–54.

Williamson, O. E. 1985. *The Economic Institutions of Capitalism*. New York: Free Press.

11
Edith Penrose's Theory of the Growth of the Firm and the Strategic Management of Multinational Enterprises

11.1 Introduction

Foss (2002, p. 148) says, 'Penrose's work is, in the crucial dimensions, at variance with economic orthodoxy. ... It should be thought of as a contribution to economic heterodoxy.' Penrose and Pitelis (2002, pp. 19 et seq.), in describing Fritz Machlup as 'Edith's supervisor' at Johns Hopkins says, 'A fascinating paradox is how Machlup, a doyen of neo-classical economics, should have been partially responsible for a work so far removed from the mainstream.' Penrose has also been claimed as a feminist economist (Best/Humphries 2003). Our argument is that Penrose sought to create a theory of the growth of the firm which was logically consistent and empirically tractable. Her subsequent adoption as grandmother of the resource-based view has only limited validity, based on a selective reading of her work and in defiance of its holistic qualities. See the debate between Rugman and Verbeke (2002, 2004) and Kor and Mahoney (2004) and Lockett and Thompson (2004), the latter based on Penrose's (1960) analysis of the Hercules Powder Company.

This chapter presents a formalisation of Penrose's model contained in the *Theory of the Growth of the Firm* (1959) and applies it to the strategic decisions of multinational enterprises (MNEs). Previous research on Penrose and the multinational firm (e.g. Dunning 2003; Pitelis 2002, 2004) has focused on Penrose's overall contributions to strategic decisions in MNEs. This chapter focuses solely on her 1959 model and compares it to the model of Buckley and Casson (1976). Interesting contrasts are found and a synthetic approach suggests that this combination is a useful basis for further theorising about the MNE and its strategic decisions.

In contrasting Penrose's theory with that of Buckley and Casson (1976), we shall see that the former's concentration on product diversification can be considered complementary to the latter's emphasis on innovation. Combining the two gives a satisfying model of the strategic management decisions within an MNE and opens up a new research agenda.

11.2   A simple formal model of Penrose's Theory of the Growth of the Firm

The key to formalising Penrose's ideas is the recognition that she reformulated the familiar cost functions used in the theory of the firm. She argued that the average cost of output is independent of the scale of production but increases with respect to the rate of growth. Thus in so far as the average cost curve is U-shaped, it is U-shaped with respect, not to the scale of production, as commonly assumed, but to the rate of growth.

The simplest way to understand this postulate is to recognise that average costs are increased by *adjustments* in the rate of output. Changing the rate of output has a bigger impact on average cost than setting *steady state* output at a higher or lower level. Changes in the rate of output dislocate the allocation of resources. This is particularly true for human resources. Employees are usually most productive when they repeat the same routines; furthermore, when their work is repetitive, productivity may improve as a result of learning on the job. As a firm grows, the internal division of labour has to change, and this forces people to change their roles. Their previous learning of job-specific skills becomes obsolete as they return to the start of the 'learning curve' in their new job.

Change is expensive in other ways too. Plant and machinery have to be reallocated to different uses, and this process needs to be managed, creating additional demands on the management team. As the management team grows, new recruits need to be trained. By leaving their previous employment with another firm, and joining the expanding firm, these recruits incur the same costs of retraining as those who have changed their jobs within the firm. Indeed, their training costs are greater because they know little about the institutional context of their job. To train recruits, experienced managers have to be diverted from their usual work, adding to the dislocation described above.

Costs of change may be related either to the absolute amount of change or the proportional amount of change. A case can be made for both, but in the Penrose model it is the proportional and not the absolute amount of change that matters. In alternative models of growth, however, the absolute amount of change is key.

The formalisation of Penrose's theory is based on Buckley and Casson's (2010) recent interpretation of her major work (Penrose 1959). The model analyses a firm that grows through diversification at a steady rate. The central point of the model is that the firm faces 'costs of growth' which increase, not with the size of the firm but with its rate of growth. The key to the model is the specification of these costs of growth.

Penrose viewed the firm as a 'bundle of resources' because she saw resources – in particular human resources – as both the key to the firm's success and the principal constraint on its growth. According to her theory, the tacitness of information on which modern resource-based theory places so much emphasis not only protects the secrets of the firm's entrepreneurial success but also inhibits the assimilation of the additional human resources required to sustain its growth. The growth rate of the firm reflects a balance between the entrepreneurial dynamism which drives its diversification and the difficulty of enlarging the firm's management team to exploit the resultant opportunities.

In the basic model, the profitability of the firm is independent of its size and depends only on its rate of growth. This leads to a simple formula for the value of a growing firm, as determined by the present value of its future profit stream. Managers serving shareholder interests will maximise this value, while managers pursuing their own objectives – such as status – may maximise growth instead. Penrose considered both objectives; the differences are small, however, because maximising profits not only maximises shareholder value but also facilitates the internal financing of growth (see also Baumol 1967, Marris 1964).

Penrose's central point is that there is, in principle, no limit to the size to which a firm can grow.

- There are limits to the extent to which a firm can grow within a single market, which are set by the overall size of the market and the existence of competitors within it. But a firm can evade any such market size constraint by diversifying into other markets.
- It is often said that because of U-shaped average cost curves, there is a unique optimal size of firm at which average cost is a minimum. However, the logic of the U-shaped average cost curve applies to physical plant and equipment rather than to a managerial unit such as a firm. A firm that cannot expand beyond optimum plant size

can expand by increasing the number of plants it operates, either through replicating plants in the same market (horizontal integration), moving into other stages of production in the same market (vertical integration) or diversifying into different markets.

- Misleading analogies have been employed to suggest that there is a limit to the size of firm. Marshall's metaphor of the firms in an industry resembling the 'trees in a forest' is misleading because it ignores the fact that firms can regenerate themselves through managerial succession. More significant still, firms can merge with each other to sustain their growth, and metamorphose into new forms, as when a small firm with highly centralised autocratic management merges with other small firms and turns into a large highly decentralised multidivisional firm. As a legal and contractual entity, a firm can in principle endure forever.

- Managerial diseconomies of scale are often said to limit the size of firms, but such limiting factors are more properly regarded as diseconomies of growth. In other words, the costs that limit the size of a firm at any time are costs that limit its continued growth, rather than costs associated with the size to which it has already grown. It is therefore more appropriate to use the concept of an optimum rate of growth of a firm than an optimum size of firm.

- In terms of international expansion, Penrose can be interpreted as considering foreign subsidiaries as autonomous companies. As such, they are beyond the reach of the firm's administrative coordination. The absence of authoritative communication would thus put them beyond the boundary of the firm. There is a potential modification of our formalisation in which the rate of growth of firms of different sizes is the same up to the extent of the reach of coordination and then zero beyond it. This is not a realistic interpretation of modern multinational firms, especially given managerial learning and technological breakthroughs in communication and control of international expansion.

When analysing growth, the natural analogue of a theory of the optimal size of firm is a theory of the optimal growth rate of the firm, and this is essentially what Penrose provides. Because size of firm does not matter, there is no reason to believe that the firm's growth rate will vary systematically over its lifetime, and so it is reasonable to postulate the existence of a steady state rate of growth. The existence of such a steady state implies that, in the limit, firms can last forever and so, with a constant rate of growth, they can eventually approach infinite size. To many observers of the corporate scene in the 1950s, it seemed as if large firms like General Motors would, indeed, continue to grow forever. Although this may now appear an extreme possibility, it was considered quite plausible at the time that Penrose was writing.

Let the size of the firm be measured by *x*. If growth proceeds continuously at a constant proportional rate *g* then the size of the firm will increase exponentially:

$$x = X \exp(gt).$$

To simplify the subsequent discussion it is useful to normalise the size of the firm on its foundation to unity, $X = 1$. In terms of Penrose's theory, size is most naturally measured by the number of markets served by the firm; the normalisation therefore means that when the firm is newly established it operates in a single market.

All variables are non-negative unless otherwise stated. Discrete variables, such as the number of markets, are treated as though they were continuous.

For expository purposes it is useful to set out the model in three stages, with the final stage representing the model actually used in this chapter.

Stage 1

Suppose that the profit generated by a representative market is *A*, where *A* is a constant independent of the size of the firm. As the number of markets grows at the rate *g*, total profit grows at the same rate:

$$\text{Profit at time } t = Ax = A \exp(gt).$$

If future profits are discounted at the rate *r*, and $r > g$, then the value of the firm at the time it is founded ($t = 0$) is

$$v = \int_0^\infty \exp(-rt)\, Ax \, dt = A/(r - g).$$

The factor $1/(r - g)$, which multiplies into the profit per market, *A*, indicates the net rate at which profit is capitalised.

The first of the firm's objectives mentioned above corresponds to the maximisation of *v*. The second objective corresponds to the maximisation of *g*, subject to a constraint that the value of the firm is sufficient to support a dividend stream of acceptable size. If the dividend stream *d(t)* grows at the same rate as the firm then

$$d(t) = D \exp(gt)$$

where D is the initial level of dividend payments. To be feasible, initial dividend payments must be less than initial profit, $D \le A$. Shareholder pressure fixes the minimum acceptable level, D, and managers then set dividends exactly equal to this level as part of their growth-maximising strategy. The value of the dividend stream is

$$v^d = D/(r - g)$$

and the managers maximise g subject to the constraint that

$$v \ge v^d .$$

If there are no costs of growth then, since A is a constant, value is maximised by setting growth as high as possible. Since g is constrained to be slightly less than r, this becomes the value-maximising rate of growth. Provided that $A \ge D$ there is no difference between growth-maximisation and value-maximisation: both objectives imply the largest possible rate of growth.

Stage 2
To avoid this trivial result, it is necessary to introduce costs of growth. Let B be a parameter measuring costs that are directly proportional to growth. It is necessary to choose the dimension of B with care: it is the average cost per unit size generated per unit rate of growth. After deducting the cost of growth, net profit at time t becomes $(A - Bg)x$, and the value of the firm at the outset becomes

$$v = (A - Bg)/(r - g)$$

It turns out, however, that costs which are directly proportional to growth do not fundamentally modify the trivial result above. If net profit is positive, $A > Br$, then value-maximising growth is just less than r, exactly as before, whereas if net profit is negative, $A < Br$, then value-maximising growth is zero. But in the latter case the firm has negative value, and so it will not be established in the first place. In the special case where profit is zero, $A = Br$, the firm is just viable and the value-maximising growth rate is indeterminate within the permitted range, $0 \le g < r$. Thus the growth rate is either just less than r, indeterminate, or the firm is not established, depending upon whether profit is positive, negative or zero.

Stage 3

To achieve a determinate value-maximising growth inside the permitted range it is necessary to introduce decreasing returns to the rate of growth through a quadratic cost term which reflects the decline of productivity as the rate of growth increases. This quadratic term, Cg^2x, represents the effects of dislocation, as described above. It is quadratic in g, the proportional rate of growth, rather than in gx, which is the absolute rate of growth, because it is the proportional rather than the absolute amount of dislocation which affects average cost.

Net profit at time t becomes $(A - Bg - Cg^2)x$, and the value of the firm becomes

$$v = (A - Bg - Cg^2)/(r - g).$$

This is the fundamental formula for the value of the firm in a theory of the growth of the firm. The formula is implicit throughout Penrose's analysis.

The first order condition for value-maximisation is

$$v_g = ((A - Bg - Cg^2)/(r - g)^2) - ((B + 2Cg)/((r - g)) = 0$$

where the subscript g denotes the derivative with respect to g. The derivative v_g measures the sensitivity of the firm's value to changes in its rate of growth, and comprises two terms. The first measures the impact of a change in growth on the capitalised value of initial profits, assuming that the profit stream remains unchanged, while the second term measures the cost of growth, which is equal to the value of the marginal reduction in the profit stream induced by growth, assuming that the capitalisation rate remains unchanged.

Placing both terms over a common denominator, $(r - g)^2$, and noting that the denominator is always positive over the permitted range $0 \leq g < r$, indicates that the first order condition is satisfied only when the numerator is zero. The numerator is quadratic:

$$(A - Br) - 2Crg + Cg^2 = 0$$

and its solution has two roots. These roots are real if

$$A - Br > 0; \quad A - Br - Cr^2 < 0$$

i.e., if growth is profitable at the margin when growth is zero, and profit is negative when growth is equal to the discount rate, $g = r$. Only the smaller of the two roots lies in the permitted range; this root determines the optimal growth rate

$$g^* = r - (r^2 - ((A - Br)/C))^{1/2}.$$

Under the assumed conditions the numerator of the derivative always declines with respect to g, and since the denominator is always positive within the permitted range, v_g switches from positive to negative as g increases in the region of g^*, which guarantees that g^* supports a maximum.

Differentiation of the growth equation shows that under the assumed conditions the partial derivates can be signed as follows:

$$g^*_A > 0; \qquad g^*_B < 0; \qquad g^*_C < 0; \qquad g^*_r < 0$$

The higher is the profitability of the representative market, A, and the lower are the cost parameters, B, C, the higher is growth. B is less important than either A or C because its impact is mediated by the rate of cost of capital, r, which is normally substantially less than unity. The key insight of the growth formula, therefore, is that growth is governed by a fundamental trade-off between the profitability of the representative market, A, and the strength of decreasing returns to growth, as measured by C. Growth is also higher when the cost of capital is lower: an increase in the rate at which future profits are discounted discourages the firm from sacrificing current profit to promote future growth.

When growth is maximised subject to a dividend constraint, growth will expand up to the point where profit is zero, which implies that

$$(A - D) - Bg - Cg^2 = 0.$$

This quadratic equation has two roots, and assuming that the dividend constraint is feasible, both are real. The smaller root is negative, and so the larger root must be taken, which is the root that corresponds to a maximum of growth:

$$g^{**} = ((B^2 + 4(A - D)C)^{1/2} - B)/2C.$$

Given the other assumptions, this root lies within the permitted range. Partial differentiation of the growth equation shows that

$$g^{**}_A > 0; \qquad g^{**}_B < 0; \qquad g^{**}_C < 0; \qquad g^{**}_D < 0.$$

Like the value-maximising growth rate g^*, the growth-maximising growth rate g^{**} is heavily dependent on A and C, but only marginally dependent on B, confirming that the optimal growth rate is basically determined by a trade-off between the profitability of individual markets, as measured by A, and decreasing returns to growth, as measured by C. Unlike the value-maximising growth rate, however, the growth-maximising growth rate is independent of the cost of capital r. The capital constraint operates through dividend commitments, D, instead. The higher is D, the less profit the firm can retain to finance set-up costs and entrepreneurial management, and hence the lower is the growth of the firm.

In view of the similarity in the results for value-maximisation and growth-maximisation, the rest of the chapter considers just the value-maximising case.

11.3 A simple multinational analogue of the Penrose model

In considering not simply the growth of the firm but also its internationalisation, it is important to note that Penrose discusses three main dimensions along which a firm can expand. While the main focus of her discussion is on product diversification, she also considers vertical integration along the supply chain, and geographical diversification which can turn the firm into an MNE. Geographical diversification can be either horizontal – the typical case where technology transfer is involved – or vertical, as exemplified by 'resource seeking' investments. In our model, as in Buckley and Casson (1976), the uni-national firm is simply a special case of a multinational firm.

Each of these three main dimensions has further sub-dimensions. Diversification can involve either different varieties of the same product, or wholly distinct products, or some combination of the two. New product varieties may substitute obsolete varieties, or complement existing varieties, or be independent of each other. Vertical integration can be either forwards – into wholesaling or retailing, for example – or backwards – into component manufacture or raw material supply. Vertical integration can also be applied to the product development process, in which the firm not only undertakes product development but integrates backwards into basic research, or forwards into quality control and warranty repairs. Finally, geographical diversification can be either local, inter-regional, international or global, depending on whether it spans regional boundaries or national boundaries, or covers the entire world.

With so many different dimensions, it is useful to focus the discussion on a single representative case. Vertical integration is therefore ignored; it is assumed that the firm concentrates on just a single stage of production. It innovates an expanding range of products which are then introduced to different national markets.

Suppose to begin with that each new product is launched simultaneously in every national market. Thus the 'markets' into which the growing firm diversifies are, in effect, global markets. While the introduction of products is sequential, their introduction to individual local markets is not.

The fact that the firm serves global markets does not necessarily make it a multinational, however. The firm only becomes a multinational if its location strategy involves production in more than one country. The firm could be simply a specialised exporter which serves all its markets from the same host-country location.

In the Penrose model, an exporter can become a multinational in two possible ways. It can serve some markets through local production, and therefore become multinational as a result of its geographical expansion; alternatively, it can serve each global market from a single plant, but locate different plants in different countries, in which case multinationality is driven by product expansion instead. Multinationality driven by geographical expansion is a response to obstacles to transport and trade connected, for example, with the perishability of the product, or the need for face-to-face delivery – while multinationality driven by product expansion exploits comparative advantage by specialising the production of each product on the location best endowed with the relevant non-tradable inputs.

When geography is the driver, the firm becomes a multinational while still a single-product firm, but when the product is the driver it becomes a multinational only when it becomes a multi-product firm. These two effects are combined in globally rationalised production, in which plants in different countries serve not only local markets but act as export platforms for particular products in the range. Case study evidence suggests that single-product firms can be multinational, which suggests that geography is a more important driver than the product. However, the interaction of the geographical dimension and the product dimension is relevant to the analysis of the globally rationalised firm.

A more refined approach to geographical expansion interprets market entry as a sequential process. Instead of entering all national markets simultaneously, the firm enters them one at a time. The basic unit of analysis is no longer an integrated global market for a product but a particular national market for a particular product. The firm expands sequentially by first introducing one product into one market, and then introducing another product into another market, and so on.

Sequential entry into national markets for individual products can be effected in several ways. Firstly, the firm can expand initially in the product dimension, selling entirely in the home market, and then, once a critical number of products have been introduced, expand the product range into foreign markets. A second method is the converse of this: the firm expands first in the product dimension and then in the geographical dimension. The firm launches its first product into a set of key markets and only introduces its second product once this process is complete, the second product is introduced into the same set of markets and then the third product, and so on. This process is illustrated in Table 11.1a, where the sequence of entry is indicated by the numerical sequence applied to the individual cells.

A more plausible process is one in which products are innovated into the home market while they are in the process of diffusing through international markets. To begin with, the firm introduces its first product into the home market. If this product is successful, it introduces the product to a foreign market in the second period and, shortly afterwards, introduces a second product to its home market to capitalise on its initial success. Next, the first product is introduced to a third country, then the second product is introduced to the second country, and then a new product is introduced to the home market, and so on. The process may be termed as 'innovation-diffusion' process, since products are innovated at the same time that established products are diffusing into national markets. This process is illustrated in Table 11.1b.

The innovation-diffusion model also predicts that the rate of introduction of new products into any given market will decline over time, even though the firm is growing at a constant proportional rate. This is because the firm is extending the geographical scope of its markets as it grows. Each stage of growth is marked by the entry of a product into another national market, rather than the innovation of another new product per se. Thus the rate of product innovation slows as the number of national markets served increases; more effort goes into diffusion, and less into innovation.

The results generated by the innovation-diffusion model seem to be broadly consistent with evidence about the growth of MNEs in the second half of the twentieth century. Furthermore, the general approach is consistent with both Vernon's product cycle theory of foreign direct investment (Vernon 1966), and with the Uppsala theory of sequential internationalisation (Johanson/Vahlne 1977), although it goes beyond both. A further development of this approach is presented below.

Table 11.1a   Sequential entry into national markets with a fixed product range

	Location 1	Location 2	Location 3	Location 4
Product 1	1	5	9	13
Product 2	2	6	10	14
Product 3	3	7	11	15
Product 4	4	8	12	16

Table 11.1b   The innovation diffusion model sequential product innovation with overlapping sequential local entry

	Location 1	Location 2	Location 3	Location 4
Product 1	1	2	4	7
Product 2	3	5	8	11
Product 3	6	9	12	14
Product 4	10	13	15	16

11.4   A contrast between the Penrose model and that of Buckley and Casson

A potential weakness of the Penrose approach to multinationals is that the growth of the firm is driven by product diversification rather than by technological innovation. Empirical evidence points to the crucial role of technology in stimulating the growth of multinational firms. Early post-war US foreign direct investment, for example, was heavily concentrated in technology-intensive industries.

Although Penrose recognised that large firms invested significantly in R&D, she regarded their entrepreneurial capabilities as the main driver of their growth. She believed that there were abundant opportunities for discovering new markets, irrespective of whether R&D was undertaken or not. The main constraint on the growth of the firm was not the need to finance expensive R&D but the difficulty of expanding the firm at a sufficient rate to exploit all of the opportunities available.

In fact, decreasing returns to R&D provides a simple explanation of how the growth of a technology-intensive firm is constrained. When market opportunities drive firm growth, as in Penrose, then decreasing returns to entrepreneurship and management will constrain growth, while if technological opportunities drive the firm's growth then decreasing returns to R&D will constrain growth instead. There is, therefore, a logical parallel between the limits to growth identified by Penrose and the limits to growth associated with R&D.

An emphasis on R&D also helps to explain why related diversifications are generally more successful than unrelated diversifications in sustaining the growth of the multinational firm. If new products are generated sequentially from a single integrated programme of research, then the cost of generating any one product can be reduced by using knowledge spillovers from other products. Furthermore, products generated in this way may also be related in terms of the materials or components from which they are produced, thereby generating supply chain economies once they are in production. Although relatedness can also be achieved through 'bundling' products for sale, or marketing different products to the same group of customers, there is little doubt that the technological relatedness of different products has been a significant factor in boosting the profits and growth of modern multinational firms.

As it happens, the link between R&D and the growth of the firm was an important part of the model of the multinational enterprise developed by Buckley and Casson (1976). This was no accident; we introduced internalisation theory in order to explain 'pattern of growth' of the MNE in terms of 'a long-run theory' (p. 59), and we concluded our exposition with 'a mathematical model of the growth of the research-intensive firm' (p. 62). Unlike the later work of Dunning (1977), our model did not assume that the firm possessed a given ownership advantage. Instead, it considered the generation of a stream of ownership advantages from a continuous process of R&D. The internalisation of the intangible knowledge flows generated by R&D established a link between the steady state *level* of R&D and the steady state *rate of growth* of production and sales. Just as in Penrose's model, decreasing returns to the growth of the management team restrict the rate of product diversification by an entrepreneurial firm, and hence limit its rate of growth. So in the Buckley and Casson model decreasing returns to the scale of R&D restrict the rate of product innovation by a technology-intensive firm, and hence limit its rate of growth. The similarity between the two theories is not surprising, since Buckley and Casson traced back their ideas, not only to Coase (1937) but also to Penrose (1959) (p. 36, fn2).

According to Buckley and Casson, R&D activity has a U-shaped average cost curve. This results from the interplay of fixed costs and increasing variable costs. R&D incurs fixed costs due to the indivisible nature of laboratory facilities and the need for a critical mass of different specialists to be combined within a research team. Beyond a certain scale, however, decreasing returns set in because the advantages of further specialisation diminish and the team becomes increasingly difficult to

Table 11.2   The Buckley and Casson model: Sequential product innovation with simultaneous local entry

	Location 1	Location 2	Location 3	Location 4
Product 1	1=	1=	1=	1=
Product 2	2=	2=	2=	2=
Product 3	3=	3=	3=	3=
Product 4	4=	4=	4=	4=

manage, as individual researchers start to pursue independent lines of research unrelated to the rest of the team. By contrast, production and marketing operate with constant average costs.

Although Buckley and Casson relate decreasing returns in R&D to the *level* of R&D activity, the output of R&D activity determines the *rate of growth* of the final output of the firm. Thus an analysis of levels in R&D translates naturally into an analysis of growth in terms of output.

In the Buckley and Casson model, R&D generates a continuous stream of new products, each of higher quality than the previous one. Once introduced, each product is sold immediately in a global market; the pattern of internationalisation is summarised in Table 11.2. National markets are highly segmented, on account of transport costs and tariffs, and so each national market is serviced by wholly owned production and distribution subsidiaries. In each market the firm enjoys market power, derived from the novelty of its product line, and so faces a downward-sloping demand curve. Both the scale of demand, and its price-elasticity, vary between markets, as do average costs.

The firm maximises shareholder value, which is equal to the value of the aggregate profit generated by the local markets, net of the costs of R&D. Sustained R&D leads to continuous improvement in quality, and this in turn maintains steady growth of demand in each market. The higher the level of R&D, the faster is the rate of quality improvement, the faster the growth of demand and aggregate profit, and the higher the cost of R&D. The optimal growth of the firm is determined by a trade-off between growing revenues on the one hand, and the higher costs of R&D on the other. This trade-off determines the rate of optimal level of R&D activity. This in turn determines the rate of quality improvement, and hence the rate of growth of output.

Each incremental improvement in quality yields the same incremental increase in profits. The discounted value of this additional profit is traded off against the marginal cost of generating the improvement in quality.

The value-maximising strategy equates the marginal value of an increase in quality to its marginal cost, and determines a rate of quality improvement which is constant over time and corresponds to a steady state level of expenditure on R&D. The optimal growth rate is an absolute rather than proportional rate, so that the growth of sales is linear in time.

The greater the optimal rate of growth, the lower are marginal costs – i.e. the lower the salary costs of researchers – and the more slowly decreasing to returns to the scale of research set in. Growth is also greater the higher the marginal value of quality improvement – i.e. the more intensive the demand for the product, the lower its price-elasticity, and the lower the cost of capital.

In both the Buckley and Casson and Penrose models, the firm faces a trade-off between faster exploitation of market opportunities on the one hand and 'costs of growth' on the other. In both cases, costs of growth increase because the productivity of human resources declines as the rate of growth they are required to sustain increases. But there are key differences too.

- In Penrose's model it is the declining productivity of the management team that limits growth, whereas in the Buckley and Casson model it is the declining productivity of scientific researchers instead.
- In Penrose's model declining productivity results from the continuous expansion of the size of the management team whereas in the Buckley and Casson model declining productivity arises from sustaining a constant rate of R&D above the scale which minimises average cost.
- The innovations made by the firm are different too. In the Penrose model, the firm diversifies into new markets, while in the Buckley and Casson model it upgrades the quality of a given product.
- Although the firm introduces new products in both cases, in the first case the new products are independent of existing products, whereas in the second case each new product replaces the previous version of the same product.

A weakness of the Buckley and Casson model is that it cannot be used to analyse the sequential nature of international expansion. Sequential entry is predicted only when new markets emerge as a result of the liberalisation of access, or a 'takeoff' in local demand stimulated by economic growth. Thus while the Buckley and Casson model can be applied to the entry into 'emerging markets' in 'transition economies', it cannot be applied to sequential entry into mature and accessible markets. It is shown below that this weakness of the Buckley and Casson model is easily overcome.

11.5   A reconciliation between the two models

The question arises as to how far it is possible to integrate the Buckley and Casson approach with the basic Penrose model. This section presents a model which attempts to do just this. It is a two-dimensional generalisation of the one-dimensional Penrose model presented in section 11.2.

The model focuses on a distinctive type of firm, founded by a Schumpeterian entrepreneur (Schumpeter 1934). The entrepreneur has identified a technological opportunity to generate a range of new products. The entrepreneur is not an inventor but an innovator; he recognises not merely a technological possibility but also a latent demand for products that embody the new technology that he plans to exploit. Although product demand is global, national markets are spatially self-contained, and so each needs to be entered separately.

Having identified an opportunity for technological innovation, two further stages are involved in bringing a product to market. The first stage is R&D and the second is market entry – first into the home market and then into foreign markets. Multinationality arises because each national market is sourced by local production.

Each stage involves its own distinctive form of sequential diversification. The firm can only develop one product at a time, and each product can only be introduced into a new market by entering one country at a time. The two stages proceed in parallel. While R&D generates a sequence of product innovations, market entry takes each product and introduces it to a sequence of national markets. Unlike the growth-diffusion model presented above, two separate sets of resources are involved – a team of researchers responsible for product innovation and a team of managers responsible for market entry. Each process is sequential because this arrangement makes the best use of the human resources involved.

Because of the two dimensions, there are two different growth rates: one associated with a growth in the number of products, g_1 and the other associated with the growth in the number of national markets served, g_2. The two growth rates are distinct, but related: the growth of the product range can be chosen independently of the speed of internationalisation, and vice versa; however, conditions which favour faster growth in the product range normally favour faster internationalisation too.

Following the general principles of the Penrose model, it is assumed that the stock of products, x, introduced by the firm grows at a constant proportional rate, g, which is chosen by the firm. These products are generated exclusively by the firm's R&D; no technology is licensed in or out to other firms. It is assumed that the firm has already developed a prototype product by the time that it is founded, so that $x = 1$ and time $t = 0$. Thus

$$x = \exp{(g_1 t)}$$

as in the one-dimensional model. To further simplify the model, it is assumed that the prototype is not sold, so that all the firm's revenue and profit is attributable to its R&D.

The rate of product innovation depends upon the number of scientists employed in R&D. Employment in R&D is n_0. Each scientist receives a fixed salary s_0. There are constant returns to the scale of R&D; other things being equal, doubling the employment of scientists doubles the rate of new product generation. Due to the real costs of growth, however, the average productivity of scientists declines with the rate of growth of R&D activity; as a result, the real cost of scientific output is $a_0 g$. The parameter a_0 measures the labour-intensity of research – it reflects the interaction between the skills of the scientists and the technological opportunities available. Thus average research productivity is independent of scale, but inversely related to growth.

When growing at rate g_1 with a cumulative stock of products x, the firm must introduce new products at a rate $g_1 x$. With real labour cost $a_0 g_1$, the firm requires $a_0 g_1^2 x$ scientists. When scientific labour is the sole input to R&D, the cost of R&D is $C g_1^2 x$, where $C = a_0 s_0$.

It is assumed that each product, once produced, has the property of a public good within the firm. This has a very specific meaning in the present context; namely that, once developed, product technology can be transferred to any country in the world. Technology is not an absolutely pure public good, because there is a positive cost of transfer to each national market. But it is a public good in the sense that a product does not need to be reinvented for every national market. In other words, R&D generates global products rather than products that can be sold only in a single national market.

National markets vary in size. A large market has a large demand for all products. The operating profit generated by each product in each national market is directly proportional to the size of the market. Each product in each market earns a uniform rate of profit per unit size, z.

Entry into each market requires an input of managerial labour which is directly proportional to market size, y. No learning takes place in the 'roll out' of the product from one market to the next, and so the cost of entry is independent of the number of markets already entered.

All markets are entered at the same speed, independent of their size. The speed of entry is chosen by the firm. Fast entry is effected by employing a large number of managers for a short period of time, and slow entry by employing a smaller number of managers for a longer period of time. No learning takes place with regard to product innovation in a given market, so that the same entry same cost is incurred irrespective of how many previous products have been introduced to the market.

Speeding up entry expedites internationalisation, by bringing forward the time of entry into subsequent markets. It also reduces the productivity of managerial labour, however. With a speed of entry h, total managerial input is a_1yh, where a_1 is a productivity parameter. When managers receive a salary s_1 the cost of entering a market at speed h incurs a management resource cost a_1s_1yh.

The optimal strategy for the firm, given a positive uniform rate of profit and a commitment to sequential entry, is to enter the largest market first, and then to enter subsequent markets in descending order of size. It is assumed, therefore, that entry is sequenced in descending order of market size.

The precise speed of market entry chosen depends upon the firm's cost of capital, r. Once the optimal speed of market entry has been determined, using the method described below, the value, B, of a new innovated product can be calculated. This value is equal to the discounted value of the operating profits generated by the growing global market for the product less the discounted value of the costs of product launch in each of the national markets. Since new products are introduced at a rate gx, the value of the output from R&D is Bg_1x.

The overall value of the firm is therefore

$$v = \int_0^\infty \exp(-rt)(Bg_1x - Cg_1^2x)\, dt = (Bg_1 - Cg_1^2)/(r - g_1).$$

The value v is finite if and only if $g_1 < r$. The first order condition for a maximum of v is a quadratic equation, which has real roots if and only if $B < Cr$. The condition for positive profit is $B > Cg_1$, and both are satisfied simultaneously only when $g_1 < r$, i.e. when the firm has finite value.

Only the smaller root satisfies this latter condition; this is also the root that fulfils the second order condition for a maximum. Optimal growth is therefore

$$g_1 = r(1 - (1 - (B/Cr))^{1/2}).$$

It can be seen that the optimal rate of growth increases with the value of new products, B and decreases with the costs of R&D, C. For a given B, g_1 is a decreasing function of r, a high cost of capital reduces the optimal rate of growth. To complete the solution of the model it is necessary to determine B.

11.6 The optimal speed of internationalisation

Consider the marketing of a representative new product which has just been developed through R&D. A sequential process of internationalisation process can be modelled in the following way.

It is assumed that there is infinite number of national markets, the largest of which has size y^+ and the smallest size zero. They are ranked in descending order of size by a continuous index m. It is assumed for simplicity that market size decreases exponentially with rank, such that the size of the mth market is

$$y(m) = y^+ \exp(-bm)$$

where y^+ is the size of the largest market, and b is a parameter that measures the rate at which size decreases with respect to rank. The parameter b indicates the inequality of market sizes, with a value close to zero indicating relative equality and a high value indicating extreme inequality.

Because there is an infinity of national markets, the internationalisation process continues indefinitely, thereby allowing the firm to expand continuously in the geographical dimension. At the same time, the decreasing size of successive markets means that the total size of the global market remains finite.

By the time the mth market has been reached, sales of the product have cumulated to

$$Y(m) = (y^+/b)(1 - \exp(-bm))$$

and so, as globalisation proceeds, total market size converges exponentially on the 'saturation level' of the global market, y/b. The size of the global market is greater the greater the size of the largest market, y^+, and the lower the inequality in market size, b.

The speed of market entry is measured by the rate at which the rank of the newest market advances over time. Since the speed of entry, h, is the same for every market,

$$m = ht.$$

Cumulative market size converges on the saturation level at a rate bh:

$$Y(t) = (y^*/b)(1 - \exp(-bht)).$$

Because markets are entered in order of decreasing size, the proportional rate of growth of the market, g_2, diminishes over time, as a higher proportion of the global market is served:

$$g_2 = bh((y/bY) - 1).$$

As noted earlier, the cost of entry into each market is proportional to its size. If the cost of entry were independent of size, it would soon become uneconomic to enter the smallest markets, and so a rational firm would terminate internationalisation at some point before the global market was saturated. If the firm persisted beyond this point, it would incur significant costs for little benefit, and the consequent drive to minimise these costs would distort the globalisation strategy.

Given earlier assumptions, the number of markets expands at a rate h, and so expenditure on market entry at any time t is

$$c_1 = a_1 s_1 y h^2 = a_1 s_1 h^2 y^+ \exp(-bht).$$

Net cash flow is $zY - c_1$ and so the present value of the product at the time of its launch, u, is

$$u = \int_0^\infty (zY - c_1)dt = (y^+/b)[(z/r) - [(z + a_1 b s_1 h^2)/(r + bh)]].$$

The first term, y^+/b, measures the size of the global market and scales the rest of the expression. The next term, z/r, is the capitalised value of the profit stream from a market of unit size. The remaining two terms – z and $a_1 brs_1 h^2$ – are deductions from profit, and both are capitalised using a rate of discount $r + bh$. This rate of discount reflects the gradual nature of the build up to the saturation of the global market, which is governed by the product of the inequality parameter, b, and the speed of market entry, h. The first term reflects the deferral of profit and the second reflects the cost of market entry.

The first order condition for a maximum of u generates a quadratic equation for the optimal speed of market entry, h. One of the roots of the quadratic is positive and the other negative. The second order conditions show that the positive root corresponds to a maximum, h^*:

$$h^* = (r/b)((1 + (b/a_1 s_1 r^2))^{1/2} - 1).$$

It can be seen that speed, h^*, increases with profit, z, and decreases with inequality of market size, b, the real cost of management time, a_1, and the salary level, s_1. It also increases with respect to the cost of capital, r: the higher the rate of discount, the more important it is to generate profits from the smaller markets as early as possible. A faster speed translates into a higher rate of geographical growth, $g_2{}^*$.

Substituting the optimal value of h into the valuation of the product gives the optimal value of the product at the time of its development as

$$B = (y^+z/br)(1 - 2(a_1s_1r^2/bz)^{1/2})$$

whence the optimal rate of growth $g_1{}^*$ becomes

$$g_1{}^* = r(1 - (1 - (y^+z/a_0s_0br^2)(1 - 2(a_1s_1r^2/bz))^{1/2}).$$

It follows that growth is an increasing function of maximum market size, y^+, and profitability, z, and a decreasing function of the inequality of market size, b, the real cost of researchers, a_0, the real cost of management, a_1, and the respective salary levels, s_0, s_1.

A high cost of capital, r, reduces the optimal rate of growth, $g_1{}^*$. The present value of the prospective revenues is reduced – especially the revenues generated by the smaller markets which are the last to be entered. Although a higher cost of capital encourages internationalisation to be speeded up, this speed-up is at the expense of higher entry costs, which further reduce the net value of the net profit stream. Thus a higher r reduces the value of B, and thereby reduces the incentive for growth, $g_1{}^*$.

In its early phase of expansion the firm expands quickly in both the product and geographical dimensions, but gradually converges to an overall growth rate g_1 as the internationalisation process matures.

11.7 Synthesis

While Penrose's dismissal of scale effects is plausible in the context of many production processes, it is not particularly plausible where teams R&D is concerned. Researchers are often motivated by personal curiosity which leads them away from their intended line of research, while the introspective nature of research activity makes it difficult to monitor. Control loss is therefore a genuine concern in large R&D teams. Furthermore, the notion that all research facilities have to start small and then grow as fast as possible is difficult to reconcile with the way that many research establishments are founded on a substantial scale. Many successful firms are able to grow large without continually expanding the sizes of their research facilities.

But while the notion of incremental expansion does not fit well with research, it fits much better with the internationalisation process, although even here the speed with which some firms internationalise has been quite high. Nevertheless the notion that the speed of internationalisation is constrained by the difficulty of enlarging the management team sufficiently fast is more plausible than an assumption that internationalisation is instantaneous.

It appears, therefore, that while the Penrose model offers a superior account of internationalisation, the Buckley and Casson model offers a superior account of innovation and R&D. This suggests that the two models should be combined by taking the analysis of internationalisation in section 11.6 and combining it with the approach to innovation summarised in section 11.4.

Following the Buckley and Casson model, let the costs of R&D be

$$C = C_0 + C_1 q^2$$

where C_0 is the fixed cost of the R&D facility, $C_2 = a_0 s_0$ a parameter governing variable costs, and q is the output of R&D. Output is measured by the rate of product innovation that it sustains. The cost function corresponds to a U-shaped average cost curve with a minimum at $q = (C_0 / C_2)^{1/2}$.

The value of an innovation exploited through an optimal internationalisation strategy is B, as derived above. The value of the firm is

$$v = \int_0^\infty \exp(-rt)(Bq - C_0 - C_2 q^2)dt = (Bq - C_0 - C_2 q^2)/r.$$

The first order condition for a maximum of value determines the optimal rate of research output, q^*

$$q^* = B/2C_2.$$

The second order conditions for a maximum are always satisfied. Substituting for B expresses q^* as an increasing function of market size, y^+, the profitability of sales, z, and a decreasing function of the inequality of market size, b, the real costs of R&D and market entry, a_0, a_1, the salaries of scientists and managers, s_0, s_1, and the cost of capital, r:

$$q^* = (y^+ z/2a_0 s_0 br)(1 - 2(a_1 s_1 r^2/bz)^{1/2}).$$

In contrast to the exponential growth of the Penrosian model, the firm now grows in the long run at a constant absolute rate q^*. Sales grow faster in the early stages of internationalisation, but converge on this level as the internationalisation process matures. Since the rate of growth is constant in absolute terms, it declines in relative terms, which is consistent with the lifetime growth pattern of a typical firm.

This model is simpler than the pure Penrosian model and offers a more realistic account of the R&D process. Because it is simpler, if offers greater scope for further development, and can therefore be recommended as a starting point for further research on this subject.

11.8   Conclusion

This chapter has shown that Penrose's *Theory of the Growth of the Firm* provides a tractable formal model which has important implications for the strategy of MNEs. Its analysis of the appropriate modes of internationalisation can be integrated with a satisfying account of the trade-off between (product) diversification and foreign market penetration. The account of speed of entry is an advance on current theories of internationalisation including 'stages' and product cycle based models. There is much profitable work to be done in extending Penrose's implicit model of multinational enterprise. For now, we can recognise the contribution of Penrose's book to the analysis of geographical expansion patterns, sequential decision making and learning in the MNE as key components of international business theory.

Notes

The authors would like to thank Christos Pitelis for his comments on earlier versions of this chapter.

References

Barney, J. B. 1985. Strategic Factor Markets. *Management Science*, 32, 10, pp. 1231–41.

Baumol, W. J. 1967. *Business Behavior, Value and Growth*. New York: Harcourt, Brace, Jovanovich.

Best, M. H. and Humphries, J. 2003. Edith Penrose: A Feminist Economist? *Feminist Economics*, 9, 1, pp. 47–73.

Buckley, P. J. and Casson, M. 1976. *The Future of the Multinational Enterprise*. London: Macmillan.

Buckley, P. J. and Casson, M. 2010. Entrepreneurship and the Growth of the Firm: An Extension of Penrose's Theory, in M. Casson, Entrepreneurship: Theory, Networks, History, Cheltenham, Edward Elgar, 60–78.

Caves, R. E. and Porter, M. E. 1977. From Entry Barriers to Mobility Barriers: Conjectural Variations and Contrived Deterrence to New Competition. *Quarterly Journal of Economics*, 91, 3, pp. 241–62.

Coase, R. H. 1937. The Nature of the Firm. *Economica*, 4, 4, pp. 387–405.

Demsetz, H. 1973. Industrial Structure, Market Rivalry, and Public Policy. *Journal of Law and Economics*, 16. I, pp. 1–10.

Demsetz, H. 1982. *Efficiency, Competition and Policy*. Oxford: Basil Blackwell.

Dunning, J. H. 1977. Trade, Location of Economic Activity and the Multinational Enterprise: The Search for an Eclectic Approach, in B. Ohlin, P-O Hesselborn and P. M. Wijkman (eds) *The International Allocation of Economic Activity*. London: Macmillan.

Dunning, J. H. 2003. The Contribution of Edith Penrose to International Business Scholarship. *Management International Review*, 43, 1, pp. 3–19.

Foss, N. J. 1997. *Resources, Firms and Strategies*. Oxford: Oxford University Press.

Foss, N. J. 2002. Edith Penrose, Economics and Strategic Management, in C. N. Pitelis (ed.) *The Growth of the Firm: The Legacy of Edith Penrose*. Oxford: Oxford University Press.

Johanson, J. and Vahlne, J. E. 1977. The Internationalisation Process of the Firm: A Model of Knowledge Development and Increasing Market Commitments. *Journal of International Business Studies*, 8, 1, pp. 23–32.

Kor, Y. Y. and Mahoney, J. T. 2004. Edith Penrose's (1959) Contributions to the Resource-based View of Strategic Management. *Journal of Management Studies*, 41, 1, pp. 183–91.

Lippman, S. A. and Rumelt, R. P. 1982. Uncertain Immutability: An Analysis of Inter-firm Differences in Efficiency under Competition. *Bell Journal of Economics*, 13, 3, pp. 418–38.

Lockett, A. and Thompson, S. 2004. Edith Penrose's Contributions to the Resource-based View: An Alternative Perspective. *Journal of Management Studies*, 41, 1, pp. 193–203.

Marris, R. L. 1964. *Economic Theory of Managerial Capitalism*. London: Macmillan.

Penrose, E. T. 1959. *The Theory of the Growth of the Firm*. Oxford: Blackwell.

Penrose, E. T. 1960. The Growth of the Firm: A Case Study: The Hercules Powder Company. *The Business History Review*, 34, 1, pp. 1–20.

Penrose, P. and Pitelis, C. N. 2002. Edith Elura Tilton Penrose: Life Contribution and Influence, in C. N. Pitelis (ed.), *The Growth of the Firm: The Legacy of Edith Penrose*. Oxford: Oxford University Press.

Peteraf, M. A. 1993. The Cornerstones of Competitive Advantage: A Resource-based View. *Strategic Management Journal*, 14, 3, pp. 179–91.

Pitelis, C. N. (ed.) 2002. *The Growth of the Firm: The Legacy of Edith Penrose*. Oxford: Oxford University Press.

Pitelis, C. N. 2002. Edith Penrose and the Resource-based View of (International) Business Strategy. *International Business Review*, 13, 4, pp. 523–32.

Rugman, A. M. and Verbeke, A. 2002. Edith Penrose's Contribution to the Resource-Based View of Strategic Management. *Strategic Management Journal*, 23, 7, pp. 769–80.

Rugman, A. M. and Verbeke, A. 2004. A Final Word on Edith Penrose. *Journal of Management Studies*, 41, 1, pp. 205–17.

Schumpeter, J. A. 1934. *The Theory of Economic Development*. Cambridge, MA: Harvard University Press.

Teece, D. J. 1980. Economics of Scope and the Scope of the Enterprise. *Journal of Economic Behavior and Organization*, 1, 3, pp. 223–33.

Vernon, R. 1966. International Investment and International Trade in the Product Cycle. *Quarterly Journal of Economics*, 80, 2, pp. 190–207.

Index

Bold page numbers indicate figures and tables.

acquisitions   12
adaptation, to local conditions   122
adversity   42–3
advertising
  and self-control   217–18
  and sex   214–15
  television   231–2
Africa, failure of technology
    transfer   154
aggregation, international business
    (IB) system   261–3
aggression   44
agricultural processing   78
alliances, political   100
Altber, A. A.   25–6
alternative strategies, key
    determinants of cost   **129**
altruism   221–2
alumni networks   22
ambiguity, of control   14–15, 16–17
analysis, new techniques   167–70
Arpan, J. S.   173
Asian countries, flexibility   157
Asian products, price
    advantage   153–4
assumptions, explicit and
    implicit   150
asymmetry   120
autonomy, of preferences   43

behaviour, modelling   118
bluffing   219–20, 221
border controls, relaxation   12
bounded rationality   49
broadcasting   230–1
Buckley and Casson model *see*
    internalisation, theory of
Buckley, P. J.   120, 134, 150, 152,
    170, 179, 180, 240, 279
business, links with universities   159

business schools   22
buy-back   59

capacity, rationalisation of   13–14
capital costs, sharing   15
capital flows   5–6
  factors encouraging   12
capitalisation rates   26
capitalism
  and civilisation   234
  and manipulation   221–2
  moral ambiguities   208–9, 219–22,
    227–8
  moral excesses   222
  and religion   206–7
  religious context   207
Casson, M. C.   120, 134, 150, 152,
    169, 170, 179, 180, 181,
    240, 279
Caves, R. E.   147–9
change
  costs of   278–9
  recognising   162–3
Chapman, M.   150
cheap labour   12
cheating   18, 44–7, 60, 62, 164
Cheung, S. N. S.   7
civilisation   234
Coase, Ronald   2, 4, 7–8
cohesion, private firms   21–2
collectivism   222
collusion   16, 60, 62, 120, 122
combinatorial complexity   242
  approaches to   243
  in IB system   259
commitment
  building   61–3
  to cooperation   50–2
  cooperation and trust   48–9
  to group   84

commodity trade, globalisation
        226–9
communication   17–23
communications
    advances in   12
    globalisation   230–3
    and prosperity   75–6
comparative advantage   157–8
comparative development   95
competence   17–18
    and innovation   104, 106
    technological   128
competition, social groups   22
competitive advantage   157
competitive individualism   75
    and voluntary association   81–4
competitiveness
    national   156–8
    restoring   158–60
    and tariff   159
complexity   240–1
    concepts of   242–5
    or confusion   241–2
complexity theory   242
comunitarianism   164–5
confusion, mistaken for
        complexity   241–2
consultation   163
consumers, protection   220
Contractor, F. J.   179
contracts
    enforcement   220
    respect for   82
control, ambiguity of   14–15, 16–17
cooperation
    commitment and trust   48–9
    commitment to   50–2
    concept of   41–2
    as input and output   48–9
    joint ventures   62
coordination
    defining   42
    under duress   42–3
    extrafirm   44
    interfirm   43–4
    selection of method   7
costs
    of doing business abroad   26
    reducing   163

costs of growth   279
creative destruction   72
credibility problems   46, 47
cultural engineering   169–70
culture
    and communication   17
    corporate   97, 115
    dependence of IJVs   130
    development and MNEs   94–5
    divergence and similarity   18
    effect of spillovers   91
    entrepreneurial   68, 73–4, 116
    and entry factors   180–1
    and geography   75–6
    homogenisation   86
    inhibiting development   80
    and innovation   115–16
    joint ventures   63–4
    low-trust   233
    multinational enterprise (MNE)
        operations   90–3
currency
    maintaining value   82
    unified and multiple   26
cyber-communities   232–3

Darwin, Charles   222–3
de-layering   156, 166–7
debt, toleration   82
decision making   249–52
decision trees   251–2, **252, 255**
decisions
    deferring   252–3, 254, 257–8
    timing of   168
deglomeration   227
demand, rate of growth   37
deregulation, domestic capital
        markets   12
development
    comparative   95
    culture and MNEs   94–5
    global   86–90
    process   73–6
    regional differences   69
diffusion, knowledge and
        technology   153, 155
disaggregation   261
disappointments   43
discounting   32

discrete choice models 134
discretion, in decision-making 49
disequilibrium 243–4
disinformation 221
disintegration, of firms 109–10, 160, 165
distribution
   channels 108
   intermediate products 9
distrust *see* mistrust
diversification 285
divestment 169
division of labour 76–7, 81
   among product users 99–100
   information processing 168
domestic capital markets, deregulation 12
downsizing 166–7
dualism 80
   in development 85
   economic 92
Dunning, John 4, 98, 152, 154, 177, 205–6, 207, 236–7
dynamic modelling 147–9
dynamic optimisation 246

e-mail 232–3
early research 5–10
eclectic theory 205
economic growth, end of golden age 152–4
economic integration 99
economic methodology 118–19
economic models *see* models
economic power, agglomeration 226
economic success, factors in **74**
economic theory of joint ventures 52–3
economic theory of teams 168
economies of scale 79
education
   and development 73
   and innovation 115
empty threats 43
enclaves 71–2
entrepôt
   cultural determinants of potential 85

geographical determinants of potential 76–9
entrepreneurial culture 68, 73–4, 116
entrepreneurial theory 69
entrepreneurship
   high- and low-level 75
   internal 111–12, 164
   moral ambiguities 219
   steps to improve 159
entry factors, and market structure 181
equilibrium 152, 243
ethnocentrism 97
evolution, theory of 222–3
exchange controls, abolition 12
exchange of threats 181
expansion 286–8
expectations 43
exporting, costs 30
externality problem 42
extrafirm coordination 44

face-to-face contact 100
factor markets, internalising 108
factor movements, globalisation 226–9
familiarisation 32–3, 38
50:50 equity joint venture 52–3
final products, markets for 8
firm size
   theory of optimal 280–1
   as unlimited 279–80
firm-specific competitive advantage 178
flagship firms 14
flattening 164
flexibility
   analysing demand for 253
   boundaries of firm 160–2
   costs 164–5
   derived demand for 165
   external 156–8
   firm and location 165–6
   firm-specific competitive advantage 166–7
   interest in 155–6
   and internal organisation 162–4
   job evaluation 111
   joint ventures 130

flexibility—(*Continued*)
  labour market   159
  R&D   161–2
  of resources   103–4
  restoring   158–60
  significance   149
Flowers, E. B.   181
forbearance   44–5, 65
  incentive to   45–7
  joint ventures   61–2
  reciprocal   49
Fordism   96–7
foreign direct investment (FDI)
  costs   31
  deferring   36
  empirical studies   177
  historical development of
      theory   178–81
  new and repeat investors   38
  received analysis of optimal
      timing   25–6
foreign market entry
  costs of alternative strategies
      compared with profit
      norm   **191**
  defining strategy set   187
  deriving profit equations   187,
      190–2
  discussion of results of example
      model   198–9
  dominance relations   192–4
  entrant   182–4
  entry strategies and variants
      188–9, 190
  historical development of
      theory   178–81
  host country rival   184–6
  joint ventures   186–7
  overview of model   181–2
  propensity to adopt strategy   195–8
  properties of solution   194–5
  rational action   246–9
  research implications of
      model   199–200
  solution   **257**
  strategies for optimising
      dynamics   253–8
  strategy set   **256**
  transaction costs   269–70

formal understandings   46–7
formulation   103
frameworks, vs models   150–2
franchising   7
freedom, of entry and exit   82, 83–4
Freud, Sigmund   208, 213–14
fuzziness   241
fuzzy boundaries   156

game-playing   49–50
game theory   246
general systems theory   241
geographical diversification   285
geography
  and culture   75–6
  and group stability   83
  and resource use   73
global capitalism
  improving moral basis   210
  and moral order   206
  moral weakness   209
  protests   233–4
global development   86–90
global economy
  dynamics of innovation   131–2
  international division of labour
      in   10–14
  and international joint ventures
      (IJVs)   140–1
global systems, information
      distribution   271–2
global trading, geographical and
      cultural aspects   85–90
globalisation   10, 172
  benefits   227
  commodity trade and factor
      movements   226–9
  communications   230–3
  effects   209–10
  international joint ventures
      (IJVs)   123
  and nation state   229–30
  winners and losers   **228**
  and world production system
      12–13
God   80
golden age, end of   152–4
goods, processing   78–9
governments, and innovation   113

Graham, E. M.   181
greenfield expansion   12
  vs mergers and acquisitions
        179–80
growth
  costs of   279, 291
  drivers of   288
  and R&D   288–90
  steady state   280–1
  theory of optimal rate   280–1
  as unlimited   279–80
guilt   212–13, 228

habits   49
Hallen, L.   179
Hayek, Friedrich von A.   4
Heckscher-Olin trade theory   5–6
High Imperialism   226
Hirsh, S.   36
hollowing out   14
honesty   18
horizontal mergers   16
Hufbauer, G. C.   36
human nature   207–8
  Buckley and Casson view   216
  evaluation of modern views   215–19,
        235–6
  Freudian view   215, 216, 217
  libertarian view   216–17
  neoclassical economist view   216,
        217
  protestant ethic   210–15
  Protestantism   216
  religious systems   236
human resources   166
Hymer-Kindleberger theory   177
Hymer, S. H.   177
hyper-differentiation   99–100

ideologies, secular   223–5
immigration   92
imperialism   223, 224
implementation   103
inalienability, of property   82
individualism   221–2
  competitive   75, 81–4
  problems of   83
  and Protestantism   210
  social cost   234

informal understandings   46–7
information
  collecting   168, 249–51
  distribution   163, 271–2
  openness   113–14
  sharing   50–1, 169
information costs   246
information technology (IT),
        implications   100
infrastructure, Asian countries   153–4
innovation
  as challenge to management   98–100
  and culture   115–16
  dynamics   131–2
  and internalisation   106–8
  management   96
  personal responsibility   108–10
  process of   103–6
  promotion of   113
  requirements for success   104
  trust in management   97
innovation-diffusion process   287
institutional trust   19
integration   160, 165, 285
integrity   17
intellectual property rights   12–13
intelligence   81
intermediate products   8–9
internal entrepreneurship   111–12, 164
internal markets, open and
        closed   160–1
internal organisation, and
        flexibility   162–4
internal production, rationalisation
        of   13
internal relations   72
internalisation   179
  and innovation   106–8
  interdependence of decisions   11–12
  non-exclusive   14
internalisation factors, strategic
        choice   127–31
internalisation, theory of   2, 289
  alternative strategies   124–7
  central role of   4
  joint ventures   14
  ownership and location of
        facilities   263–4
  and social groups   19–20

international business (IB) system
  costs and benefits   264–5
  as global network   259–61
  levels of aggregation   261–3
  location   263–7
  location costs   **265**
  location strategy costs   **266**
  network research agenda   263–7
  schematic   **260**
international business theory, current
    challenges   239–41
international development   230
international division of labour
  determinants   2
  in global economy   10–14
international joint ventures (IJVs) *see
    also* joint ventures
  alternative strategies   124–7
  application of formal model   140–1
  choice of   170–2
  conclusions drawn from formal
    model   143–5
  conditions favouring   138
  costs and benefits of
    internalisation   131–2
  cultural dependence   130
  extensions of formal model   141–3
  formal model of selection   132–4
  generalisation of results of formal
    model   143
  and global economy   140–1
  globalisation   123
  performance   180
  research assumptions   118–19
  strategic choice   127–31
  typology   119–24
internationalisation, optimal
    speed   295–7
intrafirm coordination   43–4
investment
  locations   10
  timing of decisions   34
  and volatility   168–9
invisible hand   6

Japan
  innovation   114
  joint ventures   66
job evolution, vs job rotation   110–12

Johanson, J.   179, 287
joint ventures   14–17 *see also*
    international joint ventures (IJVs)
  adaptation to overseas market   58–9
  balancing vulnerability   60–1
  bilateral monopoly of intermediate
    product   57–8
  buy-back in R&D   59–60
  collusion   60, 62
  commitment   61–3
  component quality   58
  configuration of operation   54–6
  cooperation   41–2, 62
  economic power   56
  economic theory of   52–3
  50:50 equity joint venture   52–3
  hedging against price
    fluctuations   57
  historical precedents   15
  intercultural dimension   63–4
  interlocking   160–2
  international dimension   63–4
  Japanese   66
  lack of confidence in long-term
    arms-length contracts   56–8
  management training and
    technology transfer   59
  mistrust   60–1, 65
  motivation for internalisation   56
  networks   64–5
  operational integration   58
  overview   65–6
  quality uncertainty   58–60
  rationale   3
  reputation   61–3
  symmetrical configuration   55–6
  symmetrical positioning   54–5
  symmetrically motivated   52–3
  and technology acquisition   101–2
  vs wholly owned subsidiaries   180

Kindleberger, C. P.   177
Knight, Frank   3
knowledge
  flows   260
  internalising market   107
  pooling   15
  sharing   119
  tacit   128

Kreps, D. M. 169
Krugman, P. 151–2

labour force, flexibility 166
labour market, flexibility 159
language 17
law
  recourse to 45–6
  and trust 18–19
learning organisations 166
legal systems 22
legislation, and flexibility 158
less developed countries (LDCs)
  capital-intensive technologies 71
  enclaves 71–2
  foreign divestments 71
  heterogeneity 69
  import-substituting manufacturing
    investments 70
  key issues 70–3
  lack of individualism 82–3
  MNE staffing 90–1
  protectionism 72
  resource-based investments 71
  technology transfer 71
licensing 7, 124
  costs 30–1
limit price 28, 37
literacy 210
literature, strategy 100–2
livestock 79
local conditions, adaptation to 122
local knowledge 6–7
location
  costs 268
  economics of 26
  flexibility 165–6
  of IB facilities 263–7
  research activities 179
lock ins 244–5

management
  downsizing 163
  increasing pressures 98–100
managers, capabilities and
    competencies 166
Mandeville, Bernard 219
manipulation 51
  and capitalism 221–2

of consumers 208, 219–20
  moral 234–5
  television 232
manufacturing, international
    standards 12
marginal condition 35
maritime trade 85
market entry
  dynamic modelling 170–3
  models 148
market forces 6
market imperfections 7–8
market servicing decision
  application of simple model
    30–2
  complexity 38–9
  determinants 26
  extensions of simple model 32–3
  simple model 26–30
market servicing, with set-up
    costs 33–6
market size, and volatility 134–40
market structure
  and entry factors 181
  opening up 99
mass media 235
matrix management 101
membership organisations 20, 21
mergers 124
mergers and acquisitions 13–14
  vs greenfield ventures 179–80
migration 12, 91–2
mineral processing 78
mission 84
mistrust 65, 102
  joint ventures 60–1
misunderstandings 17
modelling 118, 119 *see also*
    international joint ventures
    (IJVs)
  example of dynamic 170–3
  IJV selection 132–4
models
  applications 150–1
  overview 147–9
  static 147–9
  vs frameworks 150–2
modernisation 68–9
monitoring 162–3

moral ambiguities, capitalism 208–9, 219–22
moral decline, antecedents 222–6
moral hazard 130
moral leadership 215
moral order, and global capitalism 206
moral systems 23
  and individualism 84
  and MNEs 93
multi-component design 99
multilevel analysis 1–2
multinational enterprise (MNE)
  cultural aspects 90–3
  fundamental rationale 7–8
  heterogeneity 69
  nature of 5–10
  simple structure of early companies 13
  social consequences 92–3
multinationality, drivers of 286–8
multiple currencies 26
mutual fund effect 52
mutual insurance 130

nation state, and globalisation 229–30
national champions 153
national markets, sequential entry 286–8
net present value (NPV) 34–5
network firms 14
networking events 20–1
networks 160–2
  and complexity 240–1
  in IB system 259–61
  and information 272–4
  joint ventures 64–5
neurosis 213–14
neutrality 44
new institutional economics 18–19, 23
newly industrialising countries 13
non-equity arrangements 52
non-exclusive internalisation 14
non-production activities 179
non-profit organisations 21

oligopolistic reaction 181
opportunism 18
opportunities, exploiting 74–5

optimisation 152
organic complexity 242–3
organisational behaviour, modelling 273
ownership
  of IB facilities 263–4
  optimising patterns 267–71

partner selection 180
partners, switching 131–2
patent
  as capital asset 25–6
  protection 8
  rights 128
path-dependency 169, 244
Pearce, R. D. 179
Penrose, Edith *see also* theory of the growth of the firm
  overview 277–8
  view of firm 279
personal integrity 164–5
personal responsibility, and innovation 108–10
personal trust 19
pirating 153
Polanyi, M. 128
political alliances 100
political disruption 92
politics, populism 225–6
Pope, Alexander 207–8
populism 225–6
Porter, M. E. 151
ports 77–8
postmodernism 225
preferences, autonomy of 43
press and media 225–6
price advantage, Asian products 153–4
printing 210
private firms, social relationships 21–2
privatisation 158
processing 78–9
product cycle, post-war 38
product cycle theory 36, 177, 178, 287
  extensions 37–8
production
  intermediate products 9

joint ownership 123–4
systems view 81
production-sharing 59
products, flexibility 166
professional organisations 22–3
profit 132–4
profit equations 187, 190–2
profit maximisation hypothesis
    118
property, inalienability of 82
property rights 128
protestant ethic 210–15 *see also*
    Protestantism
Protestantism 208, 209 *see also*
    protestant ethic
    beliefs and attitudes 210–13
    human nature 216
    and individualism 210
psychic distance 179
public expenditure, East and
    West 153–4
public opinion 235
punishment, do-it-yourself 46

quality control, intermediate product
    markets 9
quality improvement 290–1

R&D
    collaboration 120, 122
    collaborative 62
    decentralisation 159
    flexibility 161–2
    and foreign distribution **270**
    and growth 288–90
    scale effects 297
rational action 118, 119, 150
    approach to modelling 240–1
    conclusions and
        recommendations 274
    decision making 249–50
    foreign market entry 246–9
    information collection 249–51
    and international business
        strategy 245–6
    and networks 273–4
    organisational behaviour 273
    under uncertainty 167–8
    uncertainty 247

rational analysis, and organic
    complexity 242–3
rationalisation
    of capacity 13–14
    of internal production 13
rationalism 222–3
rationality 211, 214–15
real option theory 246
    analysing demand for
        flexibility 253
    extensions 258–9
reciprocity 82–3
recruitment 166
    and social cohesion 21–2
regional hubs 172
regulation, mass media 235
regulatory environments, changes
    in 100
religion, and capitalism 206–7
religious systems 23, 80–1
    human nature 236
reputation, building 48, 49–50, 61–3
reputation effects 47–8
research
    and decision making 251–2, 254
    professionalisation and
        institutionalisation 98
research agenda, progressive 23–4
residual risk sharing 46
resources
    flexibility of 103–4
    obstacles to use 73–4
restructuring 10
    and joint ventures 16
reverse engineering 153
Richardson, George 4
ripple effects 155
risks, diversifying 15–16
routine, management 96–7

savings 214
scale effects 297
science, and morality 223, 225
scientific outlook 80–1
secular ideologies 223–5
secularisation 222
selection 103
self-control 208, 213–14, 228–9
    undermining 217–18

self-interest 44, 50, 152, 234
self-restraint *see* self-control
sequential entry 286–8, 291
sequential internationalisation 287
set-up costs
  optimal market servicing with 33–6
  transferring technology 36–7
sex 213
  and advertising 214–15
shocks 155
  modelling 167
sin 212–13
Smith, Adam 2, 4, 6, 219
social capital 21–2
social disruption 92
social groups 19–20
  competition 22
social networks, and
    organisations 272–4
social science
  position of international
      business 239–40
  views of human nature 235–6
social systems
  and global production systems 19
  globalisation and convergence
      22–3
socialism 209, 223, 224
sociobiology 217
source-country institutions, influence
    on performance 113–17
spillovers 91
spiritual values 206
stability
  of group membership 82–3
  political 93
stages models of entry 179
standardisation 36–7
static modelling 148
stock markets 220–1
strategic business units 101
strategic choice
  internalisation factors 127–31
  key explanatory factors **144**
strategic divestment 169
strategy
  choice of 118
  in international business
      literature 245

strategy literature, weaknesses 100–2
subcontracting 7, 108, 165
supervisory control 96
supply, flexibility 165–6
switching behaviour 32–6, 170–2
  optimal timing 38
symmetrical positioning 54–5
symmetry
  local and global 56
  partner firms 119–20
symmetry of substitution 56
synthesis 119, 150
systems integration 14
systems view 11–12, 80–1

tacit knowledge 128
tariff, and competitiveness 159
tariff reductions, multilateral 12
teams 83
technology
  acquisition of 101–2, 131
  advances in 98
  capital-intensive 71
  diffusion 153, 155
  global diffusion 230
  market imperfections 7–8
  patent rights 128
  and social systems 22–3
technology gap 6–7, 8
technology market 103
technology transfer 9–10, 59, 71,
    153–4
  set-up costs 36–7
Teece, D. J. 36
television 231–2
theoretical approaches, levels of
    aggregation 263
theory of non-cooperative
    games 169
theory of options 168
theory of the growth of the firm *see
    also* Penrose, Edith
  becoming multinational 286
  evaluation and conclusions 299
  model 281–5
  multinational analogue 285–8
  Penrose vs Buckley and Casson
      models 288–91
  reconciliation of models 292–5

reformulation of cost
functions 278
simple formal model 278–85
synthesis 297–9
toleration 81–2
trade secrets 8
transaction cost theory,
opportunism 18
transaction costs 82, 164, 267–71
transport
advances in 12, 76
and development 85
ease of 76–8
trust 17–23
cooperation and commitment 48–9
and flexibility 164–5
and individualism 75, 84
and innovation 106
in international business 3–4
joint ventures 63–4
low 233
in management 96–7
and management of
innovation 97
mutual insurance 130
sharing technology 102
Type I error 247–8, 250
Type II error 247–8, 250

uncertainty
and complexity 240
and information 249–51
and networks 272–4
rational action 247
and rational choice 167–8
reducing 162
understandings, formal and
informal 46–7
unified currency 26

United Kingdom, innovation 113–14
United States, innovation 114
universities, links with business 159
unlearning 166–7
unwarranted trust 17
utopianism 209, 223

Vahlne, J.-E. 179, 287
value-maximising 290–1
value systems, corporate 97
venture capital 103, 107
Vernon, R. 36, 177, 287
vertical integration 285
Viner envelope 27
Viner, J. 27
volatility
increase in 155
and learning 166
and market size 134–40
modelling 167–70
reflected in models 147–9
and strategic choice 138
voluntary association 74–5
and competitive individualism 81–4
vulnerability, balancing 60–1

war 223–4
warranted mutual trust 17
water transportation 77–8
Weber, Max 210
wholly owned subsidiaries, vs joint
ventures 180
Wiedersheim-Paul, F. 179
world product mandates
(WPM) 112–13
World Trade Organization, Seattle
1999 226–7, 233
World War II, effect on number of
MNEs 9